Maoists Insurgency in India and Nepal

Philosophy, Logistic Collaboration, Ideological Ties

MAOISTS INSURGENCY IN INDIA AND NEPAL

Philosophy, Logistic Collaboration, Ideological Ties

K.N. Sinha (Dy. Coll.)
(Retd.)

PRASHANT PUBLISHING HOUSE
DELHI-110094

Published by :
Prashant Publishing House
C-34, 28 Foota Road, Gali No.-3,
West Karawal Nagar, Delhi-110094
Phone : 011-22963970, Mob. : 9810396373

Maoists Insutrgency In India And Nepal

First Published 2011

ISBN 978-93-80565-14-9

PRINTED IN INDIA
Published by Mr. R.K. Jha M/s Prashant Publishing House and Published at H.S. Offset House Press, Delhi.

Preface

Compared to the Naxalbari movement of the earlier phase, the (CPI Maoist)-led armed struggle is seen by observers to be at a more advanced level. It has spread over a larger area and has survived for over two decades. The strongest guerilla zone remains the Dandakaranya forest region in central India covering eleven districts across the four states of Andhra Pradesh, Maharashtra, Chhattisgarh and Madhya Pradesh. The Maoist Communist Centre (MCC) of Bihar and Jharkhand claims that its influence in the region extends to a population of about 12 million people of tribal origin. Even though more widespread than the earlier Naxalite movement, the Maoists of today have not yet been able to build powerful country wide political movements. The overall picture is one of a relatively strong militant outfit with popular support in its strongholds in the south, central and eastern regions. Outside its core areas, the Indian state has been able to prevent Maoist entry into the national political arena.

The Maoist strategy is clearly to fish in all troubled Indian waters, and to opportunistically exploit every potential issue and grievance to generate a campaign of protests and agitations. The principal vehicles for these 'partial struggles' are 'front' or 'cover' organisations of the Maoists themselves, on the one hand, and a range of individuals and organisations best described, in a phrase often attributed to Lenin, as 'useful idiots' — well intentioned and often gullible people who are unaware of the broader strategy and agenda they are unwittingly promoting through their support to specific and unquestionably admirable causes.

There are rising doubts in Nepal that the country will have a new constitution by May 2010, and if it does, whether it will create a credible basis to cement the country as a democratic republic, as provided by the interim constitution enforced in early 2007. The party of Maoists which leads the incumbent coalition government continues to depict, by words and deeds, itself as a political force only capable of offering a revolutionary package. A striking instance of the Maoists' revolutionary zeal surfaced last week when the government enacted three ordinances - two of which pertained to fixing the reservation quotas for traditionally backward tribes and castes, and those whose names figure in the list of disappeared persons during the insurgency years (1996-2006). While the subjects taken up for action are not in dispute, the procedure adopted by Prime Minister Prachanda has attracted stiff opposition from the majority of the parties and their leaders, who see the Maoist move as a clear-cut case of evading the parliamentary process.

To regard the Maoists and strictly an external force importing change in the circumstances of the poor would be subscribe to a mechanical materialist and vulgar evolutionary theory, easily trumpted by Maoist dialectics. The Maoist Movement in India is a direct outcome of the tragedy of India ruled by her big bourgeoisie and governed by parties coopted by that class fraction.

The book analyzes almost all the terms which have been used by different scholars for charactering such movements. It examines ideology; environment; organization and strategy of the Maoist Movement

—Editor

Contents

1

India, Nepal and the Maoist Conflict

INTRODUCTION

Despite numerous similarities, India and Nepal tend to have difficulties in resolving many vital issues common to both of them, including border disputes, trade and transit issues, and matters relating to cooperation in the water sector. Successive political leaders in both countries have been unable to demonstrate the degree of farsightedness and wisdom required to cultivate and nurture a relationship that does not actually call for much hard work or a major sacrifice in order to flourish. Unfortunately, problems between India and Nepal persist and small differences become larger and then seem to be intractable.

THE BACKGROUND TO INDO-NEPAL RELATIONS

India and Nepal share not only a long and open border but also a cultural history. A sizeable population of Indian origin live in Nepal and vice versa. This is one reason why the 1950 Treaty of Peace and Friendship grants the nationals of India with national treatment in Nepal (and nationals of Nepal with Indian national treatment in India) as far as certain industrial, economic and commercial activities are concerned. However, the nature and scope of this treaty has been the subject of controversy since its conclusion. Critics argue that this treaty is based on the 'Himalayan frontier policy' of India, fundamentally a policy pursued by the British during colonial rule, which should be changed to reflect the current reality. Nepal views India's attitude towards Nepal as old-fashioned and patronising. Nepal is virtually land-locked by India and India has tended to view Nepal as its own backyard. But while India is a huge factor in Nepal's international relations, Nepal is an important, though relatively small, factor in India's own foreign policy. India has been critical of the inclination of Nepal's leaders to adopt the role of an irritating neighbour, incapable of understanding the bilateral relationship from a broader perspective. India views its dealings with Nepal in a regional context, while Nepal takes a bilateral view of relations with India.

This outlook has hindered Nepal's attempts at modernisation and economic development and the misperceptions regarding the asymmetric relationship have often prevented meaningful cooperation between the two neighbours. For instance, Nepal has huge hydroelectric potential but has yet to take advantage of this resource largely because of mistrust of India – the natural market for power.

There is little balance in the interplay between diplomacy and law in shaping the relations between Nepal and India. As a result, Indo-Nepal relations have become a "laboratory" for testing various principles of international law. While some treaties between the two countries have been unbalanced, inviting inevitable criticism, others, even those concluded ostensibly on the basis of equality, have yet to be implemented because they have also been tainted by the old mindset of "unequal" treaties. For instance, Nepal as a land-locked country has a guaranteed right to free access to and from the sea through the territory of India under international law, but India has been slow to acknowledge that fact and is often reluctant to honour the right in practice. Furthermore, the very existence of some treaties is contested. Treaties have been concluded between the two countries without being designated as such in order to avoid parliamentary scrutiny.

Indo-Nepal relations are marred by mistrust, confusion and dogmatism. It is necessary to develop an environment in both countries that is conducive to meaningful cooperation. The perception that India sees Nepal as its own backyard causes resentment in Nepal. And Nepal's tendency to denigrate its larger neighbour for any perceived ills is equally unhealthy and may ultimately block any effort by the two countries to work together.

India and Nepal need to usher their relations into a new phase, prepared for and capable of facing current challenges. They have to move away from the old dogmas and embrace transparency and democratic norms in the conduct of their relations. For this, the immediate task at hand is to:

- Regulate the Indo-Nepal border and require some sort of ID card when nationals of both countries cross the border;
- Resolve the border disputes such as those relating to Kalapani;
- Implement the Mahakali River Treaty in a manner which is satisfactory to both parties;
- Conclude a new friendship treaty to replace the 1950 Treaty of Peace and Friendship; and
- Cancel formally the 1965 Arms Agreement and any other "secret" agreements.

THE MAOIST PROBLEM AND THE ROYAL COUP

The Maoist insurgency, which began in Nepal in the 1990s, had two main political objectives:

- Abolishing the monarchy, seen as an obstacle to the economic, social and political development of Nepal; and
- Cancelling the "unequal" treaties with India in order to end the virtual control of the Nepalese economy by Indian businesses.

The Maoists began to be seen as a viable alternative to the increasingly unsatisfactory situation created by the endless squabbles among the parliamentary political parties, rampant corruption, economic mismanagement, neglect of the real concerns of the people, and unfair access to and unbalanced distribution of Nepal's resources.

To make matters worse, the King of Nepal grabbed power on February 1, 2005, and suspended human rights and democracy by declaring a state of emergency. The resumption of absolute rule in a country ridden by internal strife has further divided Nepal and complicated existing political problems. The King has tried to justify his move by arguing that he was driven by a desire to bring about peace in the country and tackle the Maoist problem. However, there are no indications of that occurring. Rather, the Maoists seem to have hardened their position and the risk is that many people standing in the middle ground may very well end up on the Maoist camp.

There can be no denying that the coalition partners within the sacked government itself were divided on the question of holding the general election under critical conditions and were unable to address the Maoist problem. But while the ousted government achieved little, the King should have taken the opportunity to build a national consensus to address the Maoist problem. His best option was perhaps to dissolve the government and call for a national convention represented by all major political forces within the country. The King could have acted as a unifying force, a mediator, a conciliator and a peace-broker, demonstrating that he himself was prepared to make sacrifices and compromise for the greater good of the country. Unfortunately, he did not take advantage of this opportunity.

In the past, various political parties, including the Nepali Congress, have taken advantage of Nepal's long open border with India and the democratic and open nature of Indian society to organise themselves in India. When the Maoist campaign within Nepal escalated, there was a tendency to look towards New Delhi for tougher action against the Maoists leaders who were supposedly operating from within the Indian territory.

The intensification of the Maoist campaign in the 1990s drew India closer into the problem. India began to supply more weapons to the Royal Nepalese Army thereby increasing the dependency of Nepal on India for the resolution of the problem. Other major powers, including the US and UK also saw things in Nepal through the New Delhi lens or were unwilling to do much for Nepal without checking first with India. International efforts to assist Nepal fizzled out due partly to the disunity among the parliamentary political parties and partly to India's resentment of any significant involvement of other countries in Nepal's affairs.

The much awaited visit by the King to India was postponed repeatedly before the Royal coup of 1 February 2005. Indian political leaders had started to increase their stake in the Maoist problem, calling it a common problem. The Indian media had started a debate about the need for Indian intervention in Nepal. The influence of New Delhi on the international media also increased.

The royal coup, however, faced criticism not only from India, but also from the UK, the US and the UN. It appears that both the UK and the US have given India the lead in putting pressure on the King to restore democracy and human rights in Nepal. Both India and the UK suspended military aid to Nepal. The US took a "wait and see" approach but was generally supportive of the Indian and the British positions. However, India has now lifted its suspension of military aid and it remains to be seen whether the UK follows suit. India is concerned both about the contagion effect of conflict on India, as well as its own arms industry. In Nepal there is a perception that India is more interested in promoting its national self-interest than in promoting democracy, requiring it to reach an accommodation with the *de facto* ruler in Nepal. During India's suspension of military aid, the King tried to give the impression that Nepal could turn to China to rescue it from international isolation but, apart from demonstrating some public support to the present regime in Nepal, it is doubtful whether China would have come to Nepal's rescue and risked its own rapidly improving relations with India. It is widely held that since 1954 both China and India have some sort of understanding whereby India would do nothing to undermine the vital Chinese interests beyond the Himalayas and China would do nothing to undermine vital Indian interests beyond the natural frontier of the Himalayas.

Indian indifference towards the Dalai Lama's claims for independence or greater autonomy for Tibet and weak Chinese opposition to India's annexation of Sikkim in 1974 are cited as examples of this détente at work. While India has provided shelter to the Dalai Lama, it has not supported his political ambitions. Similarly, China has accepted India's annexation of Sikkim. This détente makes it unlikely that China would consider replacing India as Nepal's main source of arms, or take other steps to suppress the Maoist movement. Furthermore, China has not embraced the UN human rights agenda according to which human rights violations by a despotic regime within any country should be regarded as a matter for international concern.

At present there is a stalemate in Indo-Nepal relations in terms of broader economic cooperation and a complete deadlock within Nepal in terms of resolving the Maoist problem and moving the political process forward. There does not seem to be any constructive dialogue between Nepal and India to address the whole gamut of Indo-Nepal relations and the conflict in Nepal has stalled efforts to work together for economic development.

India's claim that the Maoist problem in Nepal is spilling over to India, posing a great security threat to India itself, has gained international attention. Before the Royal coup, it was rumoured that the King was considering asking India to send troops to Nepal to fight the Maoists. Was his visit postponed to give both sides an opportunity to work out the modalities for direct Indian military intervention? Given subsequent developments, these stories seem far-fetched. It also is difficult to believe how a tiny Maoist rebel movement in Nepal would have any meaningful impact on India – a huge country with several similar rebel movements. Even if the Maoists took power in Nepal they would pose little threat to India - a regional power aspiring to become a global power. And the Maoists would face the same constraints as any Nepalese ruler. If they should want to maintain power, they would need to accept the limitations of ruling a virtually India-locked impoverished country and reach an accommodation with the larger neighbour.

A WAY FORWARD?

The government of Nepal faces two options: 1) use more military force to weaken the Maoists, forcing them to negotiate, or 2) address the issues raised by the Maoists. Option one would invite a bloodbath. Any Indian interference or direct

military assistance risks bolstering the Maoist threat. The Nepalese are fiercely nationalist and proud of their independence. The move could inflame the Gurkhas, proud of their military tradition. Furthermore, there is little guarantee that Indian interference would bring military success. India is struggling to fight its own Maoist and other insurgent movements. Any Indian interference would not only be illegal but could prove to be a costly affair, for both countries.

The second option is more sensible but would require international pressure on both the Maoists and the government. International involvement, however, would not be difficult to secure. The international community has a stake in Nepal. The international community would be abdicating its responsibility if they leave the resolution of the conflict to India alone. Gross violations of human rights and humanitarian law are taking place in Nepal. Law and order has broken down. The Maoists have not respected the rule of law and have created a lawless situation in the rural areas of Nepal. Now the royal government has created another type of lawless society in urban areas by undermining basic principles of the rule of law, democracy, and human rights. The law is confined to the books and the order that does exist is confined to the Kathmandu Valley. Outside the Valley, terror, not order, rules the day.

The forced disappearance of people is now a daily occurrence, torture is routine and the killing and suffering of innocent people caught in the crossfire is beyond belief. The protection of human rights in Nepal is as much a matter of concern for the international community as anywhere else in the world. International involvement is needed to prevent such violations of human rights in Nepal.

The Maoist problem is essentially a political problem - there are no internal territorial disputes involved, nor is the Maoist campaign based on ethnic lines. It is about political governance. The Maoists are unlikely to muster enough support to overthrow the present system of government and should know their limitations. At the same time, the army seems incapable of defeating the Maoists completely. Hence, there is a stalemate. There are, of course, beneficiaries in this conflict: recent governments (including the present Royal government) have tried to remain in power by invoking the Maoist threat; the Maoists themselves have benefited from the money collected from extortion; there is a huge INGO/NGO industry supposedly working to find a negotiated settlement, and there is a small clique which benefits from the commissions offered by the arms industry and the huge expenditure allocated to the military and the security sector.

The present Royal government has not shown any sense of urgency in dealing with the Maoist problem. Rather, it has focussed on consolidating power within the country in the hands of a small clique surrounding the King by invoking the threat posed by the Maoists and intimidating supporters of democracy. It is the marginalized – the poor, the vulnerable, the weak and those with low or no income that suffer most at the hands of the Maoists and the security forces. The international community has owes these people an obligation and should become actively involved to bring the warring sides to the negotiating table. While events in Nepal are an irritating, diplomatic disaster for India, India would benefit from a peaceful Nepal and suffers costs from having a poor and conflict-ridden neighbour. India should demonstrate greater vision and farsightedness in its dealings with Nepal, while Nepal should stop mistrusting its giant neighbour. India should let the international community, namely the UN, play a major role in bringing about a peaceful resolution to the problem. The King has a historical responsibility to show flexibility at this juncture. With the help of the international community, he should convene a broad political convention, including the Maoists, to consider the political future of the country. He should appoint a non-political caretaker cabinet, headed by a former Chief Justice or a similar figure, with the sole task of holding a free and fair general election under international supervision.

Other countries should act through the UN to facilitate a negotiated settlement in Nepal. It seems perfectly possible for a government of national unity comprising all democratic forces of the country to deal decisively with the Maoists if the international community is united behind a democratic government in Nepal. The Maoists have no popular support, believe in an outdated political ideology, and have resorted to some of the worst atrocities imaginable in order to terrorise people in the rural areas.

But in tackling the Maoists, the issues of inequality, poverty, feudal control of the country and neglect of the underprivileged classes raised by the Maoists should not be forgotten. Some of the issues raised by the Maoists should be addressed with sincerity in the negotiations. This is where India can play the role of a friendly mediator and conciliator as part of a broader international effort led by the UN to bring about peace and prosperity to the people of Nepal. In the absence of international involvement, the Maoist problem may be allowed to continue for a long time in order to justify the political ambitions of the warring sides. This will prolong and compound the suffering of the masses of innocent people rendered helpless in this brutal struggle for power.

MAOIST MOVEMENT TODAY

Compared to the Naxalbari movement of the earlier phase, the (CPI Maoist)-led armed struggle is seen by observers to be at a more advanced level. It has spread over a larger area and has survived for over two decades. The strongest guerilla zone remains the Dandakaranya forest region in central India covering eleven districts across the four states of Andhra Pradesh, Maharashtra, Chhattisgarh and Madhya Pradesh. The Maoist Communist Centre (MCC) of Bihar and Jharkhaud claims that its influence in the region extends to a population of about 12 million people of tribal origin. Even though more widespread than the earlier Naxalite movement, the Maoists of today have not yet been able to build powerful country wide political movements. The overall picture is one of a relatively strong militant outfit with popular support in its strongholds in the south, central and eastern regions. Outside its core areas, the Indian state has been able to prevent Maoist entry into the national political arena.

TOWARDS AN ALTERNATIVE STRATEGY

During the 1980s, the MHA was not just a law and order ministry but was responsible for the important subject of the development of the Scheduled Castes (SCs) and Scheduled Tribes (STs). Initiatives such as Special Component Plan for the former and the Tribal Sub-Plan for the latter were started and implemented on the ground through the state governments. The ministry also took a keen interest in the increasing violence against the SCs and STs in the country and initiated effective measures to stop the violence and to punish the offenders with 'deterrent rapidity'. The Civil Rights Cell monitored the trends of violence and prepared reports for the Cabinet and Parliament. The MHA was a strong and powerful ministry with funds and police forces to compel the state governments to follow the central guidelines and instructions on issues of violence, development and social justice.

The creation in the subsequent period of the Ministry of Social Justice and Empowerment and the allocation of the subject of the development of Scheduled Castes and Tribes to that ministry along with the issue of socio-political violence against these communities reduced the MHA to a purely law and order apparatus. As a consequence, the annual report of the ministry for the year 2005-06 reads like a strange document devoted entirely to Naxalite violence with nothing to say on the increasing number and intensity of violence against the SCs and STs in the recent period. Such a juxtaposition of the naxalite violence with the increasing violence against the SC's and ST's is necessary for appreciation of both 'violence of development' and 'development of violence' and to devise appropriate measures in coordination with the state governments. In this sense, the creation of a separate Ministry of Social Justice and Empowerment was not perhaps an altogether happy development for the Scheduled Castes and Tribes.

The process of commercialization of forest resources has reduced the access of indigenous communities to these resources. Alienation of tribal land to richer non-tribal elements from outside is a significant factor in tribal unrest. Displacement due to the construction of large dams and other industries has impoverishment of these communities, strengthening demands for tribal self governance.

Government programs for tribal development have had adverse consequences for tribal communities as documented in several studies including those conducted on behalf of the government of India (GOI, 2008). The extension of Panchayati

Raj Institutions (PRI's) to tribal areas can become an instrument of empowerment only after steps are taken to restore indigenous rights over land and forest. The setting up of the new states of Chhattisgarh, Jharkhand and Uttaranchal to enable tribal participation in governance and decision making at decentralized levels, is largely ineffective due to the unchanged character and mindset of the administrative and police setup. B. Mungekar, Member Planning Commission of India is reported to have prepared a report showing that between 1951 and 1990, 40 million people were displaced as result of development projects. Of these 40 percent were tribal people. Only 25 percent of the displaced have so far been 'rehabilitated'. The adequacy and quality of 'rehabilitation' has come into serious question especially in the context of the recent controversy over the Sardar Sarovar Project (Roy 2006). In the light of this, it is not surprising that the naxalite movement has found support among those sections of Scheduled Tribes who became victims rather than beneficiaries of development.

The issue was examined in depth by Dr. B. D. Sharma, then Commissioner for Scheduled Castes and Tribes in his 28th Report to the President of India (Sharma, 2000). The report elaborated a Constitutional schema for establishing an egalitarian society with clear provisions for countering simultaneously the inequities of tradition and the 'backlash of modernization' in the nation's development. The focus was on the dalits and the adivasis. The assessment was that the outcome of the developmental measures taken plus the adverse forces already at work was a negative one as indicated by the accentuation of deprivation and the 'relentless slide back' in the fortunes of these communities notwithstanding some token achievements such as 'reservations' in government jobs. The analysis laid bare the 'omissions, distortions, subterfuges and the studied silence on vital issues' in order to protect vested interests. The people were paying a heavy price for the so-called 'development'. All the institutions of the state, executive, legislative and judicial, had abdicated their constitutional responsibility of safeguarding the interest of the deprived sections. The executive in particular, with its distorted role perception, is working against the interests of those whose wellbeing is its sacred trust. The action taken on the report by the government amounted to undermining constitutional values and trivialization of institutions by those who had the responsibility to protect them.

However, the model that was adopted in practice legitimized divestiture of the indigenous people's traditionally recognized rights in the name of 'development'. Not merely were the immemorial customary rights of the tribals ruthlessly violated but they were made to appear as trespassers in their own lands. All this was being done in spite of the concern expressed in the Constitution's Fifth Schedule that the laws of the land should be suitably adapted in their application to Scheduled areas, a responsibility entrusted to the executive as part of its duty for the advancement of the Scheduled Tribes. To accomplish this task, the executive was conferred with special powers. The deliberate non-use of these powers resulted in not just unconstitutional and unjust governance but also in cruel and allous administration.

In the light of this analysis, the Report to the President also examined the issue of self governance at the village level and the disastrous effect of the non-recognition of command over community resources, which had resulted everywhere in disorganization, displacement and destitution of the adivasis. There could be no peace in the Scheduled Areas so long as the confrontation between the people and the state continued on the issue of self governance, particularly on the intimately associated question of the command over resources.

The current strategy of the MHA, as spelt out in its annual reports for 2004-5 and 2005-6, appear retrograde and counterproductive in the light of this analysis. The deployment of paramilitary forces on a large scale in the interior tribal areas of the country does not solve the problem but can cause immense misery to the common people. The whole policy of raising and deploying central paramilitary forces for local conflict management is based on faulty thinking and leads to serious internal security disasters. Paramilitary units as India Reserve battalions, which the Centre is encouraging states to raise to deal with internal security problems cannot be effective since their basic military type of training involves no local contact or interaction or understanding of the local population and problems. A recent visit to Chhattisgarh, where a Nagaland based IR battalion has been deployed, indicated emerging tensions between the district police leadership and the Naga battalion leadership since the latter is prioritized over the former, which is basically responsible for law and order management. A similar tension had emerged in Punjab earlier when the National Security Guard (NSG) was deployed over the head of the state DG of Police who was basically responsible for law and order in the state.

Similarly, it has been found in the northeast that lack of local knowledge on the part of the central paramilitary forces (CPFs) often led to disasters for the men, who were ambushed because they followed misleading intelligence provided to them by some interested local elements. Further, the induction of CPF's often leads to tensions between them and the local police responsible for law and order and to demoralization of central of the central forces.

THE MAOIST THREAT: THE ROLE OF RISK MANAGEMENT FIRMS

The current debate of 'people or profits', with regards to the Maoist uprising, prevents big conglomerates from investing in the mineral rich states of India. The Maoists are now in 200 districts across 12 Indian states, stretching from Nepal to the northern district of Tamil Nadu. It is a challenge to India's internal security and their growing political influence in the region will certainly have an impact on the economy. More than four decade of the left wing extremism in India has claimed approximately 20,000 lives and its reach is expanding drastically. The Maoists seek to overthrow the democratically institutionalized government through armed resurrection. They are expanding their sphere of influence by running a parallel administration with an organized military command structure in nearly 44 districts in Orissa, Jharkhand and Chhattisgarh and few districts in Andhra Pradesh.

Maoist presence in the mineral-resources rich regions scuttles India's plan to capitalize on the resources. The world biggest steel maker, Posco, yet to start their US$32 billion project in Orissa, delayed it due to agitation and protests over land. Government sources projected that recently sprung out left-wing extremism in regions rich in iron ore, coal and bauxite has stalled an upcoming project worth US$80 billion, which would have doubled the national steel input. This is despite the government assurance of additional forces, intelligence and other adequate support for the state governments. ArcelorMittal and NMDC Ltd. are reluctant to expand their projects in the resource belt due to the ongoing strife between Maoist and the Central Security Forces. Business and Investment experts believe that "the high level of risk associated with doing business in Naxal-infested regions will deter investment." If the situation continues, it will hamper India's growth rate in the future.

Even as investors are concerned, the major challenge is emerging from the public attitude mooted by eminent scholars on the 'people or profit' debate. Opposition to the TATA plant in Singur, the allegation on Posco for forceful land acquisitions and many other issues against corporate establishment in Maoist influenced areas, created enough negative agitation against the corporate establishment. Even in the Maoist-Free Zones, corporations and investors are reluctant to expand their projects due to a backlash from the local population. Arousing public sentiment can be wishfully converted into a struggle against the establishment in the poor rural regions, say leading risk advisors. Adequate safety and security to physical infrastructure merely deters the agitation group. In order to avert the risks to gain profits, big conglomerates are working on a multi-level strategy to pre-empt anti-development threats, emerging particularly from poor rural India.

Corporate Social Responsibility (CSR) plays a vital role in winning the hearts and minds of the people. Laying roads, building schools, hospitals and women empowerment are activities frequently organized by the corporations to fulfill their social responsibility role. On the political ground, corporations lack the will to fight political issues lest it hurt the good will of the company. Therefore, corporations outsource the job of analyzing socio-politico and cultural activity of a region to 'corporate security and risk consulting firms'. Leading risk consultants in India, Hill and Association (Delhi), Mitkat Risk Advisory Services (Mumbai), Mahindra Special Services

Group (Mumbai) and Orkash service (Delhi) Ltd etc. are some examples.

These firms are specifically tasked to assist corporations and investors in calculating risks and creating risk awareness in organizations by training the senior management in risk assessment programs. However, risk consulting firms' primary focus rests on crucial projects encompassing information security management to high-end physical security in vulnerable areas and instituting a security setup wherever necessary. The risk consultant helps the client in grass-root-investigation on matters ranging from money laundering investigation, asset tracing, tracking and locating individuals/absconding employees, fraud risk assessment and information forensic etc.

The recent terrorist attack on the Mumbai Taj Hotels and the uprising of people's resistance in the resource rich belt, backed by CPI-(Maoist), traumatized the corporate world with a sense of insecurity. Risk advisors primarily working on risk consultation, now shoulder more responsibility in dealing with insurgency and terrorism to caution the respective client to avoid running into a troublesome region. Corporations and investors believe that risk advisors services can mitigate possible Singur type agitations, which plunge the region into human disaster and hamper long-term investment, like it happened in West Bengal.

In conclusion, risk management firms play a vital role for investors and corporations in an emerging security threats environment. The risk advisor by conducting early investigation in an area foresees possible risks and threats to the investor in the region. This creates a conducive environment for the corporation/investor to expand the project without disturbing the state apparatus. At the same time, the role of private actors investigating Maoist and people resistance activities is sometimes exposed to vulnerable situations, like abduction, harassment and a threat to life etc. Although, so far no such incident has been reported, risk advisory firms should be cautious while operating in such a dangerous environment. Nevertheless, corporate security and risk management firms are committed to playing a crucial role in the emerging security environment.

THE MAOIST INSURGENCY IN INDIA

The Indian government is puzzled by one fundamental problem that has become desperate to its own security. With its officials eyeing Pakistan and the funnelling of terrorism through its borders, and the concern with international jihadi movements, it has ignored its own, Maoist grown revolt. Anywhere up to 6,000 people have perished in the Naxalite insurgency of the last 20 years, and the Indian Prime Minister Manmohan Singh has decided to place the Maoist movement's threat to Indian security at the forefront of public and official debate.

Near the end of 2009, the central Indian government began implanting forceful measures to combat the Naxals, who now have a presence in 180 of Indians 626 districts (Guardian, Dec 6, 2009). The establishment of this Red Corridor is certainly a far cry from the origins of the movement, which sprouted from the Naxalbari area of West Bengal in 1967. Then, they were a motley crew, discordant and incoherent, susceptible to internal vendettas and feuds. With a marriage of Marxist-Leninist ideology and Maoist tactics, the movement staggered and stuttered through near annihilation to emerge as a highly dangerous force.

In December, government forces commenced operations with Operation Green Hunt, a military engagement with little fuss and even less activity. The rebels, reports suggested, had simply melted into the jungles. The military solution is now all some officials can talk about. The logic of force, rather than the force of logic, prevail in these circles.

Union Home Minister P. Chidambaram has insisted that the Maoist ultras will be crushed. His most recent comments, quoted in the Indian press, suggest that he has little time for their revolutionary antics. The Naxals were 'cowards enacting dramas', lethal thespians who went about the business less of protecting the poor than destroying schools, railway lines and vital infrastructure links. 'If they have courage they should take part in democratic processes and face elections. Who is stopping them from winning elections?'

The attacks by the Naxals on schools are certainly doing it no favours. Violent attacks in such states as Chhattisgarh, involving the dynamiting of scores of school buildings, must surely alienate their core support. But its members undoubtedly feel that the state has to be attacked at vital centres, endings that require demolition and severance. Education is inevitably one of the targets in this Maoist appraisal.

Truth has not merely been a casualty of this war, but a sure corpse, lying in state for all to witness it. Paramilitary forces have backed militias and classes who have been ruthless in perpetrating what Manmohan Singh admitted were grave acts of 'social and economic abuse'. Atrocities are committed by all participating forces in this conflict. Martyrs are created in numbers, such as those of Kursam Lakhi and Sukki Modiyam of the village of Pedda Korma, raped and killed by the forces of the Salway Judum militia and their police counterparts on February 6, 2005 (The Observer, Mar 29, 2009). The Naxal messages of land and wealth redistribution hold a natural attraction.

Chidambaram is confident that the insurgency will be put down in two or three years. This will be difficult, given the Naxalite rise from conventional guerrilla force to something approximating to an army. But the refusal to deal with a whole series of reforms, the continuing poverty in the North Eastern states and the perennial problem of ethic conflict, will allow the Naxal flame to burn that much longer. Military force will simply perform its own dramatic role of obfuscation. The diplomatic tables will be left empty that much longer.

NEPAL'S MAOISTS PREPARE FOR FINAL OFFENSIVE

There are signs that Nepal's Maoist insurgents may be preparing to wage a final offensive in accordance with their understanding of Maoist ideology. Bertil Lintner explores the methods, capabilities and resources of the group, and the government's attempts to counter the threat.

Two attacks launched by Nepal's Maoist insurgents in September have dashed hopes that the government's nine-month state of emergency had succeeded in crushing the country's militant movement. In the first attack on 7 September, Maoist rebels overran a police station in Sindhuli district,

85km east of the capital Kathmandu, killing at least 49 policemen and wounding 22 others before escaping with a haul of guns. The following day, insurgents attacked Sandhikharka, headquarters of the Arghakhanchi district, 300km west of Kathmandu. As many as 200 policemen, soldiers and civilians may have died in this attack. The government is now considering reimposing the state of emergency lifted on 27 August, a decision that could undermine public support for Prime Minister Sher Bahadur Deuba, the armed forces and the king, boost the insurgents and derail the political process leading up to general elections scheduled for 13 November.

The Maoists' strategy

In orthodox Maoism, there are three phases of protracted war: the strategic defensive, the strategic stalemate and the strategic offensive. According to this model, the Communist Party of Nepal-Maoist (CPN(M)) has, in its battle with the government, reached strategic stalemate: it is not as powerful as the government in terms of troop strength and military equipment, but is almost equal in terms of actions, initiatives and control of the countryside. The question, therefore, is one of when the Maoist leadership will decide that the group will be ready to move into its strategic offensive, the final stage of the protracted war. "The Maoists appear to have decided that the time is ripe for their war ki par ['do or die'] moment", says Puskar Gautam, a Nepalese newspaper columnist and himself a former Maoist commander. According to Gautam, the CPN(M) leadership has carefully studied experiences from South America, especially what went wrong in Peru after the 1992 arrest of Abimael Guzman, leader of Sendero Luminoso (Shining Path). "In their analysis, the Shining Path and the Colombian revolutions failed because they let the strategic balance drag on for too long. In Nepal, the Maoists think a quick push when the state is vulnerable will take them to victory," he says.

There are signs that the rebels may indeed be preparing to make their final push. In April, during the height of the state of emergency, the insurgents began to target infrastructure in order to paralyse the government. Hydroelectric power plants, bridges, telecommunications centres and government building were blown up. Since the emergency was lifted in August, even

Kathmandu itself has been hit by almost daily bomb blasts targeting shopping centres and other public places.

Rebel arms and men

In order to launch their final offensive, the Maoists will have to further strengthen their forces and, more importantly, acquire more sophisticated automatic weapons. Military analysts in Kathmandu estimate current CPN(M) strength at 3,000-4,000 'hardcore militants', or regular troops, and 10,000-15,000 men organised in various local militias. In addition, there are thousands of activists and other cadres who work openly in the countryside, or through front organisations in the towns. Initially, the insurgents had only hunting guns, mostly muzzle-loaders collected from local people and a few home-made rifles and pistols, which they had obtained from illegal gun factories in the neighbouring Indian state of Bihar. Their tactic of raiding police armouries has allowed them to expand their arsenal to include .303 rifles, 12-bore shotguns and pistols, while attacks on army camps have yielded hauls of Sten-guns and Indian-made self-loading rifles.

These small arms have been supplemented by bombs made from explosives smuggled into the country, mostly by sympathetic Nepalese labourers working on road construction projects in India.

Thus far, the Maoists have not used sophisticated automatic rifles, but there is evidence suggesting they are trying to obtain such weapons from abroad. On 2 November 2001 - just a few weeks before the rebels broke a six-month long ceasefire - a large consignment of 200-400 weapons was seized by the Myanmar authorities near their country's border with India. The United Wa State Army (UWSA) had trucked the shipment across Myanmar, an ethnic-minority force that has a ceasefire agreement with the ruling junta in Yangon that effectively allows it to move drugs, guns and contraband along government-controlled roads. This consignment was intercepted because, while most of the weapons were purchased by the UWSA from private arms dealers in China, some had been bought from poorly paid Myanmar soldiers. It would have been a major embarrassment for Yangon if its weapons had fallen into foreign hands. It is still not entirely clear whom the guns were destined for. The buyer was identified only as 'Ariya', and could have been any of the local insurgent groups in India's northeast.

However, the United Liberation Front of Assam, the biggest group in the area, has more weapons than soldiers while other, smaller groups in Nagaland, Manipur and Tripura are too poor to afford a consignment of such magnitude. This, combined with the timing of the seizure, suggests that the Nepalese Maoists were the most likely buyers.

Financing the revolution

A string of bank robberies and extensive collection of 'revolutionary tax' from people in the areas under its control as well as in all major towns and overseas has made the CPN(M) one of the wealthiest rebel movements in Asia. It has netted between an estimated five and 10bn Nepalese rupees (US$64m-$128m). Considerable amounts also derive from 'collections' from Nepalese abroad, particularly the several million Nepalese who work in neighbouring India.

The main organisation among them, the Akhil Bharatiya Nepali Ekta Samaj (All-India Nepalese Unity Society), was banned in July for links to the CPN(M). The Indian authorities arrested its secretary, Bamdev Chhetri - thought to be the most important contact for the Nepalese Maoists in India - on 7 September and extradited him to Nepal.

Poverty and social and political unrest have forced tens of thousands of Nepalese to emigrate. There are reports of a small but very active Maoist cell among the approximately 20,000-strong Nepalese community in Hong Kong as well as forced 'revolutionary tax collection' there.

In Belgium, some Nepalese expatriates have linked up with the Workers' Party of Belgium, one of the few remaining Maoist parties in Europe, where they are reportedly trying to use the Belgian courts to block the sale of arms to the Nepalese Army. However, the CPN(M) is not supported by any foreign power or major group abroad. Even China has assured the Nepalese government of its support, branding the Nepalese Maoists ultra radicals and not 'true Maoists'.

The government response

The state of emergency can claim few successes, and there is now Maoist-related violence in nearly all of Nepal's 75 districts, according to a 2002 report by the Informal Sector Service Centre for Human Rights and Social Justice, a Nepalese non-governmental organisation. In the western districts, including Rukum, Rolpa, Salyan and Jajarkot - the Maoist heartland in the hills - the government controls little more than district headquarters and strings of checkpoints on the roads leading down to the lowlands in the south. Even in Kalikot, Dailekh, Surkhet, Dang and Pyuthan, adjacent to the Maoists' main strongholds, the government's presence is negligible outside major towns. The Nepalese Army did not enter the conflict until the state of emergency was introduced. Previously, the insurgency was considered a law and order issue, which fell to the 28,000-strong police force to control. The policy changed when Maoist forces broke a six-month ceasefire and attacked military positions in November 2001, prompting the government to call in the army.

When the insurgency began, the army had 47,000 men. The figure is set to rise, with an immediate goal to field a 60,000-strong fighting force. In addition, a paramilitary police force was set up to counter the Maoists. Its current strength is 9,000, but the plan is to boost numbers to 25,000. In July, the government announced a 25% increase in the defence budget to fight the insurgency. Despite being home to the renowned Gurkhas, considered some of the best soldiers in the world, the country's regular army has no experience of combat. In the past, it was used mainly to guard national parks at home and for UN-sponsored peace missions abroad.

It is also poorly equipped, and attempts to buy weapons from abroad have run into unexpected problems. For example, an arms deal with Belgium was almost overturned when a government minister resigned arguing that according to Belgian law weapons cannot be exported to countries in conflict. In the end, the centre-left Belgian government survived a no-confidence vote in parliament, but the sale of 5,500 automatic weapons will be permitted only after 'free and fair' general elections have been held in November.

Other international help has been promised, however. Some assistance is coming from India, and US Secretary of State Colin Powell promised US$20m in aid during his visit to Kathmandu in January. But a further militarisation of the conflict could lead to more resentment in the hills, while the expansion of the army and the concomitant need for arms means that Nepal will divert more of its limited resources to the military, instead of development. This will exacerbate the already grave situation in the countryside. Government activities have made little impact in the countryside, where state-mandated violence has alienated many. According to official figures, 744 policemen and 150 soldiers died during the emergency, compared to 2,850 Maoists - a far higher death toll than occurred during the previous five years of the insurgency, which broke out in February 1996.

As Kanak Mani Dixit, editor of the monthly journal Himal, asks: "Who really are the 'Maoist' dead?" According to Nepalese human rights organisations and journalists in the field, most of them may have been ordinary civilians who were caught in the crossfire or mistaken for Maoists by the security forces. For example, on 24 February government forces gunned down 34 labourers working at an airport site in Kalikot, having mistaken them for Maoists. In other places, members of local branches of perfectly legal leftist parties have been shot. "The army shoots first and asks questions later," says Mohan Mainali, director of Nepal's Centre for Investigative Journalism.

As a result, in the countryside at least, support for the Maoists has grown rather than diminished since the imposition of the emergency, according to Padma Ratna Tuladhar, chairman of the Forum for Protection of Human Rights in Kathmandu. Tuladhar says that: "Many have turned to the Maoists for protection against excessive violence by the security forces." Government restrictions on the transportation of grain and medicines into western Nepal, meant to prevent such materials from falling into the hands of the insurgents, has led to a severe shortage of food in the area. Famine now looms over several impoverished districts in the northwest.

The government has made some progress in curbing insurgent activities in the towns, however. Newspapers and

periodicals sympathetic to the Maoists have been closed down and several journalists, intellectuals and others were detained during the emergency, although most of them were later released. The Maoists have also lost some support from the urban middle class due to their extreme violence and constant requests for 'donations', from government officials as well as shopkeepers and others in the towns.

Prospects for peace

The Nepalese government continues to pin its hopes on some sort of peace process. Both government officials and the Nepalese media speculate that there is a serious rift within the CPN(M) between 'softliners' such as Baburam Bhattarai (once the leader of the United People's Front, the Maoists' front organisation in Kathmandu); hardline followers of party chairman Pushpa Kamal Dahal; and the 'extreme hardliners' led by Ram Bahadur Thapa (alleged to be chief of the People's Liberation Army). Bhattarai is supposedly in favour of negotiating a settlement with the government, while Thapa wants to continue the armed struggle and Dahal is somewhere in between.

However, there is little to substantiate these assumptions, which sources close to the Maoist leadership say indicate just how little the authorities understand Maoist strategy. CPN(M) leaders see no contradiction between armed struggle and occasional appeals for a 'dialogue' with the government. In an interview on 28 May 2001 interview published in A World to Win, a magazine published by the Revolutionary Internationalist Movement, a worldwide network of Maoist parties, Dahal said that: "Our guiding principles on the question of negotiations are the experiences of the Brest-Litovsk Treaty under Lenin's leadership and the Chongqing negotiations under Mao's leadership" - instances in which Lenin's Bolsheviks and Mao's communists talked peace while regrouping and preparing their forces for an offensive. He went on to quote Mao's dictums that "without a people's army, the people have nothing"; and that "political power grows out of the barrel of a gun". In other words, Maoist requests for peace talks do not mean that they are about to give up their armed struggle to take part in elections. If they did so, they would cease being Maoist revolutionaries and become just one of several dozen leftist parties in Nepal, sources close to the CPN(M) say.

The government appears to be caught in a classic catch-22 situation. Until there is substantial social and economic development in the areas of the countryside where the Maoists hold sway, the insurgency will continue. Development cannot happen until the government gains even limited access to these areas, and access can only be achieved by using highly unpopular and potentially counterproductive military means. Nepal is caught in a difficult dilemma. This may be why the Maoists believe the time is ripe to move into the strategic offensive, their 'do-or-die battle' that they hope will decide the future of the country.

NEPAL'S MAOISTS CRY INDIAN FOUL PLAY

For any Indian who ever felt intrigued as to why South Asian neighbors often dislike his country, the past fortnight offered clues. Like in a Tennessee Williams play, painful to watch as the plot thickens slowly and invidiously, as protagonists begin tearing each other apart in quiet despair after love begins to drain or threatens to flee, India and Nepal are still locked in an embrace.

Someone must do the merciful act of separating them; of making them behave as they should - as two sovereign countries. Indian papers are full of interviews by Nepal's former prime minister Prachanda, who claims he was deposed in a concerted conspiracy by the Indian bureaucratic establishment. He repeatedly claimed that at a time when the seasoned Indian politicians who by instinct understood Nepali politicians and their native ways have been out of Delhi on the grueling campaign trail in the current parliamentary elections, the mandarins of the Indian bureaucratic establishment settled scores with him and his Maoist party. According to the Maoists, the Indian establishment has forced them out of power in a virtual coup by rallying disparate political elements and vested interests opposed to them in Kathmandu on various counts, including the Nepalese army and Nepal's deposed king.

The Indian establishment is not generally known for such neat planning or efficiency. But what matters is that in Nepali public perceptions, the allegation resonates. Any Indian diplomat who has served in India's neighborhood can tell that India carries the burden of a larger-than-life profile. There is a wealth of misconceptions among India's neighbors about its capacity to harm. The common perception is that India can be a ill-tempered, self-righteous bully. But the ungainly truth, as often happens, gingerly lies somewhere in the middle. True, India can probably muster a quick temper and may even be capable of doing mischief if its feathers are ruffled, but then, if its neighbors are clever enough, they can pay back in the same coin.

Take Sri Lanka. In the early 1980s, Delhi took a deliberate decision to start a quarrel with Sri Lanka's Western-oriented leadership in Colombo. Several complicated factors led to the quarrel, including vanities at the leadership level, but it overtly wore the look of a pale Indian variant of the Monroe Doctrine. Delhi wanted the unhelpful leadership in Colombo to be put in its place - like the Maoists in Kathmandu who showed the audacity to warm up to China's friendly overtures. Books have been written which graphically describe that Delhi fostered the Sri Lankan Tamil insurgent groups as an instrument of foreign policy to pressure the then Sri Lankan government under president J R Jayewardene.

If so, Delhi truly underestimated the tenacity of the Colombo political elite to hit back. The grit of small countries, which depend paramountly on their wits rather than muscle to safeguard their autonomy, is something too hard to believe. Before Delhi could count to ten, Jayewardene sought and won an Indian military intervention in Sri Lanka to put down the very same Tamil insurgency it thoughtfully fostered in the first instance. And, amazingly, in no time, Delhi agreed to do the unthinkable - dispatch an expedition to intervene in a neighbouring country's civil war. But Colombo soon made yet another neat somersault and the Indian military expedition in Sri Lanka found itself to be the common target of the Tamil insurgents and the Sri Lankan security forces alike. The result was that after the loss of a few thousand Indian soldiers and the assassination of a former Indian prime minister, Delhi wound up its expedition in Sri Lanka in shame and ignominy and sailed home. But the story didn't end there. The Colombo elite, having tasted blood, allowed Delhi a brief respite before working on its vanities again and getting the Indian elite on its side even as another bloody chapter of the civil war was unrolling. Some say the Indian establishment was not so dumb-witted as made out to be, but was probably on a brilliant Machiavellian act in assisting Colombo to vanquish the Tamil insurgent army. Time will tell. At any rate, if the Maoists are clever, they would do a Colombo act on Delhi. It seems they may do just that. They are reaching out to a political formation at the other end of Nepal's fragmented political spectrum comprising Nepalis of ethnic Indian origin who are commonly seen as Delhi's proxy on the Nepalese democratic chessboard - the Joint Madhesi Democratic Front (JMDF).

Quite possibly, the Maoists may have calculated that with their 230 members in an alliance with the 83 members of the JMDF, they can be a force in the 601-member parliament that can spike the incipient plans of a ganging-up by Nepal's status quo parties as a new non-Maoist coalition government. At the very least, the Maoists are seeking to avoid political isolation. But it could presage something more. The Maoists are evidently reaching out to Indian public opinion as well over the head of the Indian bureaucratic establishment. They are doing what the Colombo elite would have surely done in similar circumstances.

At the very minimum, one has to be truly moronic to miss the point that the Maoists want to play by the democratic rules; that they do not want to return to the jungles and become guerillas again; that they are pragmatic enough to cross ideological divides; and, quite probably, they want to be Delhi's favourites in the corridors of power in Kathmandu. So, what is the problem? The problem seems to lie in a five-letter word - China. The malaise bears a striking similarity with the early 1980s when the Jayewardene government in Colombo took to the free market with gusto, was favourably inclined to accede to the setting up of a Voice of America transmitter within earshot of India, was reportedly allowing in Israeli intelligence specialists, and was toying with the idea of leasing out Trincomalee's fine natural harbour and its vast "oil farm" built by imperial Britain during World war II as a naval base for the Americans.

The supreme irony is that today Delhi is not going to lose sleep over any of those daredevil things that Jayewardene likely contemplated. Today, a quarter century later, India has not only taken to the market, but the current government in Delhi, which is about to complete its term, subscribed to the Washington consensus even after the Americans began losing faith in it. The Israelis of course are all over India, with the visiting Israeli army chief taken to Kashmir last September on a counter-insurgency tour and Indian space scientists launching away Israeli "spy" satellites. India today not only desires a strong US naval presence in the Indian Ocean (as a "counterweight" to China) but aspires to be the US Navy's preferred partner. If Indians don't care to listen to Voice of America, it is merely because they have chosen to watch CNN.

Alas, the Indian strategic community's ire about the Nepalese Maoist dalliance with China is a replay of the xenophobia that was prevalent in Delhi in the early 1980s. True, China is taking an excessively high degree of interest in Nepal. But that isn't because Nepal's biggest political party subscribes to Maoism or because Beijing wants to add yet another "pearl" to its "string" around India, to borrow the famous words of a minor analyst working for the Pentagon which have become the hot favourite idiom among Indian strategic thinkers. The fact is that China is keen to plug the infiltration route of Tibetan militants who travel to and from India via Nepal. It is a crucial issue for Beijing. Unsurprisingly, China will go the extra mile to ensure there is a friendly government in Kathmandu that dissociates itself completely from the "low-intensity war" waged in Tibet by militants coming in from outside. Just as China pays enormous attention to its Central Asian neighbors to ensure that Uyghur militants from the outside world do not infiltrate the Xinjiang Autonomous Region.

Kyrgyzstan may have a population less than five million, but when a Kyrgyz dignitary comes calling, Beijing rolls out a red carpet as if US President Barack Obama had arrived. That shows an acute sense of national priorities, as a sizeable

Uyghur community lives in Kyrgyzstan. Therefore, it shouldn't come as a surprise that China has begun assiduously courting the democratic leadership in Nepal. Or, that the Maoist government began cooperating with China to clamp down on the activities of the Tibetan activists who operated out of Nepalese soil through the past half-century.

China will not be deterred from befriending Nepal on the crucial question of tranquility and stability in Tibet, no matter what it takes. The time is not far off before Beijing offers Nepal a berth in the Shanghai Cooperation Organization. Indeed, China has the political will and the financial capacity to offer to Nepal what Delhi could have offered through the past six decades and failed to do - staking a common future as partners in economic development and regional stability. China's reach is enormous today. It has just replaced the United States as Brazil's top trade partner. Countering the Chinese challenge in Nepal needs imagination, a coherent game plan and a sustained approach on India's part. Muscle-flexing is not the answer. Nor is diplomatic one-upmanship the answer or the pretensions by the right-wing Hindu nationalist outfits in India that Nepal is their sequestered pasture.

Antagonizing the Maoists will not be a smart thing to do, as they represent historical forces that are on the ascendance and they will be around as the dominant political force in Nepal, sure as the sun rises in the east. But there are pragmatic ways in which the Maoists could be made to view Delhi as their preferred partner. Arguably, the Maoists are themselves already intensely conscious that they cannot do without India's cooperation. Contrary to the Indian security establishment's earlier doomsday scenario, the Maoists are not messing around with the radical left movements professing to follow Mao Zedong's ideology which are active in something like 160 out of India's 600 districts. That shows a high degree of sensitivity to India's national-security concerns.

But what Delhi should scrupulously avoid is any interference in Nepal's internal affairs. Let the Nepalese settle their squabbles themselves over drawing up a new constitution and charting out their future. Leave it to the Nepalese political parties to carve out their space on the democratic arena. Political parties begin to die when they cease to be relevant. The forces, which Delhi might have favoured when Nepal was a "Hindu kingdom", may no more be capable of representing the people's aspirations. India cannot resurrect them. Let them die. Of course, it will be dangerous to encourage the Nepalese army to harbour Praetorian instincts, either. South Asia has had enough of armies.

India will always enjoy a huge advantage over China in cultivating Nepal - of history, geography, culture, ethnicity, economy and social bonds and kinship. Where India loses is that it cannot get its act together as a driving force for Nepal's emergence out of abject poverty. That is the leitmotif of China's challenge to India. The entire sub-Himalayan region will incrementally feel gravitation toward China as Tibet surges forward at its present level of economic transformation and Beijing shows a willingness to share the cake.

MAOISTS RHETORIC ON INDIA-NEPAL RELATIONS

India's External Affairs Minister SM Krishna will undertake a three-day official visit to Kathmandu from January 15, 2010. According to the Indian Embassy in Kathmandu, at least five memorandums of understanding will be signed during Krishna's visit. The possible MoUs include construction of a National Police Academy at Panauti in Kavre district, Indian assistance for the Nepal Stock Exchange, construction of roads in the Terai, establishment of a science learning centre and a solar electrification project. Krishna will also take up issues related to Indian security and counterfeit currency issues.

Though the visit is timely and significant, uncertainties over the future of the peace process continue due to differences between the political parties on contentious issues like federalism, rehabilitation of Maoist combatants, and the nature of Constitution. The UCPN-Maoist leader Prachanda has accused the ruling parties of being puppets of the Indian ruling class, accused the Indian establishment of intervening in Nepal's internal affairs and trying to derail the peace process. He also said that the UCPN-Maoist should hold direct talks with New Delhi since the ruling parties are guided by remote control and talks with them to establish civilian supremacy have been failing.

The Maoists have made elaborate arrangements to express displeasure during Krishna's visit. Recently, they declared the fourth phase of their nationwide agitation demanding restoration of civilian supremacy and formation of a Maoist-led national government. As part of the fourth round of protest programmes, senior party leaders will visit those locations along the open border with India where India has reportedly occupied Nepal's territories. The Maoists will organise mass rallies at several bordering regions 'encroached' by India and torch the copies of the various treaties with India. They will hold demonstrations outside the Indian Embassy and Singha Durbar on January 19.

Krishna's visit is taking place at a time when the Maoist sponsored anti-India feeling is at an all time high in Nepal. Maoists have been consistently branding the 1950 treaty as unequal, raising issues such as illegal encroachment and the recruitment of Nepalse Gurkhas into the Indian Army. But none of these demands are genuine and valid. The Maoists, in fact, do not want to resolve these issues since these give them huge political dividends to retain public support. Pushpa Kamal Dahal alias Prachanda, during his nine month tenure as prime minister, did not take any steps to withdraw from the 1950 treaty though clause 10 of the agreement cleanly mentions that the "Treaty shall remain in force until it is terminated by either party by giving one year's notice." The issue figured prominently during his visit to New Delhi in September 2008. On this occasion, Prachanda had agreed with India's Prime Minister to "review, adjust and update" the 1950 Treaty of Peace and Friendship and other agreements, while giving due recognition to the special features of the bilateral relationship. Why did Prachanda not use clause 10 of the treaty and agreed to review the same during his visit?

Regarding the Gurkha recruitment issue, Pracahnda preferred to remain tightlipped during his visit to India. On the eve of the visit, Deepak Bahadur Gurung, chairman of the Nepal Ex-Servicemen's Association, warned that his organisation would start a new 'People's War' if the Maoist government stopped the recruitment. Most importantly, Maoists' argument about Gurkaha recruitment being colonial is illogical because Gurkha Nepalese have been joining the Indian Army purely on a voluntary basis. This is not forced recruitment or conscription by the Indian Army.

Given the geographical dynamics in the border region, "encroachment" is more a natural phenomenon than man-made. Rivers flowing from Nepal to India frequently shift their course during the monsoons. As a result, certain portions of the border region either come to Nepal or to India depending on the shifting of the river course. Since farmers from both countries find that part of the land fertile, they encroach upon it for agricultural purposes. In fact, Prachanda during his last visit to India acknowledged the problem of inundation in the border areas and agreed to take up necessary work for its effective prevention on the basis of bilateral consultation. Both countries have already (unofficially) agreed that 98 per cent of the border is demarcated except two disputed areas in Kalapani and Susta. India's former external affairs minister Pranab Mukhrjee during his official visit to Kathmandu in November 2008 talked about it before the media. Interestingly, then the Maoist-led government in Kathmandu did not contradict his view on border demarcation. The issue rose to prominence again only after Prachanda's resignation. The Maoists have accused encroachment of Nepalese territory by Indian security forces in the Dang district.

The problem is not only with the Maoists. India has consistently given space to the Maoists to take advantage of the faultlines in India-Nepal relations. Till date, India has hardly clarified its stand on these controversial bilateral issues in a public forum. All discussions have taken place only at the official level, which have been tampered with and then highlighted by the pro-Maoist or Royalist Nepalese media. One such faultline is the absence of high-level political engagements from the Indian side while Nepal is passing through political turbulence. In the last 13 years, seven Prime Ministers of Nepal have visited India in return for one Prime Ministerial visit from India to Nepal. Prime Minister I. K. Gujaral visited Kathmandu in June 1997. The political imbalance in the relationship has been gradually eroding India's traditional leverages in Nepal. If the vacuum continues, other countries including China may consolidate in near future. Another major faultline is unnecessary statements from various agencies of India about internal developments in Nepal. Third, India has a very good relationship with many leaders of Nepal cutting across party lines. But it is yet to introduce a comprehensive policy towards Nepal.

India's options in Nepal

1. Stability in Nepal is extremely important for India. It has to acknowledge that the present political stalemate is an internal matter of Nepal and encourage the stakeholders to hammer out their differences. India should strike a neutral stance and play the role of an honest negotiator to bring the various factions together.
2. Existing controversial treaties, border disputes, encroachment issues and the Indian Embassy's alleged support to certain groups in the Terai region and personal level support to Nepali Congress leaders are major irritants in India-Nepal relations. These issues have been generating huge anti-India feelings and thus need immediate attention. This will help prevent the growing Chinese role in Nepal. India needs to come out with a clear policy on these issues and express positive views to resolve them.
3. India should focus more on socio-economic and development programmes. India's assistance to Nepal should be enhanced and directed towards projects which benefit the Nepalese people directly.
4. Hydro-projects and dams situated on the Indo-Nepal border should be maintained and managed by the Union Government under the Ministry of External affairs.
5. Border crossing should be mechanized. People crossing the border should be treated with dignity.
6. India should realize that the monarchy is gone for ever although the pro-monarchy sentiment remains. India needs to acknowledge the emergence of new forces in Nepal and learn to deal with them.
7. India should enhance and upgrade co-operation with Nepalese agencies to patrol and manage the border.

Anti-India feeling is a permanent phenomenon in India's neighbourhood including in Nepal. India should not deterred by these activities. This visit is a golden opportunity for India to reactivate its relationship and reassure both the ruling and opposition parties about India's positive contribution to the peace process. During the visit, India should come out with some official statements that India is interested more in people to people relations and the prosperity of Nepal. If possible, India should seriously engage and talk to the Maoists. They may have their own ideology which may not be comfortable to India. But there is no harm in talking to them and learn about their concerns. Similarly, India should make its concerns in Nepal clear to the Maoists. It should clarify through actions and declare that India has no intention to interfere in Nepal, that it respects Nepal's sovereignty and that it is ready to work with any dispensation in Nepal for furthering mutual security and economic concerns.

2

Philosophy of Maoism

Maoism or Mao Zedong Thought, is a variant of Marxism-Leninism derived from the teachings of the Chinese communist Mao Zedong. It should be noted that the word Maoism has never been used by the Communist Party of China in its English-language publications, except pejoratively. The term Mao Tse-tung Thought has always been the preferred term. Likewise, Maoist groups outside China have usually called themselves Marxist-Leninist rather than Maoist, a reflection of Mao's view that he did not change, but only developed, Marxism-Leninism. However, some Maoist groups, believing Mao's theories to have been sufficiently substantial additions to the basics of the Marxist canon, call themselves "Marxist-Leninist-Maoist" (MLM) or simply "Maoist." The Maoist Internationalist Movement is an example of this usage.

In the People's Republic of China Mao Tse-Tung Thought is part of the official doctrine of the Communist Party of China, but since the 1978 beginning of Deng Xiaoping's market economy-oriented reforms, the concept of "socialism with Chinese characteristics" has come to the forefront of Chinese politics, Chinese economic reform has taken hold, and the official definition and role of Mao's original ideology in the PRC has been radically altered and reduced. Outside the PRC, the term Maoism was used from the 1960s onwards, usually in a hostile sense, to describe parties or individuals who supported Mao Zedong and his form of communism, which was in staunch opposition to the communism practiced in the Soviet Union. Since the death of Mao and the reforms of Deng, most of the parties explicitly defining themselves as "Maoist" around the world have disappeared, but various communist groups, particularly armed ones like the Communist Party of Nepal (Maoist) and the New People's Army of the Philippines, continue to advance Maoist ideas and get press attention for them. These groups generally have the idea that Mao's ideas were betrayed before they could be fully or properly implemented. Since Mao was an ardent supporter of the brand of socialism advanced in the Soviet Union before the rise of Nikita Khruschev, it is usually accepted that Maoists follow an anti-revisionist rather than a "Reform Communist" political line.

MAOIST THEORY

Unlike the earlier forms of Marxism-Leninism in which the urban proletariat was seen as the main source of revolution, and the countryside was largely ignored, Mao focused on the peasantry as a revolutionary force which, he said, could be mobilized by a Communist Party with their knowledge and leadership. The model for this was of course the Chinese Communist rural insurgency of the 1920s and 1930s, which eventually brought the Communist Party of China to power. Furthermore, unlike other forms of Marxism-Leninism in which large-scale industrial development was seen as a positive force, Maoism made all-round rural development the priority. Mao felt that this strategy made sense during the early stages of socialism in a country in which most of the people were peasants. Unlike most other political ideologies, including other socialist and Marxist ones, Maoism contains an integral military doctrine and explicitly connects its political ideology with military strategy. In Maoist thought, "political power comes from the barrel of the gun" (one of Mao's quotes), and the peasantry can be mobilized to undertake a "people's war" of armed struggle involving guerrilla warfare in three stages.

The first stage involves mobilizing and organizing the peasantry. The second stage involves setting up rural base areas and increasing coordination among the guerrilla organizations. The third stage involves a transition to conventional warfare. Maoist military doctrine likens guerrilla fighters to fish swimming in a sea of peasants, who provide logistical support. Maoism emphasizes "revolutionary mass mobilization" (physically mobilizing the vast majority of a population in the struggle for socialism), the concept of New Democracy, and the Theory of Productive Forces as applied to village-level industries independent of the outside world. In Maoism, deliberate organizing of massive military and economic power is necessary to defend the revolutionary area from outside threat, while centralization keeps corruption under supervision, amid strong control, and sometimes alteration, by the revolutionaries of the area's arts and sciences.

A key concept that distinguishes Maoism from other left-wing ideologies is the belief that the class struggle continues throughout the entire socialist period, as a result of the fundamental antagonistic contradiction between capitalism and communism. Even when the proletariat has seized state power through a socialist revolution, the potential remains for a bourgeoisie to restore capitalism. Indeed, Mao famously stated that "the bourgeoisie [in a socialist country] is right inside the Communist Party itself", implying that corrupt Party officials would subvert socialism if not prevented. This was the main reason for the Great Proletarian Cultural Revolution, in which Mao exhorted the public to "Bombard the [Party] headquarters!" and wrest control of the government from bureaucrats (such as Liu Shaoqi and Deng Xiao Ping) perceived to be on the capitalist road.

Mao's doctrine is best summarized in the Little Red Book of Mao Zedong, which was distributed to everyone in China as the basis of revolutionary education. This book consists of quotations from the earliest days of the revolution to the mid-1960s, just before the beginning of the Cultural Revolution.

MAOISM IN CHINA

Since the death of Mao Zedong in 1976, and the reforms of Deng Xiaoping starting in 1978, the role of Mao's ideology within the PRC has radically changed. Although Mao Zedong Thought nominally remains the state ideology, Deng's admonition to seek truth from facts means that state policies are judged on their practical consequences and the role of ideology in determining policy has been considerably reduced. Deng also separated Mao from Maoism, making it clear that Mao was fallible and hence that the truth of Maoism comes from observing social consequences rather than by using Mao's quotations as holy writ, as was done in Mao's lifetime.

In addition, the party constitution has been rewritten to give the pragmatic ideas of Deng Xiaoping as much prominence as those of Mao. One consequence of this is that groups outside China which describe themselves as Maoist generally regard China as having repudiated Maoism and restored capitalism, and there is a wide perception both in and out of China that China has abandoned Maoism. However, while it is now permissible to question particular actions of Mao and to talk about excesses taken in the name of Maoism, there is a prohibition in China on either publicly questioning the validity of Maoism or questioning whether the current actions of the Communist Party of China are "Maoist." Although Mao Zedong Thought is still listed as one of the four cardinal principles of the People's Republic of China, its historical role has been re-assessed. The Communist Party now says that Maoism was necessary to break China free from its feudal past, but that the actions of Mao are seen to have led to excesses during the Cultural Revolution. The official view is that China has now reached an economic and political stage, known as the primary stage of socialism, in which China faces new and different problems completely unforeseen by Mao, and as such the solutions that Mao advocated are no longer relevant to China's current conditions.

Both Maoist critics outside China and most Western commentators see this re-working of the definition of Maoism as providing an ideological justification for what they see as the restoration of the essentials of capitalism in China by Deng and his successors. Mao himself is officially regarded by the Chinese communist party as a "great revolutionary leader" for his role in fighting the Japanese and creating the People's Republic of China, but Maoism as implemented between 1959 and 1976 is regarded by today's Communist Party of China as an economic and political disaster. In Deng's day, support of radical Maoism was regarded as a form of "left deviationism" and being based on a cult of personality, although these 'errors' are officially attributed to the Gang of Four rather than to Mao himself.

Although these ideological categories and disputes are less relevant at the start of the 21st century, these distinctions were very important in the early 1980s, when the Chinese government was faced with the dilemma of how to allow economic reform to proceed without destroying its own legitimacy, and many argue that Deng's success in starting Chinese economic reform was in large part due to his being able to justify those reforms within a Maoist framework.

Some historians today regard Maoism as an ideology devised by Mao as a pretext for his own quest for power. The official view of the Chinese government was that Mao did not create Maoism to gain power, but that in his later years, Mao or those around him were able to use Maoism to create a cult of personality.

Both the official view of the Communist Party of China and much public opinion within China regards the latter period of Mao's rule as having been a disaster for their country. The various estimates of the number of deaths attributable to Mao's policies that have been offered remain highly controversial. For more discussion of this period, see the article Cultural Revolution. There is also a strain of Chinese Neo-Leftism in the country that seeks to return China to the days after Mao but before Deng; for more on that current's beliefs, see its article. Some Western scholars argue that China's rapid industrialization and relatively quick recovery from the brutal period of civil wars 1911-1949 was a positive impact of Maoism, and contrast its development specifically to that of Southeast Asia, Russia and India.

MAOISM INTERNATIONALLY

From 1962 onwards the challenge to the Soviet hegemony in the World Communist Movement made by the Chinese Communist Party resulted in various divisions in communist parties around the world. At an early stage, the Albanian Party of Labour sided with CPC. So did many of the mainstream (non-splinter group) communist parties in South-East Asia, like the Burmese Communist Party, Communist Party of Thailand, and Communist Party of Indonesia. Some Asian parties, like the Communist Party of Vietnam and the Workers Party of Korea attempted to take a middle-ground position.

In the west and south, a plethora of parties and organizations were formed that upheld links to the CPC. Often they took names such as Communist Party (Marxist-Leninist) or Revolutionary Communist Party to distinguish themselves from the traditional pro-Soviet communist parties. The pro-CPC movements were, in many cases, based amongst the wave of student radicalism that engulfed the world in the 1960s and 1970s.

Only one Western classic communist party sided with CPC, the Communist Party of New Zealand. Under the leadership of CPC and Mao Zedong, a parallel international communist movement emerged to rival that of the Soviets, although it was never as formalized and homogeneous as the pro-Soviet tendency.

After the death of Mao in 1976 and various power-struggles in China that followed, the international Maoist movement was, in rough terms, divided into three. One portion supported — although not necessarily with great enthusiasm — the new Chinese leadership under Deng Xiaoping. Another portion denounced the new leadership as traitors to the cause of Marxism-Leninism Mao Zedong Thought. A third portion sided with the Albanians in denouncing the Three Worlds Theory of the CPC. The pro-Albanian category would effectively start to function as an international tendency of its own, led by Enver Hoxha and the APL. That tendency was able to amalgate most of the groups in Latin America, such as the Communist Party of Brazil. The first category was extremely heterogenous.

The new Chinese leadership had little interest in the various foreign factions supporting Mao's China, and the movement fell into disarray. Many of the parties that had been fraternal parties of the Chinese government before 1975 either disbanded, abandoned the Chinese entirely, or even denounced Marxism-Leninism and developed into non-communist, social democratic parties. What is today sometimes referred to as the "international Maoist movement" evolved out of the second category- the parties that opposed Deng and claimed to uphold the legacy of Mao.

During the 1980s two parallel regroupment efforts emerged, one centered around the Communist Party of the Philippines, which gave birth to the ICMLPO, and one that birthed the Revolutionary Internationalist Movement, which the Shining Path communist guerrilla group and the Revolutionary Communist Party USA played a leading role in forming.

Both the International Conference and the RIM tendencies claimed to uphold Marxism-Leninism-Mao Zedong Thought, although RIM was later to substitute that ideology with what they termed 'Marxism-Leninism-Maoism'.

Today the Maoist organizations grouped in RIM have their strongest hold in South Asia, and are at the forefront of the armed struggles taking place in Nepal, India and Bangladesh. There are also lesser struggles going on in Peru and Turkey. In the Philippines, the Communist Party of the Philippines, which is not part of the RIM, leads an armed struggle through its military wing, the New People's Army. The largest Maoist group in the USA is the RIM-affiliated Revolutionary Communist Party, USA. In Germany the ICMLPO-affiliated MLPD is the largest Maoist group in the country.

MILITARY STRATEGY

The military aspects of Maoist theory have garnered much more universal respect than his political or economic ideas. Mao is widely regarded as a brilliant military strategist even among those who oppose his other ideas. His writings on guerrilla warfare and the notion of people's war are now generally considered to be essential reading, both for those who wish to conduct guerrilla operations and for those who wish to oppose them.

As with his economic and political ideas, Maoist military ideas seem to have more relevance at the start of the 21st century outside of the People's Republic of China than within it. There is a consensus both within and outside the PRC that the military context that the PRC faces in the early 21st century are very different from the one faced by China in the 1930s.

As a result, within the People's Liberation Army there has been extensive debate over whether and how to relate Mao's military doctrines to 21st-century military ideas, especially the idea of a revolution in military affairs.

MAOISM AND THE CHINESE REVOLUTION

The history of the CCP as the leadership of a peasant based and largely guerrilla army began with the historic defeats of the Chinese proletariat in the years 1926-30. The CCP had entered the Nationalist Party, the Kuomintang (KMT) in a subordinate role in 1923-24 having been under pressure to do so from representatives of the Communist International (CI) since 1922.

On 20 March 1926 Chiang Kai-shek led a coup d'Ètat in Canton, at that time the centre of CCP influence. Through the coup Chiang, with communist compliance, disarmed the workers' militia controlled by the CCP-led Hong Kong-Canton General Strike Committee. He also forced the CCP to relinquish its posts in the government and KMT administrations. In March 1927, Chiang's troops entered Shanghai, after the workers had seized the city. Again Chiang disarmed the workers and again the CCP called for acceptance of this measure. On 12 April Chiang's troops aided by the underworld gangs of Shanghai, unleashed a pogrom against the workers' districts in which thousands were killed.

Under CI instructions, the CCP launched a series of insurrections. Each of these, at Changsha, Nanchang, Canton and Haifeng was put down by Chiang's troops with great loss of life amongst the CCP and the workers. The CCP responded to these defeats by withdrawing the remnants of its forces to the isolated and mountainous Chinese interior. The changed material circumstances of the communist forces after they had fled from the towns, together with the disastrous consequences of attempted urban insurrections (e.g. Changsha 1930), were the material basis for the development of that variant of Stalinist class collaboration identified with Mao Zedong.

The Maoist current, initially centred on the Front Committee in the Soviet Base Area in the Jing Gang Mountains and opposed to the Shanghai based Central Committee, rationalised the rural and distinctly non-proletarian base of the CCP. They developed a strategy for fighting the imperialists and "compradors" that centred on the mobilisation of the peasantry, rather than the proletariat, within the framework of the Stalinist policy of the bloc of four classes.

From November 1930, Chiang led a series of five extermination campaigns against the communist-held Soviet Base Areas. The first four of these failed signally but the fifth, with the assistance of German advisers such as Von Seeckt (later Nazi commander of Belgium) and a force of a million well armed men, forced the CCP to leave the Jiangxi Soviet and undertake the perilous Long March.

This 8,000 mile trek across some of the worst terrain in China under almost daily attack, in which 70,000 of the original 100,000 communist troops were lost, brought the remaining 30,000 to the future Maoist stronghold of Yenan in North West China. After the confused and demoralising first stage of the Long March the Maoist current gained control of the Party from the clique around Stalin's protege Wang Ming at the Zunyi Conference of January 1935.

The establishment of the Maoist forces in the already existing Yenan Base Area marked the consolidation of the hold of the Maoists within a continuing period of territorial dual power in China that constantly threatened to develop into civil war and which lasted until 1949. Although land reform and other much needed reforms were carried out in the Base Areas in the early 1930s and later in Yenan, private property as such was protected. This was an essential element in the Maoist strategy and conception of the Chinese Revolution: "the spearhead of the revolution will still be directed at imperialism and feudalism, rather than at capitalism and capitalist private property in general. That being so, the character of the Chinese Revolution at the present stage is not proletarian-socialist but bourgeois democratic."

This commitment to a "stagist" conception of the revolution, the first stage being purely "bourgeois-democratic", defined the CCP's relations with the KMT and the Chinese bourgeoisie.

Following the policies pioneered by Stalin and Bukharin in the mid-1920s, the CCP viewed the bourgeoisie as a fundamentally revolutionary class, which was committed to a struggle against imperialism. It would therefore make an important component of a long term political alliance involving the proletariat, peasantry and petit-bourgeoisie athe "bloc of four classes" which were welded together by their common hostility to imperialism. However as sections of the bourgeoisie were clearly colluding with the imperialists, it was necessary to distinguish between "good" national sectors of the bourgeoisie and "bad" comprador or bureaucratic sectors. Which of these sectors a bourgeois grouping or party belonged to depended largely on whether it was willing to enter into an alliance with the CCP.

Trotsky attacked this notion of the revolutionary nature of the bourgeoisie in imperialised countries in his polemics on the Chinese question. He pointed out that the bourgeoisie of an imperialised country might well enter into a struggle with the imperialists in defence of its own interests, in order to "deepen and broaden its possibilities for exploitation", but such actions would be sporadic and aimed at compromise.

The willingness of the bourgeoisie to enter such a struggle depended on the degree of threat to its power posed by the proletarian and peasant mobilisations necessary to confront the imperialists. Without the masses behind it this bourgeoisie had no chance of defeating imperialism. With the masses aroused its very power was threatened, inevitably leading it to go scuttling back into the arms of imperialism.

It was this understanding of the cowardly and feeble nature of the bourgeoisie of the imperialised countries that led the still revolutionary Comintern to develop the Anti-Imperialist United Front, not as a long term, general agreement with the bourgeoisie, but as a series of episodic, practical agreements with definite aims. Agreements entered into which did not for one moment mean abandoning the independent position and programme of the communists the overthrow of capitalism and the expropriation of the bourgeoisie.

In contrast for the CCP, (as for all the Stalinist parties in the imperialised world) the "united front", the bloc of four classes, meant precisely abandoning, "for the time being", the communist programme in order to woo the bourgeoisie into an alliance. It meant holding back the peasantry from pursuing too radical reforms and explicitly committing the CCP to defend capitalism, to limit its fight to the goal of a bourgeois democratic phase. This of course was not a united front but a popular front, an alliance which subordinated the independent demands of the workers and peasants, and the programme of socialist revolution, to an alliance with the bourgeoisie on its programme. That this alliance was not completely fulfilled in China was not the fault of the CCP, which conscientiously carried out its side of the bargain, but because of the hostility and treachery of the KMT.

In September 1931, the Japanese began an invasion of Manchuria from bases established in the 1920s. On 9 March Pu Vi, the last Chinese Emperor and himself a Manchu, was installed as the Japanese puppet in "Manchuguo". During the following five years repeated incursions and raids into North China signalled Japan's intentions but Chiang refused to send his troops to the defence of North China, preferring to maintain his blockade of the CCP held areas. This antagonised many nationalists in China. The long expected full-scale invasion of China by Japanese imperialism in 1937 provided ample proof of the continuing Stalinist nature of the Maoist CCP.

As in the 1920s the CCP strategy was to subordinate everything to the formation of an alliance with Chiang Kai-Shek and the KMT. To this end the CCP dropped all the radical elements of its programme, including land reform, renounced the class struggle against the KMT, accepted the dissolution of its armies into the Nationalist Army and recognised the leadership of the KMT in general and Chiang in particular.

In the original version, later withdrawn, of Mao's report to the sixth plenum of the Central Committee, he wrote: "Without the KMT it would be inconceivable to undertake and pursue the war of resistance. In the course of its glorious history, the KMT has been responsible for the overthrow of the Oing (Ch'ing Dynasty-Eds), the establishment of the Republic, opposition to Yuan Shih-kai, establishment of the three policies of uniting with Russia, the communist party and with the workers and peasants, and the great revolution of 1926-27. Today it is once more leading the great anti-Japanese war. It has had two great leaders in succession. Mr Sun Yat-sen and Mr. Chiang Kai-shek."

So important was Chiang in the CCP's schema that, in Xian in December 1936 they saved him from execution by his own troops who were enraged by his refusal to move against the Mongolian allies of the Japanese and his attempt to send them into battle against the CCP. In exchange for acceptance by Chiang of the self-effacing "united front" of the CCP, Zhou Enlai secured his release.

THE POPULAR FRONT AGAINST JAPAN

The Second United Front between the CCP and the KMT was used by Chiang in precisely the same way as the first, to prepare his forces for an attack on the CCP and the workers and peasants of China. Once again the CCP maintained the alliance and kept quiet about Chiang's "excesses". In Spring 1939, for example, Chiang attacked the CCP bases in Hunan, Hubei and Hebei. In early 1941, the new Fourth Army (a renamed communist unit) attacked and defeated the Japanese in Anhui, thereby allowing access to the lower reaches of the Yangzi, China's largest river system. Chiang, commander in chief of all forces, ordered them to retreat through enemy held territory and, when they nonetheless managed to return to their base, attacked with his own forces killing several leading commanders and cadre. Despite its policy toward the KMT the CCP did wage a determined and increasingly effective war against Japanese imperialism. By the end of the war the Party and its forces controlled nineteen regions of China, led an army of three million regular and militia troops drawing support from a population of some 100 million in a total area of 950,000 square miles an area approximately twice the size of France.

Although the CCP opposed land redistribution in its areas during the Second United Front, its policies of reducing rents and interest rates, of establishing a new, efficient and honest local administration, of strengthening traditional forms of seasonal cooperation in agriculture into mutual aid teams throughout the year, of basing its anti-Japanese militia on these teams and of elected local government, won the support of the vast majority of the population in these areas.

Communist control of these elected bodies was ensured by the "three-thirds" system whereby one-third of the elected had to be party members, one-third supporters and the remaining third, "middle of the roaders". By comparison with the KMT-held areas where punitive taxation went alongside blatant corruption and even collaboration with the enemy, the "liberated zones" were a shining example of the "New China" and attracted considerable numbers of youth and intellectuals to the communist ranks. With the surrender of the Japanese in August 1945 the CCP continued to pursue its aim of an alliance with the bourgeoisie.

Now, with the defeat of the Japanese, this meant the priority was to establish a Popular Front Government. All efforts were bent to establish a stable coalition with the KMT, with the Americans acting as mediators. The CCP launched its political offensive under slogans calling for internal peace and national reconstruction. By October 1945 the Chongqing Negotiations had achieved an agreement. The CCP would withdraw from eight liberated zones in the south and reduce its army to twenty divisions (a tenth of its strength). In return it was agreed that a Political Consultative Conference would be convened, which would be open to the Communists and centre parties e.g. the Democratic League.

This policy was fully endorsed and encouraged by the USSR which was firmly convinced of the need for the Chinese to make virtually any compromise to achieve a coalition with the KMT. At the end of the war the Government had immediately signed a friendship treaty with the KMT. A delegation of CCP leaders who went to the USSR at the end of the war were told in no uncertain terms by Stalin what was expected of them, as he later recounted to Dimitrov: "after the war we invited the Chinese comrades to come to Moscow and we discussed the situation in China. We told them bluntly that we considered the development of an uprising in China had no prospects, that the Chinese comrades should seek a modus vivendi with Chiang Kai Shek, that they should join the Chiang Kai Shek government and dissolve their army."

Stalin even complained, when the CCP was forced by KMT attacks to take up arms, that they had not followed his instructions. But in 1948 when the conversation with Dimitrov took place and the communists were clearly winning the civil war he could ruefully admit: "Now in the case of China we admit we were wrong." Again it was the KMT, with American connivance, which reneged on the agreements. The Japanese were ordered in August to surrender only to the KMT and to "keep order" until KMT forces arrived. In Autumn 1945 shortly after the Political Consultative Conference met, Chiang reissued his 1933 Manual on the Suppression of Communist Bandits and launched offensives against several communist bases.

Political repression continued, student meetings were broken up, Democratic League offices were raided, Communists newspaper offices were destroyed. In March 1946 the KMT central committee disavowed the Consultative Conference resolutions which called for a democratic constitution and the convening of a national assembly. Despite this the CCP clung to its policy of alliance until the summer of 1946 when the KMT started moving its troops into Manchuria, in clear violation of the agreements, as Russian forces withdrew.

After the failure in June 1946 for a joint commission including American representatives, when the KMT demanded the CCP hand over all the areas it controlled first, the CCP was subject to an all-out attack by Chiang's forces. The Americans stepped up their aid to the KMT considerably. After the war, in what the American supremo, Wedemeyer, called "the greatest air and sea transportation in history" the US transported 540,000 KMT troops into formerly Japanese held territory. In addition all the supplies and munitions of the 1.2 million strong Japanese army were handed over to Chiang. On top of this 56,000 US marines joined the KMT armies as advisors. Between 1945 and 1948, the US gave Chiang some three billion dollars in direct cash aid.

With this support Chiang's armies rapidly gained control of former Soviet Areas, even including their capital, Venan, as the CCP withdrew before them. This policy of retreat did allow the CCP to avoid great losses and to regroup in Northern China. Despite US warnings of the consequences, Chiang followed the retreating communist forces, thereby severely over-stretching his lines of supply and communication. In preparation for what would be the final offensive of the civil war, the CCP now reintroduced land reform which had been held back during the agreements with the KMT. Although the expropriation of the landlords was most extensive in the communist held North, it was not confined to this area, and was not, even in the North entirely under Communist control.

In June 1947, the CCP led People's Liberation Army (PLA) now reinforced with new recruits and the Japanese armaments seized by the armies of the Soviet Union when they entered Manchuria in 1945, abandoned guerrilla warfare and began to advance southwards. By this time disaffection had penetrated into the KMT itself. A number of prominent generals, such as Li Jishen had left the KMT and fled to Hong Kong, there to establish the Revolutionary Committee of the KMT on a programme of coalition with the CCP to oust Chiang and the establishment of a republic based on a mixed economy.

Indeed, General George Marshall, the US special envoy, expressed the opinion that, No amount of military or economic aid could make the present Chinese Government capable of re-establishing and then maintaining its control over China. Demonstrations and strikes swept all of Nationalist China at this time. In Shanghai, a virtual general strike raged as workers fought to maintain a sliding scale of wages to protect them from hyperinflation. The price index that had been 100 in 1937 rose to the staggering level of 10,300,000 by mid-1947 and was to continue upwards until it reached 287 million before the final victory of the CCP/PLA in 1949.

KMT repression kept pace with the escalating militancy and inflation: "Suspected communists and others believed to be conspiring against the state were dragged before drum head courts and then out to some public place to be shot through the back of the head. Scenes of this kind were a daily occurrence in Shanghai, the busiest street corners being invariably chosen for the execution of the victims, who were nearly all young men."

At the same time the corruption of the Four Great Families (the Soong, Kung, Chen and Chiang families owned a large proportion of modern industry in China) became ever more blatant. In October 1947, one of Chiang's principal economic advisers (and brother-in-law) T. V. Soong, bought the governorship of Canton Province with a donation of ten million dollars to the KMT (of which, of course, he was a leading member). A resolution passed by the National Federation of Chamber of Commerce in November 1948 summed up the feelings of those capitalists who were excluded from the inner circle of the KMT: ... our people have lost confidence in our government leaders who are only interested in their personal gain at the expense of public welfare. We businessmen stand firm and united in fighting against corruption and despotism."

In a clear attempt to win over the petty bourgeoisie of the cities and to hold back the tide of peasant revolt, the CCP reversed its policy on expropriation of the landlords. In a report to the Central Committee in December 1947, Mao criticised the land reform already taking place as, "Ultra left and adventurist." In February and May 1948, further directives were issued which called for greater moderation in the newly conquered areas of central China. The movement for land reform was stopped entirely when the CCP/PLA took control of Southern China where the landlords were, traditionally, verly closely connected to the urban bourgeoisie.

On 1 May 1948, the Central Committee of the CCP formally called upon all anti-Chiang parties to take part in a new Political Consultative Conference at which the form of a future coalition government could be discussed and decided upon. The call was primarily aimed at the Revolutionary Committee of the KMT and the Democratic League. Both these parties accepted the invitation and preliminary work began. An agreement was signed in November 1948 which provided for a preparatory committee to be established prior to the convening of a national conference.

THE CHINESE DEGENERATE WORKERS' STATE

By Spring 1949, the PLA had reconquered China North of the Yangzi river. After the collapse of the KMT armies in Manchuria in late 1948, most KMT-held territory and towns were surrendered without any fighting. Fu Tso-yi, for example, surrendered Peking in January 1949 as soon as the PLA advanced towards the city, indeed, he joined them in the march South.

In April 1949, after the expiry of a last deadline for Nationalist surrender, the PLA crossed the Yangzi and entered South China. They met little resistance and disarmed some two million KMT troops in a period of six months. In September, the Political Consultative Conference met in Peking and established a central government headed by Mao Zedong, leader of the CCP, Zhu De, a principal commander of the PLA, Soong Ching-ling (the widow of Sun Yat-sen and sister in law of Chiang Kai-shek), Li Jishen, leader of the Revolutionary Committee of the KMT (and the butcher of the Canton Commune in 1927) and Zhang Lan, President of the Democratic League.

The CCP had achieved its aim of establishing a popular front coalition government. Mao Zedong had outlined the policy that such a government would follow in 1945: "The task of our New Democratic system is to promote the free development of a private capitalist economy that benefits instead of controlling the peoples' livelihood, and to protect all honestly acquired private property."

This was the policy which was followed between 1949 and 1952, which meant both defending capitalism and containing and if necessary repressing the demands of the workers and peasants. When in 1952 the CCP decisively struck out at the bourgeoisie, expropriating their property, it was a moment not of the CCP's choosin. It was a vital defensive measure forced on the Stalinists by the onslaught of US imperialism. As Mao was to declare in 1957 "socialism": "came to our country too suddenly."

The economic life of China at the time of the accession to power of this government was only one step away from complete paralysis. The collapse of the central administration, soaring inflation and the displacement of millions of people from the areas of military operations were accompanied by floods and droughts that affected 20 million acres and threatened 40 million people with starvation. Coal production stood at 50 per cent of its previous highest point, iron and steel were down by 80 per cent, cotton goods down by 25 per cent, grain 25 per cent, raw cotton 48 per cent and livestock 16 per cent.

To make matters yet worse the railway network was out of operation with 50 per cent of the track destroyed and most of the maritime fleet was in Hong Kong, Taiwan or Singapore. The first priority of the People's Government was expressed in the Common Programme of October 1949: "A policy that is concerned with private and public interests, that benefits the bosses and the workers, that encourages mutual aid between our country and foreign countries in order to develop production and bring prosperity to the economy."

In other words, the existing framework of capitalist property relations was to be maintained. The policy of tolerance and encouragement extended to the "national" capitalists was not extended to the "bureaucratic" capitalists. Their possessions were immediately nationalised, giving the state control of nearly one-third of all industrial production.

While the state had majority holdings in heavy industry (70 per cent of coal, 90 per cent of steel and 78 per cent of electricity) heavy industry was historically chronically underdeveloped in relation to light industry, much of which was often dependent on imported materials. It was in light industry that the "national" capitalists now dominated along with the distribution and transport networks. This group owned two-thirds of all industrial capital in 1949.

The modern sector of the economy was, however, a small percentage of the economy as a whole. In 1945 it had been calculated at between 10 and 15 per cent. Largely because of its years of control in the "liberated zones" the CCP/PLA already had within it a relative experienced administrative cadre. However, with the partial exception of those who had been in Manchuria this cadre lacked experience of urban and industrial administration. This lack was partly made up by the entry into the CCP of ex-officials of the KMT regime and educated elements of the middle classes in the cities. At the time of liberation, a sample of 6,000 cadres had the following composition: 2,500 middle class, 1,150 ex-KMT officials, 400 liberal professionals, 150 members of the privileged classes, 140 from the working class. Workers made up a mere 2 per cent of party members in 1949.27 With a membership of this sort it was possible for the CCP-dominated government to take state capitalist economic measures such as nationalisation and statification, primarily aimed at the universally hated "bureaucratic" capitalists, so long as this remained within the general framework of capitalist property relations.

In March 1949, the state formed six major trading corporations for the distribution and procurement of Food, Textiles, Salt, Coal, Construction materials and "miscellaneous" goods. In addition, a network of state owned retail outlets was established. These two measures, coupled with the introduction of a new currency, a sliding-scale of wages linked to the monetary value of essential foods, an enforced loan at 5 per cent interest from capitalists and the state distribution of goods that had been hoarded by the KMT and its supporters, allowed a rapid improvement in the living conditions of the masses and brought inflation under control. By mid-1951 it was down to 20 per cent and prices were essentially stable in 1952.

That, despite this statification of essentials, the popular front government was anxious not to scare the "national" bourgeoisie into fleeing, can be seen from the assurances given them by Chen Yun the Chairman of the Financial and Economic Commission, in August 1950, "... industrial investments undertaken for a long time by the national capitalists, if they remain progressive in character, will be useful to the state and the people." The Agrarian Reform of June 1950 shows the same clear intention of maintaining friendly relations with the capitalists in order to maintain production. Article 4, dealing with whose lands could or could not be expropriated, said:

"Industry and commerce shall be protected from infringement, industrial and commercial enterprises operated by landlords, and the land and other properties used by the landlords directly for the operation of industrial and commercial enterprises, shall not be confiscated."

The new land reform was only applicable in the south where, as we have noted, the ties between landlords and the urban bourgeoisie were stronger than in the north. In addition to the strictures on landlords' lands, it was also expressly forbidden to confiscate all the "surplus" lands of the wealthiest peasants and that of the "richer middle peasants" was to be left alone entirely. Mao explained why at the third session of the Central Committee, 6 June 1950: "... our policy towards the rich peasants ought to be changed. Their excess land must no longer be confiscated, but their life must be preserved to speed up the restoration of production in rural areas."

Despite these limitations imposed by the state, the land reform did involve a massive transfer of land in South China, some 7 million acres out of a Chinese total of 17 million. On average all individuals over sixteen held one-third of an acre after the reform. As in the country generally, so in the cities the chief priority of the new government was to re-establish order Far from utilising the entry of the Liberation Army to ensure a proletarian takeover of the towns and industrial plant, Un Biao, commander of the Fourth Army, issued the following proclamation in January 1949:

"The people are asked to maintain order and to continue their present occupations. KMT officials or police personnel of provincial, city, county or other level of governmental unit district, town, village, or Bao Jia personnel are enjoined to stay at their posts".

In addition, whilst granting statutory rights to workers' organisations the People's Government showed in its Labour Law of 1950 that its interest lay solely in regularising the labour-capital relationship, not in abolishing it. With regard to disputes, for example, it laid down the following procedures: "the first step in procedure for settling labour disputes shall be consultation between the parties the second step shall be mediation between the parties by the Labour Bureau [a state department-Eds] and the third step shall be arbitration by the arbitration committee established by the Labour Bureau."

The nature of the unions set up by the government, and modelled on those of the Soviet Union, can be judged from the fact that one of the Vice Chairmen of the All China Federation of Trade Unions was Chu Xuefan, previously the head of the yellow unions of the KMT, the Association of Labour. In addition, the Minister of Labour, U Lisan was simultaneously vice-president of the ACFTU. The Chairman of this body made perfectly clear what the priorities of the government were: "The immediate and sectional interests of the working class must be subordinated to the long term and over all interests of the state led by the working class."

That "subordination" was to be taken absolutely literally was shown by Un Biao when he sent his troops against the workers of the Sun Sun Textile plant in Shanghai who had occupied their plant to prevent its removal to Manchuria, under the government's policy of thinning out industry. Ten workers were killed or wounded in the clash. While capitalist representatives shared the government with the CCP, between 1949 and 1951 and the policy of that government was clearly to defend capitalism, the repressive apparatus of the state-the police, army, secret police etc., remained firmly in the hands of the Stalinists.

This special form of dual power already witnessed in Eastern Europe and Yugoslavia, continued to exist until it was resolved decisively against the capitalists. The popular front period played an important role for the Chinese Stalinists in demobilising the aroused workers and peasants. At the time when capitalism was at its weakest and the mobilisations of the workers and peasants at their strongest, the CCP acted to limit those mobilisations and to restrain them within the limits of capitalist property relations. The dangers of this policy of maintaining and strengthening the capitalists swiftly became apparent. The utopian goal of the Stalinists a stable New Democracy where capitalists and Stalinists worked in harmony was never a possibility. The onslaught of American imperialism in the Korean war produced a growing threat of capitalist counter-revolution inside China amongst sections of the remaining bourgeoisie. America and Chiang Kai Shek were ready to act as their heavily armed allies.

This forced the CCP towards the close of 1951 to move swiftly to resolve the situation of dual power in its favour through a bureaucratic, anti-capitalist workers' government. As in the other Stalinist social overturns this necessitated striking out at both the capitalists and suppressing the last remnants of the independent workers' movement.

The immediate cause of the change of policy and, eventually, the nature, of the government, was the outbreak of the Korean war in June 1950. As American armies (supposedly UN) advanced towards the Yalu River (the border between Manchuria and Korea) under the rabid anti-communist, MacArthur, the People's Government was forced to change its policy both internationally and domestically.

The initial victories of the PLA under Peng Dehuai, which forced the US back beyond the 38th parallel, were met by Washington with the rearmament of Chiang Kai-shek and the delivery of considerable economic aid to Taiwan. The US Seventh

Fleet took up station between Taiwan and the mainland, thereby forcing the Chinese to divert troops from Korea to the coastal province of Fujian. In addition a total economic blockade of China was instituted. The New York Times, 5 April 1951, reported that, "MacArthur favours a Nationalist second front on the Chinese mainland and is convinced that the fate of Europe will be decided in the war against communism in Asia." Now, under both economic and military pressure from imperialism and fully aware of the potential alliance between foreign, Taiwan based and domestic capital, the CCP took steps to mobilise the masses against the "national" capitalists. In the countryside, the Agrarian Reform was accompanied by the building of the People's Tribunals, organised by the Party cadres with the purpose of applying a degree of terror and intimidation to the landlords. Although the campaign was limited to the terms of the Agrarian Reform, the wave of executions, fines and expropriations both broke the class power of the landlords and served to bind the peasantry yet closer to the regime.

At the same time the control of the CCP ensured that this did not go beyond its own predetermined limitations. Indeed, so bureaucratic was the procedure for ratifying redistribution of land that, in Canton province it still had not been completed by December 1952. A parallel movement was set in train in the cities for similar purposes. The so called "three anti's" campaign, introduced alongside the "five anti's" campaign at the end of 1951, was aimed at CCP and government functionaries. The masses of members who had been recruited to the CCP on the basis of its popular front programme, were now considered unreliable a massive purge took place in the party, involving the expulsion of over one million members (a fifth of the party) between 1951 and 1952. It was also in this period that the Stalinists struck out against the left. Chinese Trotskyists, many members of the 'nternationalist Workers Party had been active leading strikes in Canton and Shanghai. They had suffered repression before 1952 at the hands of the CCP, but at the end of that year a nation wide raid by the secret police completely decimated the Chinese Trotskyists two or three hundred were thrown into gaol. Leading members Cheng Ch'ao-Un and eleven others were only released 27 years later in June 1979. The "Five anti's" campaign which ran parallel with the "three" was aimed at weakening and intimidating the bourgeoisie. Mass meetings were held throughout the country to whip up feelings against the capitalists. Businesses were investigated for fraud and corruption. In the first six months of 1952 nearly half a million businesses were inspected and over three quarters found guilty of infractions.

Many were heavily fined, contributing $850m to state coffers. Those who could not pay were nationalised instead. By these bureaucratic methods, albeit backed up by mass mobilisations and denunciation sessions, the CCP-led government, a bureaucratic anti- capitalist workers' government came to control 64 per cent of wholesale trade and 42 per cent of retail trade by mid 1952. Initially, this led to a fall in production as the bourgeoisie retaliated by closing down plants. Between January and February 1952, at the height of the campaign, production fell by 34 per cent and the state was obliged to slow down the campaign.

Once again Chen Yun offered reassurance: "Private factories will, according to concrete conditions, be guaranteed a profit of around 10, 20 or up to 30 per cent on their capital." Once again private capital survived in China, but it was now severely curtailed in its freedom, state control of orders placed with private industry, for example, was a powerful weapon for ensuring that the capitalists did not step out of line. This respite was short lived however and in 1953 at a government convened National Congress of Industry and Commerce the remaining capitalists were told that the first aim of the government was to have a fully socialist economy in which private industry would have no place.

After 1951 primarily under pressure from imperialism, the popular front government was transformed into a bureaucratic, anti-capitalist workers' government which removed the foundations of the class rule of the capitalists, "not by decree but by relentless, high-pressure gradualism". In this way it ensured that its prime enemy, the independently organised revolutionary working class, remained firmly excluded from political power within China. Because the fundamental bastion of the bourgeois state its bodies of armed men had already been smashed, the CCP was able to carry out the military-bureaucratic overthrow of the Chinese bourgeoisie relatively peacefully.

It was against a background of economic blockade by the West, majority state control of heavy industry and effective control of trade in the modern sector that the government of the People's Republic moved against the essential foundations of capitalism with the introduction of planning in 1953. At first this took the form of annual plans for 1953 and 1954, these were then incorporated into, and used as a basis for, the First Five Year Plan 1953-57. This was not published until late 1955.

The introduction of planning in 1953 on the clear basis of subordinating the operation of the law of value, marks the establishment of a degenerate workers' state in China. The plan was modelled on the Five Year Plans of the Soviet Union. Planners exhorted plant managers to take careful heed of the "advanced experience" of the Soviet system. The ability of the plan to even begin the industrialisation of China was, in a large measure, due to the aid provided by the USSR. Since 1950 China had been in receipt of an annual $300m loan from the Soviet Union. In March 1953 this was added to by a commercial agreement with the USSR, supplying China with many of the materials necessary for industrial expansion.

The plan revealed the dynamic lodged within the post capitalist property forms, and, at the same time, the way in which the bureaucracy acts as a fetter on the full realisation of this dynamic. The bureaucracy claimed that 1953 saw a 13 per cent increase in industrial output over the 1952 level, while in 1954 output rose a further 17 per cent higher than the total for 1953.

However, the exclusion of the masses from political control of the plan meant that these advances were undermined by the bureaucracy's tendency to plan blind. In 1955, when the collection of statistical data took place on a national scale, the figures often disguised the problems of the plan. In 1956 these surfaced. On March 18th 1956 the People's Daily was forced to admit that only just over 50 per cent of the capital construction programme had been fulfilled. Shortages, particularly in construction materials, began to block the fulfilment of targets. Inflationary pressures mounted and the bureaucracy was forced to reduce its targets in heavy industry.

As usual with bureaucratic plans the fulfilment of targets did not mean that the goods produced were of a high quality. The tyranny of the "target" in fact meant that workers often took little care with their products, and ended up producing shoddy goods, but at a faster rate! These features of bureaucratic planning have been apparent in the Chinese economy since 1953. They are an inevitable product of a regime under which the working class is excluded from political power. In China the economic power of the bourgeoisie was destroyed, bureaucratically, through induced bankruptcies and, after 1955, by state purchases of majority shareholdings. In 1956 the modern sector of the Chinese economy was virtually 100 per cent nationalised, and the bourgeoisie as a class was eliminated. But perched at the top of this workers' state was a Stalinist bureaucracy, ruling over the working class.

The independent base of the CCP, built up over years of war, provided the Chinese Stalinists with the means to pursue their own policy, independently of Stalin, at certain decisive moments. This did not mean that the CCP was not Stalinist. It merely confirmed the ability of certain indigenous Stalinist parties to prosecute Stalinist polices in spite of the wishes of the Kremlin. The initial hostility of Stalin to Mao's seizure of power was in reality a hostility to an independent Stalinist force, similar to Tito's YCP. The Sino-Soviet split in 1963 brought these hostilities once more to the surface. It illustrated the tendency of Stalinism to fracture along national social patriotic lines. In no way was it a sign of the CCP's transformation into a non-Stalinist party.

3

Rise of Naxalism and Maoism in India

The Prime Minister Dr. Manmohan singh has said that the recent brutal killing of policemen, blowing up railway tracks and burning of vehicles by the Naxalites and the Maoists alike can not be equated to terrorism! what else do you require to qualify for a label like Terrorists? Its very immature of a national leader to say something like this instead of coming down heavily with an iron hand against all those who take up arms and hold the machinery to ransom? Its time that India takes lessons from the neighbouring country China in handling such terror activities. The politicians say something sitting in a heavily guarded chambers in the capital and its the poor front line police constables and the security forces who bear the brunt of the brutal attacks and make their families suffer silently. The Government on their part console the families by sending a Wreath and announcing some relief!

What is the reason for this uprising of disgrunt led elements in the society?

While Unemployment can be assigned the first and the foremost reason, the main reason can be attributed to the ever rising divide amongst the rich and the poor without any justification for equality. In India, the rich are getting richer and the Poor, poorer day by day! The government should pay prime attention to this problem and take effective steps to develop all other states in the Country which is also part of India. For the politicians, India means only Delhi and all the developmental activities centre around the capital and nothing beyond! Thanks to some regional parties emerging stronger whereby some kind of developments happen elsewhere in states like Maharashtra, Karnataka and Tamil Nadu due to sheer bargaining power of the political alignments. The states in the North East remains totally ignored and underdeveloped and it touches your heart when you see people from those states taking up odd jobs like performing Watchmen duties or assisting in Beauty Parlours in the few mentioned front line states. There are no proper roads or infra structure leave alone industries in the North East which forms an integral part of the country! Except during the elections or inauguration of some festivals or games where you can see the central politicians dancing with the locals, there is absolute neglect of these states despite 60 years of independence!! Unemployment and backwardness forces the young, unemployed youth to take up arms and term themselves as Naxals/Maoists and different labels in different states!

Its time that the central government in Delhi distributes the benefits of independence equally amongst states and be a cause for development thereby bringing cheers to the local people and make them come into the mainstream. To set an example that the government cares, they should first distribute industrial formation equally amongst states and also distribute the venues of the Common Wealth Games equally amongst the states. The country will prosper only if there is all round prosperity and a sense of fulfilment amongst the entire population and this can be achieved only by equal distribution of Prosperity so that there is peaceful life for the future generations??

THE RISE AND RISE OF MAOISTS IN BENGAL

It all started on November 2, 2008 when Maoists made an attempt on the life of Chief Minister Buddhadeb Bhattacharjee—a land mine ripped off a vehicle of his convoy. Moments later, his car went past the incident spot near Bhadutala in the Salboni police station area. What followed was a massive operation by the police where the tribals claimed their women had been assaulted during raids on November 4 at Lalgarh — nearly 40 km away from the blast site.

The police arrested school students and locals from Lalgarh for their alleged involvement in the blast. The tribals began an agitation to not allow the police to enter the Lalgarh area. The agitation gradually spread to various parts of the district, particularly to Jhargram sub-division, Goaltore, Salboni, Sarenga in Bankura and in the forest areas of Purulia in the first week of November.

The tribals demanded an unconditional apology from district police superintendent Rajesh Singh and closure of the police camps at Lalgarh and Ramgarh. The movement took a new turn on November 21 after a press statement from Kanchan — state secretary of CPI(Maoists). According to Kanchan, Maoists supported the tribal agitation in Lalgarh and they would convert the same into a bigger one in the forest areas of West Midnapore, Bankura and Purulia.

Chhatradhar Mahato, a local youth from Lalgarh, came up as a leader of the tribals in November last week and a committee was formed called the People's Committee Against Police Atrocities (PCAPA). The emergence of Mahato established the direct involvement of Maoists with the PCAPA — Mahato is the younger brother of Sasadhar Mahato, the most wanted Maoist. According to police, Sasadhar has been operating from Belpahari and Binpur for long. He was responsible for several killings in the last few years, said West Midnapore SP Manoj Verma.

On November 30, the PCAPA gave a deadline of 24 hours to the Lalgarh police to remove their camps. On December 1, the West Midnapore district police closed down two police camps at Lalgarh Ramakrishna High School and Lalgarh Saradamoni Girls' High School. On December 7, tribals from the Lalgarh area temporarily withdrew their agitation after signing an agreement with the district administration. But Chhatradhar warned that the movement would continue as the administration had not met their demands — the SP would have to visit Lalgarh and apologise for police excesses on the tribals.

Meanwhile, the Maoist outfit reportedly moblised armed cadres in the Lalgarh area and the CPM allegedly formed resistance committees in various areas of Binpur and Belpahari to counter them. During the agitation, Sudhir Mandi, who played an important role in anti-Maoist protests in Belpahari, was shot dead at West Midnapore's Jordanga on December 11.

This was the first killing by the suspected Maoists during the Lalgarh episode. The Maoists continued to kill CPM cadres at Lalgarh, Salboni, Binpur and Belpahari. From January to April 2009, 14 people were killed in West Midnapore, Bankura and Purulia. The state government, meanwhile, announced various development projects for the affected areas to woo tribals. As the Lok Sabha elections were scheduled for April, the government did not initiate police operation against the Maoists. The CPI(Maoist) gave a call for vote boycott during election in West Midnapore, Bankura and Purulia. Voters in Lalgarh and Banspahari in West Midnapore boycotted the poll. After the election, the Maoists and PCAPA organised their movement to remove remaining police camps from Lalgarh and its adjoining areas.

On May 3, thousands of tribals — carrying shovels, axes and hammers and led by CPI(Maoist) cadres — demolished a police camp at Kalaimuri near Lalgarh. On May 23, the Maoists forced six CPM cadres to walk for 8 km after being garlanded with shoes at a people's court held at Salboni's Madhupur village. A total of 32 CPM men were forced to quit the party in a similar manner. On June 15, PCAPA cadres demolished the palatial house of a CPM leader, Anuj Pandey, with crowbars and hammers at Lalgarh. Maoist leader Bikash claimed his outfit was leading the tribal agitation. The PCAPA members ransacked several police outposts, offices of the CPM and the house of a local leader.

On June 16, the CPM party office was set on fire when the CPI(Maoist)-backed PCAPA held a "victory" rally at Lalgarh. Following such developments, the Central government agreed to deploy paramilitary forces and the state government decided to carry out the Central-state joint operation in the area. On June 18, the Central-state joint forces launched counter-offensive to oust the Maoists.

Meanwhile, Kishenji appeared before mediapersons at Lalgarh and said Maoists would establish a free-zone there. As the state launched a counter-offensive against CPI(Maoist), the Maoists killed four CPM activists — including a local leader at Goaltore— when joint operations started to proceed from Midnapore town. The joint forces succeeded in taking control over Lalgarh on June 29. Around 1,600 personnel of the paramilitary forces, police and Cobra reached Kantapahari from Lalgarh and Ramgarh, and established its control over the area. The forces faced resistance on various occasions during the 12-day operation to capture Lalgarh. Maoists opened fire from the forests and triggered landmine blasts on several occasions.

During the joint operation, the Maoists retaliated by killing two CPM cadres at Sirsha village — 25 km from Lalgarh — on July 10. A squad of around 50 armed CPI(Maoist) cadres, including women armed cadres, reportedly held a procession and people's court in the village, along with PCAPA members. The 12 CPM supporters were summoned to the court. Gurucharan Mahato and Baren Mahato — local CPM leaders — were killed. The remaining were brutally assaulted and forced to quit the party. As the joint operation continued, Maoists continued to kill CPM cadres. According to CPM district committee of West Midnapore, 57 CPM activists have been killed since the operation.

On the other hand, six activists of Jharkhand Party (Naren) were killed allegedly by CPM cadres, as they supported the PCAPA movement, said Chunibala Hansda, party MLA from Binpur. Two activists of Jharkahan Janamukti Morcha were killed at Binpur in September. According to the police, over 110 people — more than 90 civilians, seven security personnel and 10 Maoists — were killed this year in connection with the Maoist violence in West Bengal. Recently, six more companies of paramilitary forces reached West Midnapore as the state government intensified the joint operation in the forest areas of Goaltore, Salboni and Lalgarh. According to a CPM leader, Maoists are desperate to capture Goaltore and Salboni.

The Maoist activity had come to the surface in the forest area of West Midanpore, Bankura and Purulia in 1999-2000. They allegedly killed CPM leaders Sudhir Singh Sardar, Baridbaran Mondal, Rampada Majhi, Rabi Das, Anil Mahato, Palaram Tudu and Rabindranath Kar and his wife between

2001 to 2005. According to a report of the Union Home ministry that was prepared in 2006, 12 police stations have been affected by the Maoists. Now, the Maoists are active in 18 police stations in these three districts.

In West Midnapore, Maoists are active in the police stations of Jhargram, Binpur, Belpahari, Lalgarh, Salboni, Jamboni, Goaltore, Sankrail. Their presence has also been noticed in Gopiballavpur, Nayagram and other areas of West Midnapore. A total of 37 companies of security forces — including 23 Central paramilitary forces — continue with its offensive to oust the Maoists from West Midnapore.

MAOISTS GAIN STRENGTH IN ORISSA

The Red terror has spread its wings to 22 out of 30 districts in Orissa throwing a serious challenge to the state authority even as chief minister Naveen Patnaik has come back to power in Assembly poll marketing his king-size image of honesty and good governance. The Leftwing insurgency has grown and the situation has gone out of control now because of the neglect of the deprived section by the state government over the years. The people, largely, have lost faith over state mechanism due to the factors like absence of civil administration in remote areas, collapse of the justice system, exploitation of tribals by contractors and rich people and failure of police to provide minimum security to civilians.

When Naveen led BJD Government banned CPI (Maoists) and few of its frontal wing including Daman Pratirodh Manch, the Revolutionary Democratic Front, the Chasi Mulia Samiti, the Kui Lawanga Sangh, the Jana Natya Mandali, the Krantikari Kisan Samiti and the Bal Sangam on June 9, 2006, the annoyance of Leftwing insurgency was very negligible. But after 2006, the Red Ultras have expanded their network in at least 22 districts out of 30. The situation is almost alike an all-out war where both the State and the extra-constitutional forces seem to be interlocked in a deadly fight. In fact, BJD Government did not take any steps in the last two-terms to provide employment opportunity to the educated tribal youth, who are currently with the Maoists, resulting the entire situation more critical.

On September 21, 2004, the Maoist Communist Centre of India (MCC), People's War Group (PWG) and the Communist Party of India (Marxist-Leninist) had merged to form the outfit, which has since been wrecking havoc in Orissa and all its neighbouring States including Andhra Pradesh, Jharkhand, Chhattisgarh and West Bengal. Likewise, the People's Guerrilla Army and People's Liberation Guerrilla Army – the two organisations also unified and became a strong People's Liberation Guerrilla Army, the militant wing of the outfit. Taking advantage of Naveen Patnaik Government's easygoing response to the growth of the Left wing insurgency, the CPI-Maoist) has not only carried out a number of high profile attacks in the State, but has established a precise process of consolidation, what they called 'Liberated Zone'.

Official data indicates that, while the total number of Maoist-related incidents in Orissa increased to 129 in 2008 from 67 in 2007, fatalities suffered by security forces rose sharply to 76, from just two in 2007. Six south-western districts – Malkangiri, Koraput, Raygada, Kandhamal, Nayagarh and Gajapati – accounted for almost 60 percent of all incidents in 2008. In 2009 till October 15, several attacked have been took place and dozens have been killed including security forces. In 2006 and 2007, according to security experts of New Delhi based Institute of Conflict Management and Institute of Defense Studies and Analysis, the Leftwing ultras quietly went about with the tasks of political mobilization and expansion of their area of operation, in 2008 the Maoist 'takeover' of several areas in south-western Orissa had evidently been completed. This has allowed the extremists a corridor of easy transit between Andhra Pradesh and Chhattisgarh. The movement of armed Maoists was noticed along the Ganjam-Kandhamal border in South Orissa.

The dense jungle and hilly terrain of this region proved conducive to Maoist movement. As a result, it was hardly surprising that, when pressure mounted on Maoists in Andhra Pradesh and Chhattisgarh, they found it convenient to step up activities in Orissa. But reports of Maoist incidents from districts like Jagatsinghpur, Jajpur, Khurda, Angul, Dhenkanal, all along the eastern region of the State and far from borders along

States like Jharkhand, Chhattisgarh and Andhra Pradesh, as well as the arrest of a substantial number of Maoists, points at a steady strengthening of their base in the State. The augmentation of Maoist capacities in Orissa was most dramatically manifested in several high profile Maoist attacks in 2008, three of which targeted on elite anti-insurgency security forces. The first of these was the near simultaneous raids on the district Armoury and the Police Training College at the District Headquarters town of Nayagarh, at the Mahipur Police on February 15, 2008.

The second high profile attack occurred on June 29 when 38 security force (SF) personnel, including 36 belonging to the elite anti-Maoist Greyhounds from Andhra Pradesh, were killed in the Chitrakonda reservoir of Malkangiri District, close to the Andhra Pradesh border. The third major incident occurred on July 16, when CPI-Maoist cadres killed 17 personnel of the Special Operations Group (SOG) of the Orissa Police in a landmine blast, once again in the Malkangiri District in the same year.

They have killed dozens of police informers in Rayagada and Malkangiri districts in recent months. Moreover, the new tactic is being adopted in Malkangiri because Andhra Orissa Border Special Zonal Committee secretary, Sudhakar, has taken the leadership of the Mottu armed squad, which operates in Mottu region of Malkangiri district for the past several months. The rebels have been virtually running parallel Government by creating political vacuum either by killing village headmen or driving out influential persons from the villages.

Interestingly, the leftwing ultras also do not allow Construction of Bridge on the Sileru River which will connect Dantewada district of Chhattisgarh and Malkangiri. The rebels have been prohibiting construction of these two bridges because of police access to the Chitrakonada region, one of the 'Liberated Zones' of the leftwing guerrillas. The entire game plan reported to have been prepared by Sabhyasachi Panda aks Sunil, who heads the outfit in Orissa. Maoist movement is gaining momentum gradually also in various industrial hubs of the State." The Maoists use "pandemonium in South and assault in North" tactics," Around 70-80 Naxalites in three groups are roaming around in K Bolang border areas of Sundargarh district and Karampada area close to Sarenda forests of Jharkhand.

Similarly, another group has been moving around Baunsjor area of Jharkhand closer to Biramitrapur police station of Sundargarh. The third group is camping near Raikera of Jharkhand just 10 kilometers away from Nuagaon area of Sundargarh district. It is believed that the Maoists may capture the Mohanadi Coalfields Limited (MCL) mines, sources close to CPI (Maoists) reveal. Interestingly, the Jajpur division was formed near the industrial corridor. There are around 15 armed cadres in that division. Similarly, the Sambalpur division manages operations in Sudargarh and Keonjhar districts, where both the POSCO and Mittal groups have applied for their proposed steel plants captive area. Apart from Mittal more than 48 mining companies are also active in Keonjhar district. Recently, Maoists activity has also increased in many places like-Anadapur, Ghasipura, Ghatagaon, Badbil, Harichandanpur, Daitari, Telkei and Joda area of Keonjhar district. Out of 20 police stations in the districts, Maoists have presence in nine police stations. The rebels' organized a meeting at Atei and Rebna forests in April, 2008. Strategically, the rebels have identified Keonjhar districts as funding zone. "It seems the situation is out of control now. Over the years, Leftwing insurgency violence growing because of the failure of the State Government," alleged former Orissa DGP Amiya Bhusan Tripathy. The Government must ensure sustainable development in tribal areas, he added.

Another former State Police chief Sarat Chandra Mishra said the police while maintaining balance between security and human rights put in back foot as the rebels did not care for the Human Rights while referring to the historic judgment of Andhra High Court, which says any encounter by police would be, treated a murder.

The issue needs a deeper sociological study to find out a solution, he suggested. "I am admitting that the situation is very tough but steps have been taken to challenge the Leftwing guerrillas," present DGP Manmohan Praharaj added. Undoubtedly, these incidents reflect strong support base of the CPI-Maoist vis-a-vis poor intelligence of Orissa police. The state police has been consistently failed to collect intelligence in southern Orissa due to complete lack of police-public relationship.

The CPI-Maoist took a decision at the 9th Congress in January 2007 to develop the movement to from present guerilla warfare to mobile warfare and urban warfare as central policy. It is learnt that the central committee has deputed around two hundred Maoist cadres from Chhattisgarh and Andhra Pradesh to Orissa for organization building in Malkangiri, Koraput, Kalahandi, and Nawarangpur. They have been trying to set up a corridor from Kalahandi-Nuapada and Bastar. Hence, it is clear that Maoists are consistently working overnight to tighten their hold in the state of Orissa. The State government should not treat this issue as a merely law and order problem. Instead, it should be first considered a social and economic problem. A holistic development of the State both in terms of geography, individuals and groups can only offer a permanent solution to this problem.

THE ROLE OF MAOISTS IN INDIA TODAY

If we have to understand the present role of Maoists, we have to go back a bit into the history of the Maoist movement in India. Right from the beginning, the Naxalite movement which emerged in the late 60s, claimed that it was the genuine marxist revolutionary force in India and it was the only Marxist Leninist organisation which can mobilise the people to overthrow the Indian state and liberate the Indian people from feudalism and imperialist exploitation.

When we look back at the 40 year history of Naxalism in India, we should not be surprised that such a phenomenon arose in India. Because in every country where the left movement has existed or grown, we have seen the emergence of left sectarian and left sectarian anarchist trends and much before all these happened in India, in the world in the 1960s and 1970s, Lenin, analysing the rise of left sectarianism in the international communist movement had zeroed in to the essence of the problem and it was Lenin who had said, 'A petty bourgeois driven to frenzy by the horrors of capitalism is a social phenomenon which like anarchism is characteristic of all countries'. So, particularly in countries like India, which are predominantly petty bourgeois in character, where capitalism had begun to develop, you had this phenomenon of some strata of the petty bourgeoisie who, having experienced the horrors of capitalism, get into a frenzy of activity, which generally ends up in sectarian adventurist violence and it is very important to understand this. Because now in our country, when the activities of the Maoist party are being talked about, the tendencies of our recent experiences with terrorism is to characterise these organisations as terrorist. Yes, in some sense, this organisation resorts to terroristic attacks and violence. But it is fundamentally wrong to label the Maoist groups and parties into a terrorist organisation.

First of all, what is their ideology and what is their world view? They situate themselves within the Marxist framework, they claim. And it is on the basis of a Marxist approach that they view our society and the world. But what is their worldview today? ... they think that South Asia is on the verge of a great revolutionary upsurge. That the national liberation movements in South Asia are forging ahead and they draw a comparison – they say that today in the world, West Asia is the focus of the national struggles against imperialism. And next to West Asia, South Asia is the centre – the hotbed.

But what is the reality today? What is happening in South Asia? We have Pakistan... which everybody knows is a subordinate ally of the USA. The Pakistani state at present, cannot survive without sustenance of the US of A. The US has gained India as a major strategy ally... it is entrenched in Bangladesh, it is entrenching itself in Sri Lanka and so on. And imperialism and NATO is waging a war in Afghanistan. But apart from that, is this South Asia a focal point for resurgent fight against imperialism and are the people in these countries on the verge of overthrowing their comprador ruling classes and thereby also imperialism?

The essence of Maoist ideology and polity today is that they are divorced of reality. That is why when they talk of West Asia, they see the Islamist fundamentalist forces... they see the Taliban and the other forces that are there in West Asia and in Afghanistan as their allies in the fight against imperialism. In fact they say it is a setback.. the offensive against Islamic/jehadist forces in Swat Valley in Pakistan.. and the Pakistani Army actions in FATA and South Waziristan... all these places are considered as centres for the anti-imperialist national liberation struggle. And that is why the Maosits are very upset when the LTTE was militarily defeated and crushed and their leader Prabhakaran was killed. They see that as another setback in South Asia in their fight against imperialism. So this is a very warped view to consider the LTTE as a national liberation struggler against imperialism. An LTTE which went about systematically eliminating all democratic and left struggles within the Tamil polity and society within Sri Lanka...which decided to institute an authoritarian military setup within the Tamil speaking areas. Its downfall is seen as a great setback.. while we view it as something which was necessary to start rebuilding a strong democratic movement within the Tamils in Sri Lanka.

So, just as their worldview is totally distorted and warped, as far as India is concerned they have always talked about the comprador ruling classes of India.. But what has actually happened is that their ideology is comprador and their outlook is comprador. They borrowed wholesale what was being put out by the Communist Party of China in a period when the CPC was itself in the grip of left sectarianism. In the period of the so called, Great Cultural Revolution. If you look at all the concepts which they have, they find their origins in the period of left sectarianism and adventurism. It is that outmoded and warped and distorted ideology which still drives them.

What is the outcome of that? When you say India is a semi-colonial, semi-feudal country, you deny what happened in India, what exists in India in terms of classes; and you deny that India has one of the strongest bourgeoisies of all the countries that got liberation in the 20th century. India has developed a strong capitalist base and state; it denies that state. It denies the development of capitalism in agriculture. Here's a party which talks about being the revolutionary vanguard which has no place for the working class!

Theoretically also, it cannot conceive of that working class because they don't recognize that that type of capitalism has developed in India. Neither will you see in all their political pronouncements, statements and practice, any place for the working class. Of course, sourcing themselves, basing themselves from Maoism, they talk about the peasantry, how the peasant classes are marching toward the revolutionary path.

But if you look at them carefully, there is hardly any place where they have developed a strong peasant movement. The only place where they have been active and they have been able to succeed in mobilising some people are in the tribal areas in the most remote, hilly and thickly forested terrain. Which are most backward in terms of development, communication and where it is possible to maintain or sustain to some extent armed squads and guerillas taking shelter in this type of terrain. But where is the great revolutionary movement based on the working class and the peasantry? That is outside their realm of thinking. In fact they make no distinction when they are talking about the annihilation of the class enemies, which is not new and present since the original Naxalite movement, particularly after they failed to mobilise the peasantry of West Bengal. And you find that their main targets are ordinary policemen and many of the people whom they kill are those they claim are agents of the state or informers to the police, are ordinary people.

What has happened is, over a period of years and years of this style of sectarian adventurist politics, they rely purely on their armed squads and their guns and other weapons. And today if they are able to operate in these areas, they have also tried these earlier in Andhra Pradesh. It is after their debacle in AP, when the state and police effectively snuffed out their bases and their shelters and their squads, they were moved out into Chhattisgarh and then the Dandakaranya. You can see a pattern... they have spread out to around AP. From AP to Orissa, Chhattisgarh, to pockets in Maharashtra and in Jharkhand and from Jharkhand to adjoining areas in West Bengal.

The claim that they make that they are the only party or force which is taking on the ruling classes and the state is hollow. Because the very people who are subject to class exploitation and oppression are not in the picture at all. They are not part of their strategy to mobilise the people against the state. If you look at the recent history, in the 80s they had more or less disintegrated (what was known as the Naxalite movement) but ever since the merger of the Peoples War Group (mainly based in AP) and the MCC in 2004, they have acquired a striking power in terms of the armed squads, in terms of the weapons they possess, in terms of knowhow- planting explosive devices etc. which they got from the LTTE. Training and collaboration with/from the LTTE people in camps in AP that time, this is what got them their striking power. Therefore the loud claims that they are making, that they have spread all over and the "spring thunder of revolution is approaching because the masses are being roused" – even the terminology is reminiscent of what was there and used in the Great Cultural Revolution. This is the worldview and ideology of the politics of the Maoists today

MAOISTS' DREAM CAN BECOME INDIA'S NIGHTMARE

The 'Red Corridor', extending from 'Tirupati to Pashupati' (Andhra Pradesh to Nepal), has long been passé in the Indian Maoists conception. Maoist ambitions in India now extend to the farthest reaches of the country, and this is not just a fantasy or an aspiration, but a strategy, a projection, a plan and a programme under implementation. A multiplicity of Maoist documents testify to the meticulous detail in which the contours of the current and protracted conflict have been envisaged, in order to 'intensify the peoples' war throughout the country'.

These documents reflect a comprehensive strategy, coordinating all the instrumentalities of revolution — military, political, economic, cultural and psychological — harnessed through the 'three magic weapons' Comrade Mao spoke about: the Party, the People's Army, and the United Front.

After a great deal of dissembling and vacillation, India's security establishment, both at the Centre and in the 'affected' states, appears to have conceded, finally, that the Maoist threat is, in Prime Minister Manmohan Singh's words, the country's "single biggest internal security challenge." But the threat is still restrictively envisaged as afflicting only parts of those states where Naxalite violence is visible, and is assumed to follow the erratic trajectory of incidents and fatalities from year to year. However, as the Chhattisgarh Director General of Police, O P Rathor, recently observed at a conference in Raipur, 'Statistics of incidents never give a real picture of the ground. Whatever is visible is only the mere tip of the iceberg. Unless caution is exercised, volcanoes can erupt.'

It is necessary to recognise, crucially, that the phase of violence, which is ordinarily the point at which the State takes cognisance of the problem, comes at the tail end of the process of mass mobilisation, and at a stage where neutralising the threat requires considerable, if not massive, use of force. Within this context it is, consequently, useful to notice not merely the current expanse of visible Maoist mobilisation and militancy, but the extent of their current intentions, ambitions and agenda.

Significantly, the Maoists have established regional bureaus across a mass of nearly two-thirds of the country's territory and these regions are further sub-divided into state, special zonal and special area committee jurisdictions where the processes of mobilisation have been defined and allocated to local leaders. As these maps indicate, there are at least five regional bureaus, 13 state committees, two special area committees and three special zonal committees in the country. This structure of organisation substantially reflects current Maoist organisational consolidation, but does not exhaust their perspectives or ambitions. There is further evidence of preliminary activity for the extension of operations to new areas including Gujarat, Rajasthan, Himachal Pradesh, Jammu & Kashmir and Meghalaya, beyond what is reflected in the scope of the regional, zonal and state committees. A 'leading team' recently visited Jammu & Kashmir to assess the potential of creating a permanent party structure in the form of a state committee to take the Maoist agenda forward in the state.

In 2004, moreover, the Maoists also articulated a new strategy to target urban centres in their 'Urban Perspective Document', drawing up guidelines for 'working in towns and cities', and for the revival of a mobilisation targeting students and the urban unemployed. Two principal 'industrial belts' were also identified as targets for urban mobilisation: Bhilai-Ranchi-Dhanbad-Kolkata; and Mumbai-Pune-Surat-Ahmedabad.

Within this broad geographical spread, the Maoists include, in their inventory of 'immediate tasks', among others, the following:

- 'Coordinate the people's war with the ongoing armed struggles of the various oppressed nationalities in Kashmir, Assam, Nagaland, Manipur and other parts of the Northeast.
- 'Build a broad UF (United Front) of all secular forces and persecuted religious minorities such as Muslims, Christians and Sikhs...
- 'Build a secret party apparatus which is impregnable to the enemy's attacks...
- 'Build open and secret mass organisations amongst the workers, peasants, youth, students, women and other sections of the people...
- 'Build the people's militia in all the villages in the guerrilla zones as the base force of the PGA (People's Guerrilla Army). Also build armed self-defence units in other areas of class struggle as well as in the urban areas.'

The Maoist strategy is clearly to fish in all troubled Indian waters, and to opportunistically exploit every potential issue and grievance to generate a campaign of protests and agitations. The principal vehicles for these 'partial struggles' are 'front' or 'cover' organisations of the Maoists themselves, on the one hand, and a range of individuals and organisations best described, in a phrase often attributed to Lenin, as 'useful idiots' — well intentioned and often gullible people who are unaware of the broader strategy and agenda they are unwittingly promoting through their support to specific and unquestionably admirable causes.

As the political and organisational review of the erstwhile Communist Party of India, Marxist-Leninist – Peoples War (CPI-ML-PW), also known as the Peoples War Group, which merged in September 2004 with the Maoist Communist Centre to create the Communist Party of India – Maoist noted, 'Cover organisations are indispensable in areas where our mass organisations are not allowed to function openly...There are two types of cover organisations: one, those which are formed on a broad basis by ourselves; and two, those organisations led by other forces which we utilise by working from within without getting exposed.'

This strategy has already contributed to the 'eruption' of a few unexpected 'volcanoes' in the recent past, with the role of Maoist provocateurs often discovered much after the event. Two of the most recent and impeccable causes that have been embraced in this cynical strategy include the caste conflict in Khairlanji and the escalating tensions and violence over the displacement and Special Economic Zones issues, including Singur and Kalinga Nagar. Sources indicate that current Maoist debates and documents condemn the 'second wave of economic reforms' as a 'violent assault on the right to life and livelihood of the masses', and call for 'an uncompromising opposition to the present model and all the policies that are coming up.' Internal debates on the issue have further underlined the 'need to build a huge movement against displacement and the very model of development itself', and to unite all 'genuine democratic and anti-imperialist forces... to create a tornado of dissent that forces the rulers to stop this juggernaut'.

The issues at stake envisaged for potential mobilisation comprehend 'development driven through big dams, super highways and other infrastructural projects... gigantic mining projects, Special Economic Zones, urban renewal and beautification'.

Within the same pattern, United Fronts and Joint Action Committees have focused on 'burning issues of the peasantry such as for water, power, remunerative prices for agricultural produce, against exploitation by traders, against suicides by the peasantry, against the World Trade Organisation, and on worker, student, women, Adivasi and Dalit issues.' Thus, 'Issue-based joint activity with other forces has been the general form of UF (United Front) undertaken by our Party at various levels...' Suitable 'issues' are not picked up randomly or opportunistically, but are based on extensive 'investigations' into 'social conditions and tactics', and are meticulously reconciled with the broader Maoist strategy and agenda.

These various causes, as already noted, are impeccable, and no one can be faulted for extending support to demands for greater equity, justice and access in these various spheres. For the Maoists, however, these various causes, whether they relate to 'oppressed nationalities', minorities, caste excesses, or other social and economic issues, are an integral component of their strategy of political consolidation, leading to military mobilisation. In Maoist doctrine, these 'partial struggles' are no more than a tactical element in the protracted war, and they have no intrinsic value of their own. These 'struggles' create the networks and recruitment base for the Maoist militia and armed cadres.

Where partial struggles thrive, an army is being raised. These 'peaceful' or sporadically violent movements are eventually and inevitably intended to yield to armed warfare and terrorism. Their objective is to 'isolate the enemy by organising the people into various cover organisations and build joint fronts in order to mobilise the masses into struggles to defeat the enemy offensive.' Army formation, the Maoists insist, 'is the precondition for the new political power', and 'all this activity should serve to intensify and extend our armed struggle. Any joint activity or tactical alliances which do not serve the cause of the peoples' war will be a futile exercise.'

Moreover, the integrity of the 'partial struggles' and the overall aims of the protracted peoples war is underlined by the fact that cadres of the Peoples Guerrilla Army are required to engage in these agitational programmes as well. As the PGA's 'programme and constitution' notes: 'The PGA will participate in the propaganda and agitations programmes as directed by Party Committees. It will organise the people. The PGA will extensively employ people's art forms in its propaganda. It will try to enhance the consciousness of the people.'

The Maoists' Urban Perspective Document, moreover, envisages the formation of 'Open Self Defence Teams' and armed 'Secret Self Defence Squads' in urban areas. The document notes, moreover, that for the Secret Self Defence Squads, 'One significant form of activity is to participate along with the masses and give them the confidence to undertake militant mass action. Other tasks are to secretly hit particular targets who are obstacles in the advance of the mass movement.'

It is useful to recall, in this context, that when talk of the 'Red Corridor' was first heard at the turn of the Millennium, most security, intelligence and political analysts simply scoffed, dismissing the very idea as a pipe dream and a propaganda ploy. Since then, however, the Maoist consolidation has occurred precisely along the axis of the then-projected 'Red Corridor'. If the State is to prevent a further consolidation of Maoist subversion and violence across the country, it is crucial that the futile debate on, and disputable enumeration of, 'affected' states, districts and police stations, be abandoned, and the scope of the state's defences be extended to cover the contours of the Maoist projections.

The Maoists are — and have long been — working to a plan, and have explicitly rejected the 'Left Opportunism' which they believe led to the failure of the original Naxalite movement (1967-73). This gives the movement great strength — but to the extent that this design is well known — makes it enormously vulnerable. Regrettably, while there is a handful of officers in the security and intelligence establishment who are aware of the details of this design, the general grasp in the security and political leadership in the affected and targeted states (the latter category now comprehends the entire country) and at the Centre is, at best, poor. There is, moreover, the added constraint that the Maoist strategy exploits the vulnerabilities of constitutional governance and its freedoms to the hilt, and the security apparatus has only limited instrumentalities of containment available in the initial stages of subversion and mass mobilisation.

The Maoists believe that there is, at present, an 'excellent revolutionary situation in India', and have clearly declared that 'the seizure of State power should be the goal of all our activity'. Building bulwarks against their complex strategy is a challenge, it would appear, that is yet to be imagined by the national security establishment.

The fire-fighting responses of the past, the 'battalion approach' of deployment of Central Paramilitary Forces from one theatre to another, and the preferential allocation of financial resources to 'disturbed' states and areas, may help fitfully contain the violence of Maoist armed cadres. However, if the nation-wide campaigns of subversion are not addressed, and if prevention, rather than containment, does not become the sheet-anchor of national policy, there will be a tipping-point beyond which national capacities for emergency management will begin to fall disastrously short. That is the Maoist dream; it could become the country's nightmare.

INDIA: THE NAXALITE MOVEMENT

India has a long history of peasant uprisings. From the 1930s onwards, communist-inspired organizations and movements have been in the forefront of the struggle for land and tenancy reform. The agitation was especially powerful during the last years of colonial rule and during the first years of independence when the government of India dragged its feet on land reform and compromised with the feudal landlords. In 1946, Bengal witnessed a large-scale tebhaga ("three shares") movement among sharecroppers, which demanded the reduction of the landlords' share in the crop from a half to one-third. Landlords had been using force to take at least half the harvest. The peasants, guided by the kisan sabhas (peasant unions), forcibly seized two-thirds of the harvest, leading to violent clashes. The landlords fled and the kisan sabhas temporarily established control in many rural areas.

In subsequent decades, the popularity of the communist peasant leaders declined in some areas, such as Punjab and Andhra Pradesh, but the movement has endured in Tripura, Kerala, and West Bengal, three states where communist parties have repeatedly headed popularly elected governments. When this happened for the first time in 1967 in West Bengal, a populous state plagued by feudal forms of exploitation and suppression in agriculture, a section of the leftist communist party, the Communist Party of India–Marxist (CPI–M), broke ranks and opted for a radical alternative. They rejected participation in multiparty governments, and electoral politics in general, and opted for a nonconciliatory attack on the landed classes. While a left-dominated front was forming the government in Calcutta (in 1967), three sharecroppers with the help of 150 members of the breakaway wing of the CPI–M, armed with sticks, bows, and arrows, removed the entire stock of grain from a landlord's granary.

This happened in the village of Naxalbari in the narrow corridor between Nepal and what is now Bangladesh that connects mainland India with the northeastern states. Peasants and tribals have continued to be oppressed by unscrupulous landlords and moneylenders, and the local leaders in Naxalbari considered government intervention too slow, too legalistic, and too moderate. Their revolt signaled the birth of a new armed struggle.

The struggle, inspired by the Chinese Communist Party, was initially led by the Communist Party of India–Marxist-Leninist (CPI–ML) under the chairmanship of Charu Mazumdar. Very soon, dissent erupted and gradually the party disintegrated into numerous breakaway factions, all claiming to be less revisionist in ideology and more revolutionary in practice than the others. Since then, all forms of armed struggle by such groups that have taken up the cause of socioeconomic development of the downtrodden rural masses have come to be termed "Naxalite."

In West Bengal itself, where the government has been quite successful in implementing land reforms, the movement did not endure beyond the late 1970s. In many other areas in eastern India, semifeudal conditions have remained. The semifeudal conditions have been exacerbated by the failing government machinery and by the formation of senas (armed squads) by the upper castes and classes to safeguard their socioeconomic and political interests.

Today, a dozen Naxalite groups operate primarily in the states of Bihar, Jharkhand, and Andhra Pradesh (AP), and in pockets in the neighbouring states of Madhya Pradesh, Uttar Pradesh, Chattisgarh, and Orissa, although other states may also be incidentally affected. Most groups are disorganized, lack popular support, and continuously face splits, but the People's War Group (PWG) in AP and the Maoist Communist Centre (MCC) in Bihar and Jharkhand are the two best-organized, and most ruthless, Naxalite groups in India.

Conflict Dynamics

In Andhra Pradesh, the revolutionary peasant movement was of great significance at the time of independence. An armed struggle emerged as early as 1946 in the princely state of Hyderabad. The movement, first against the Nizam and then against the government of India, is known as the Telengana Armed Struggle. It started as a revolt against the continuation of feudal land ownership and the oppression of the poor peasantry and tribals by landlords. The communist-led movement "liberated" more than three thousand villages, but, ultimately, after more than four thousand revolutionaries lost their lives, was suppressed by the Indian army. Again in 1961, a violent movement under the banner of Srikakulam Armed Struggle sought to liberate the deprived hill people from the clutches of the plainsmen who had alienated them from their land and oppressed them economically. Coordinated police action resulted in the collapse of this movement. Extremist activities in AP began once again with the formation of the People's War Group in 1980. Presently, fifteen of the twenty-three districts in AP are affected. The two parties to the conflict are the government, represented by the police, and approximately nineteen Naxalite groups. The PWG is predominant among them in terms of party organization, network, manpower, and striking capabilities: it has about one thousand full-time underground cadres, three thousand overground militants who are organized into four military platoons and further into dalams (forest squads).

In the last couple of years, activities have intensified after a decline in the mid-1990s. In October 2001, the Coca-Cola plant was attacked. The attack, in response to the U.S. bombing of Afghanistan, caused substantial damage without affecting the production process. One month earlier, in a single action, the PWG killed nine policemen in Guntur district. The aim of the PWG is to capture power through the strategy of protracted armed struggle and an areawide seizure of power by initially building bases in rural and remote areas. These bases would eventually be transformed into guerrilla zones and later into liberated areas that would ultimately encircle the urban centres of power.

The security forces as well as police and government offices have been the main targets of the PWG, but most victims have been civilians. Of the nearly three thousand casualties since extremism started, less than five hundred are policemen, the rest being civilians. Analysis of the casualty list shows that only a quarter of the civil victims belonged to the high castes. The others belonged to the lower classes, "scheduled castes," and "scheduled tribes," the very sections whose cause the Naxalites are supposedly championing. Naxalite activities thus also appear to be associated with the struggle to eliminate the political influence of other organizations such as the parliamentary communist parties, among others.

In Bihar, similar conditions exist as in the most backward areas of AP. The feudal nexus of big landowner, rack-renting, and market control has left millions of poor peasants, sharecroppers, and agricultural labourers in abject poverty and oppression. Communist parties had been reasonably strong in some pockets of the state and mass movements were active, but revolutionary violence erupted only after the developments in Naxalbari. From West Bengal, revolutionaries went over into Bihar and assisted locally in the organization of revolutionary cells. The CPI–ML was formed at Musahari in 1967 under the leadership of S. N. Singh. After Singh left the organization in 1971, as in the neighbouring West Bengal, the movement very soon underwent various splits. In the early 1980s there were at least three major Naxalite parties: the CPI–ML (Liberation), MCC, and CPI–ML (Party Unity).

CPI–ML (Liberation) is said to be active in thirty-six districts and to have five thousand full-timers and a membership of more than two hundred thousand. It runs five organizations: the All-India Students Association, Bihar Pradesh Kisan Sabha, All-India Coordination Committee of Trade Unions, All-India Progressive Women's Association, and Jan Sanskriti Manch. Dipankar Bhattacharya is the Liberation's national general secretary. In 1977, the organization, then under the leadership of the influential Vinod Mishra, decided on a "rectification" program.

This program resulted in the creation of the Indian People's Front (IPF) and the decision to participate in elections. The first initiative (the IPF, meant to unite all anti-feudal and anti-imperialist forces) failed to attract other groups and the IPF was discontinued in 1994. The second initiative was reasonably successful. Particularly in Bihar, some of its candidates were elected to parliament. The other two major segments of the Naxalite movement (Party Unity and the MCC) have not "rectified" their political line and have continued to operate as underground movements.

The rectification by CPI–ML Liberation resulted in the MCC emerging as the most radical and militant of the Naxalite groups in Bihar. The Maoist Coordination Committee was originally established as the Bengal–Bihar Special Area Committee in the early 1970s, but was renamed the MCC in 1975. It became very powerful during the second half of the 1980s. The first major massacre in which the MCC was involved took place in 1987 when it brutally killed forty-two persons belonging to upper-caste Rajput families in the Aurangabad district of Bihar. The MCC has been fighting the upper-caste/class landlords in Bihar and their private armies (senas) ever since. It is said to be active in thirty districts, and to have three hundred professional revolutionaries, sixty armed squads, and thirty thousand members. Like the CPI–ML Liberation, it has various front organizations such as the Krantikari Chhatra League (students), Communist Yuva League (youth), Naari Mukti Sangh (women), and Mazdoor Mukti Sangh (workers). The organization has been banned since 1987.

The CPI–ML Party Unity was formed in 1978; after the mid-1980s it went through a number of splits and in 1999, it merged with the People's War Group. It is active in twenty-five districts, and has various front organizations including the Majdoor Kisan Sangrami Parishad (agricultural labor), Shramik Sangharsh Manch (workers), and Bharat Naujawan Sabha (youth). The most gruesome killings in Bihar have been related to the ongoing caste-war, in which the sena is one of its opponents. In March 1999, thirty-five upper-caste villagers were killed in Jehanabad in retaliation for thirty-three lower-caste killings by the sena earlier in the year. Other attacks, such as the attack by the MCC in Jharkand in September 2001, killing thirteen policemen, were aimed at the security forces.

It should be emphasized that the differences between these Naxalite groups that continue along the nonparliamentarian path have to do more with personal clashes among the leadership and less with their ideology. Invariably, all the Naxalite groups work toward the same objectives, and use the same methods.

The Naxalite groups have enough weapons to operate at the local level, but they do not pose a threat at the supralocal level. Some groups in Bihar, Jharkhand, and AP are equipped with sophisticated arms including AK-56s. These weapons, however, are few: according to a news report, the MCC possesses one thousand weapons, including more than a dozen AK-47s and AK-56s. Most of the weapons have been looted from licensed holders or snatched from the police during raids on police convoys. Interestingly, there may also be a nexus between established political parties and some Naxalite groups.

It is generally known that there is a nexus between leaders of several political parties and the rebel outfits, both in Bihar and AP. In return for votes or support in general, some leaders of the Bharatya Janata Party (BJP), the main party in the government coalition in New Delhi, may have gifted AK-47 rifles and money to Naxalite outfits. On the other hand, they are also supporting the private armies of the landlords, the so-called senas. Reports from other areas in the country also suggest that this may be the case. A report tabled in the Maharashtra assembly in December 2000 established that in the Naxal-affected districts (Gondia, Chandrapur, and Gadchiroli), forest contractors and local businessmen are being forced to fund Naxalites in their area. The report also suggested that most of the businessmen actually exploit tribals and consider funding the Naxalite groups operating in the region a good investment.

The Naxalite groups exploit the vacuum in the administrative machinery to attract the masses by their campaign against various social evils such as the dowry system, exploitation of lower castes by the upper castes, theft, rape, and prostitution. The failure of the government administration and the armed power of Naxalite groups such as the MCC and the CPI–ML "People's War" in a number of areas (for example in Palamu and Daltonganj in Bihar, and in Warangal, Adilabad, and Karimnagar in AP) has created a different type of law and order.

According to Arjun Prasad Singh, joint-secretary of the All-India People's Resistance Forum, law and order in the Naxalite-infested areas is far better than in other areas. Even some landlords have started supporting the Naxalites. According to a report in The Week (20 April 2000), out of the 3,207 villages in Palamu district, Naxalites operate in 1,700. There are only three big landlords left in the district, which once had nine kings, 2,100 zamindars, and six thousand landlords. Bonded labor has been abolished and no employer dares pay less than the wages fixed by the state government. The exploitation of tribal women and collection of tolls by local goons have also stopped. But it is a fact, the local reporter adds, that the ultra outfits collect money from forest contractors, traders, and landlords in exchange for peace. The contractors are only too happy to contribute to the Naxalite coffers. A contractor was quoted as staying: "Before the Naxalites came I had to grease the palms of policemen, forest officers and local criminals. Today I have to go to only one place." Top Naxalite leaders defended this by saying they have not used the money for committing crimes but for people-oriented schemes.

The MCC and Party Unity hold jan adalats (people's courts). Jan adalats are usually held at night after a notice is issued to the villagers. These "courts" are gaining in popularity since the settlement of cases in government courts is costly and time-consuming. Moreover, the Naxalites are able to deliver on their verdicts, which the government courts often fail to do. Similarly, in the field of education, Naxalite groups in a number of areas have taken over the educational system and have made sure that it works. They are often the people's only insurance against demanding policemen, criminals, and landlords, and against upper-caste teachers who had been drawing salaries without doing any teaching.

Official Conflict Management

In general, government intervention has concentrated on military efforts to eliminate the "Naxal problem" rather than focus on the demands that the revolutionary groups have raised.

Extrajudicial executions by security and police forces have been documented by international human-rights organizations and Indian civil-liberties groups. The police routinely claim that the killings occur in so-called encounters. Moreover, the Naxalite threat has been used to justify state violence against all forms of peasant resistance and against other critics of state policy. A Human Rights Watch report has stated: Police have also repeatedly engaged in excessive use of force when dealing with Naxalites. Under the pretext of seeking out Naxalite militants police have conducted raids on Dalit villages and falsely arrested those accused of harboring Naxalites. In some cases, federal paramilitary forces have been deployed. Like the private militias, police have sexually assaulted women and attacked children who remained behind after the men fled the villages.

The official response to the Naxalite problem takes place at three levels, first at the state level in which the individual states deal with the problem; second at the union level, in which the union government provide funds and security forces to tackle the Naxalite groups; and third at the intrastate level, where the states cooperate with each other to deal with the situation.

The government of the state of Bihar has banned all Naxalite organizations, except for CPI–ML Liberation, and has provided financial assistance to the families of the victims. The state government launched a number of centrally assisted schemes aimed at providing better infrastructure and communication facilities, and at providing employment, but ineffective administration, corruption, and class interests made them unproductive. In December 2000, the governments of Bihar and Jharkhand mounted a coordinated offensive against the Naxalites; Bihar also put together a special task force with 150 commandos for anti-Naxalite operations and deployed them in hypersensitive areas. Additional policemen are undergoing specialized commando training. They appear, thus, to be addressing the situation more as a security problem than as a socioeconomic problem.

The government of Andhra Pradesh has adopted a multipronged approach to the Naxalite problem. Since the issue has its origins in socioeconomic underdevelopment, attempts have been made to address this by special programs for youth, the formation of cooperative societies of tribals, the improvement of primary health centres, village water-tank repairs, the provision of drinking water, roads, schools, youth clubs, etc.

The police have formed a special anti-Naxal force (the Greyhounds), which is specially trained in guerrilla warfare and equipped with sophisticated weaponry. A coordinated and consistent police action has resulted in the elimination of most of the top leadership of the movement and the year 2000 saw extremist-related killings decrease by around 20 percent. The enforcement agencies are positive that the two-decade-old problem will soon be solved.

The AP government has also tried to win back the peasantry by redistributing some of the land in the north Telengana region and has initiated programs to lure the Naxalites into surrendering by helping them to reintegrate into the mainstream society. Since 1993, when the program started, nearly four thousand Naxalites have surrendered and more than one thousand have been rehabilitated. During the last couple of years, the government has approached the left-wing extremist problem less as a police (law-and-order) problem and more as a socioeconomic issue. Those who surrender are rehabilitated. The rewards include the distribution of Jeeps, tractors, and auto rickshaws along with financial assistance to start shops. For this purpose, rehabilitation mela (fairs) are organized, attended by politicians and officials.

The Naxalites are opposed to any form of representative government under the present constitution and have issued poll boycotts. In the last ten years nearly 250 political leaders belonging to various political parties have been killed. Since other leftist parties, particularly the parliamentary parties, are catering to the same classes, it is not uncommon for leaders of these parties to be targeted.

Still, some understanding exists between the Naxalites and some political parties: it is not uncommon for right-of-center parties to seek the help of the Naxalites for getting elected in Naxal-dominated areas in return for the release of

Naxalites or their sympathizers from prison and stopping police action against them. In Bihar and Jharkhand, leaders of almost every political party, including some leaders of the BJP and of the Samata Party, have been making efforts to keep the Naxalite leaders on their side. The parties do not openly condemn the Naxalites at public meetings and refer to them as misguided brethren.

The extent of support accorded to the Naxalites by the main political parties in AP remains unclear as the policy keeps fluctuating. The Congress government banned the PWG in 1992. Four years later, all curbs were lifted and the PWG was permitted to operate freely and hold meetings without any restriction, before it was banned again. N. T. Rama Rao, founder of the Telegu Desam Party, which then came to power, offered the Naxalites a "red salute" and called them "true patriots, who have been misunderstood by [the] ruling classes." The current TDP chief minister Chandrababu Naidu has expressed his willingness to hold talks with the outlawed PWG or any other Naxalite group and help them to reintegrate in society. The underground leadership of the PWG had recently said that it was ready for talks with the government. However, the PWG had laid several preconditions for the talks, including the withdrawal of the ban on the group and action against police officials involved in "fake encounters." The role of regional and international organizations in this issue is minimal. The regional organization—South Asian Association of Regional Cooperation (SAARC)—has no mandate to deal with these issues. India traditionally has been against any external involvement in its domestic issues. Besides, none of the other countries in the region or elsewhere has anything at stake in this ongoing conflict.

MULTI TRACK DIPLOMACY

Whenever a massacre is perpetrated by the Naxalites, there is widespread condemnation of both the Naxalites and the governments for their inability to come to a negotiated solution, but on the ground improvements over the last quarter century seem to have been minimal. The media do play an important role in reporting whatever gruesome murders have taken place, but otherwise by and large are silent on the various social and economic issues underlying the conflict. The state governments' response has varied according to the policies of political parties in power and the scale of the problem. While AP has banned the PWG, formed an exclusive counter-Naxal police force, and made it a punishable offense to provide food or shelter to the Naxalites, Madhya Pradesh is keen to negotiate with the Naxalites in order to solve the problem.

A result of these disparate responses is that Naxalites committing crimes in one place flee to another where government policy is favourable to them. Following the killing of a high-profile minister from AP in March 2000, the union home affairs ministry has set up a coordination committee of the seven states most affected by leftist extremism. Their police chiefs have been meeting regularly. The central government has already granted several proposals submitted by the states for developmental activities that would help tackle Naxalism at the social and economic levels.

In some areas, the Naxalites have been able to muster public support among the downtrodden people. The polarization between the have-nots and the landed elite is sharp in areas in Bihar and Jharkhand where the Naxalites operate. The upper section of civil society, the upper classes and castes, finds the Naxalites hostile to its social and economic interests, and it has organized private militia called senas, particularly the Ranvir Sena, to safeguard their interests.

As defenders of the interests of the poor villagers, Naxalites can count on a more sympathetic response from the villagers themselves. They give them shelter against the forces of law and order. NGOs such as the People's Union for Democratic Rights (PUDR) have taken sides in this caste and class conflict. In one of its reports, the PUDR considers the birth of Marxist-Leninist organizations and their growing support among the peasantry a direct outcome of the social order and the failure of the state to implement its own laws. A similar position is being taken by the People's Revolutionary Front. This ideological alignment with the Naxalite movement has somewhat diminished the neutral status of the PUDR, but it remains one of the foremost human-rights organizations in the country.

In AP, the Committee of Concerned Citizens (CCC), People's Union for Civil Liberties (PUCL), Association for the Protection of Democratic Rights, AP Civil Liberties Committee (APCLC), and United Struggle Committee Against Fake Encounters are some of the organizations that have also raised their voices against police/government action against the Naxalites. They have frequently voiced their concern about the number of Naxalites who are killed in "encounters," labeling them "false encounters." In the wake of an "encounter" that left three central-committee members of the PWG dead in December 1999, civil-liberty activists were able to mobilize as many as forty-six different organizations and coordinate rallies protesting the police action.

The CCC and PUCL for years have been trying—unsuccessfully—to negotiate a settlement between the government and the Naxalites. However, as in Bihar, their position as a mediator is impaired by their focus on misbehavior by government staff and institutions, passing over terrorist acts by Naxalites. They have also tended to remain oblivious to the hardships caused to the people and damage to property by the Naxalites. The government therefore sees them as front organizations of the Naxalites. Consequently, their decade-long talks with the government have yielded little result. However, the reports they bring out and the press campaigns they organize are invaluable as sources that document the human-rights violations involved.

At the international level, Human Rights Watch (HRW) has been monitoring the problem for a long time and has made recommendations to the state and central governments. It has carried out a number of studies and investigations, and has approached the state government directly with a list of suggestions. These include the prosecution of senior officials found to be complicit in the attacks, the provision of full security to villagers, placing police pickets away from upper-caste areas, and creating independent commissions of investigation.

Prospects

The extremist communist movement is often analysed as a highly fragmented and splintered movement without a proper road map, intent only on violence and destruction. Yet, in a number of districts, it has survived for many decades. The reasons for its endurance are related to a number of factors. First, land reforms have not been properly carried out and landlords have been left in effective control of land, credit, and labor markets.

The major Naxalite outfits thrive on the issue of land redistribution and proper wages and labor treatment. Second, the governments, which are often controlled by the urban upper-class elites and the rural landlord class, have not extended infrastructural facilities to the remote and backward areas. Many villages in Jharkhand and Bihar are without even basic necessities such as schools, health centres, roads, electricity, and water. The government's failure has resulted in the growth of the Naxalite movement with its parallel governments there. In North Telengana, conditions are somewhat better, and the issue is more a law-and-order than a socioeconomic problem. The extremist groups operating there have become more interested in extortion than in the socioeconomic improvement of poor tribals and peasants. Finally, the collusion between vested political interests and extremist politics may be an added reason.

Some progress has been made. In West Bengal, the cradle of the Naxalite movement, extremist tendencies have been brought under control through an effective socioeconomic program, including land reforms, and an effective (police) administration. The success achieved by counter-Naxalite operations in AP registering an 18 percent decline in the year 2000 is a pointer to the general optimism that the movement can be brought under control.

Leftist extremism in the 1960s could be tackled more effectively due to a strong centralized authority and because basically the same party (the Congress Party) was in power at the center and in the states. With political fragmentation and with decentralization, law and order being a state subject, the effective response to the problem has been lacking. The states with a Naxalite problem have woken up to the need for concerted action and have had a series of interstate meetings beginning in December 1999. With the states' responses getting more organized than in the past two decades, the extremist movement will face greater challenges.

Recommendations

An effective response to Naxalism would have to include strategies at three levels. The Naxalite movement can thrive in an environment where economic development is lagging, where the old exploitative classes (feudal lords, contractors, and traders) have not been dislodged by modernization and development, and where the government machinery has not been made transparent by the pressure of a functioning democracy.

At the first level, the lack of socioeconomic development provides a breeding ground for discontent and extremist solutions. The implementation of tenancy reforms, protecting the rights of sharecroppers, and the payment of minimum wages require urgent attention. In some of the areas, land redistribution should help to create sustenance for landless labor families and curtail the power of landlords. Governments must ensure that existing facilities are properly utilized: schools, primary health centres, and government extension facilities should be run in such a way that the most downtrodden people have unhindered access. A basic-needs strategy, including a network of roads that makes the areas more accessible, will help to open the remote and backward areas to the outside world. If these conditions are fulfilled, the breeding ground for violent resistance will be reduced.

Second, law and order being a state responsibility, efforts at countering the Naxalite problem have until recently been undertaken only at the state level. There is a need for coordinated and uniform policies and for coordinated police action, including resource and intelligence sharing across the states, to tackle the problem from a law-and-order angle. There is also a need for evenhandedness by the police and administration, who tend to come down heavily on Naxalites yet remain inactive when private armies of landlords (senas) resort to violence.

A case could be made for the modernization of the police force in order to increase their effectiveness and morale. The problem, however, is to distinguish between terrorist activities and poor-people's movements, and it is imperative for the police to be evenhanded. All too often repressive behaviour by the elite has not been curtailed or punished, and this permissiveness had been a breeding ground for terrorist reactions. Citizens' vigilance committees should be given an official status so that they can help in separating legitimate action against terrorist and criminal outfits and human-rights abuse in actions against rightful political activities.

The often repressive onslaught, of which genuine Naxalite organizations have been the target, often in fake encounters, should be considered as a human-rights abuse, and should be allowed to be investigated as such. On the other hand, the various Naxalite outfits should also allow civil-society organizations, other than the human-rights groups associated with them, to investigate cases of manslaughter and large-scale killings. Their extremist political stand continues to prevent a united front of all organizations and political parties fighting for the poor and thus in fact sustains the very power of exploitative classes and castes.

Social and economic rehabilitation programs to bring the discontented Naxalites into the mainstream would be helpful. Currently, only AP has a comprehensive package for rehabilitating surrendered Naxalites. The problem with such programs is that it may reward those who have held villages at ransom, and who continue to do so in alignment with mainstream political leaders. The programs have also been utilized by mainstream politicians in a secret understanding with Naxalite leaders. Development finances meant for the general good of the poor people in the affected areas should not take second position to the individual buying out of Naxalites willing to surrender.

INDIA, BETWEEN NUCLEAR EUPHORIA AND NAXALITE INSURRECTION

India is the second most populous country in the world and at the same time one of the most unknown. While on the one hand China and Russia are courting India so as to create a real counterweight to the United States, the country's oligarchy want to break with that proposed alliance and to do so are using the issue of nuclear power. Still, US proposals to share technology and nuclear fuel with India lack India's agreement on a crucial matter : whether or not to carry out new nuclear tests. The US opposes them, while India thinks that agreeing to US demands would limit its right to process depleted uranium fuel, a key step to obtain plutonium and, thus, would limit its sovereignty.

This is not only the official government position but that of the opposition, on both Right and Left, and of scientists, who demand that the agreement not be ratified unless Parliament does so beforehand. On that, both the Communist Party of India (Marxist), with 44 seats of the New Delhi Parliament's total of 543, and the right-wing Bharatiya Janata (138 seats) agree and without them it is impossible to get a parliamentary majority. The pressure is such that if Prime Minister Manmohan Singh ratifies the agreement without parliamentary approval it would bring down his coalition government. It is worth noting that the government is made up of a centrist three party alliance led by the National Congress Party of India (145 seats), the Rashtriya Janata Dal (21 seats) and the Dravida Munnetra Kazhagam (16 seats), supported from outside government by the Left Front (Marxist Communist Party of India with 44 seats, and the Communist Party of India with 10 seats) together with other regionalist and ethnic parties.

The Bush administration began the process of agreement with India on the nuclear issue in March 2006, at the same time as the beginning of the nuclear crisis with Iran. That rapprochement consisted of the recognition by the US of India's nuclear capacity, justified as part of an effort by Bush to prevent proliferation of nuclear weapons, avoid an arms race between India and Pakistan and reinforce India-US ties. It put an end to the 30-year embargo on nuclear material imposed on India in 1974 when India-which is a non-signatory of the Nuclear Arms Non-Proliferation treaty, while Iran is-carried out its first nuclear test. In accordance with the agreement, which is up in the air for now, India would accept the presence of International Atomic Energy Authority (IAEA) inspectors in 14 of its nuclear installations and would clearly separate the civilian and military aspects of its nuclear programme. But the agreement went even further : it sought to have India break off all its energy and military agreements with Iran. The US offer included stronger trade links with Kazakhstan and Turkmenistan, two Central Asian states with large energy reserves, especially gas, and likewise with Afghanistan and Pakistan to make good India's energy deficit if it were to break with Iran.

Both India and Pakistan have signed an agreement with Iran to build an oil pipeline, "the oil pipeline of Peace" worth US$7bn, to distribute gas to the three countries and this is expected to be formally signed on June 30th. This is something the US is trying to avoid at all costs since at the end of June it intended to return to the UN Security Council asking for a new set of harder sanctions against Iran for not halting its nuclear programme. Already early pressures are being applied by the US to the member countries of the UN Security Council so as to include gas companies within the sanctions. As usual, US foreign policy carries an undeniable element of coercion and in this case more than usual : in exchange for the signing of a nuclear agreement, the Bush Administration would support India's entry into the Security Council as a permanent member, although without veto rights.

According to the UN reforms timidly initiated by Kofi Annan, the UN Security Council would be enlarged taking into account new global realities and would include as permanent members, without right of veto, Germany for Europe, Nigeria or South Africa for Africa, Brazil or Mexico for Latin America and India or Japan for Asia. The criterion used by Kofi Annan was demographic and economic weight, dressing it up with criteria of greater representation in the UN's executive body for different peoples and cultures.

MAOIST INSURRECTION AND THE STRUGGLE FOR LAND

India aspires to become an unrivalled regional power by 2015. But, to achieve that, guaranteeing its energy needs (oil and, preferably, gas) is vital and it is in this regard that nuclear energy plays an important role. Since its independence from

Great Britain, India has tried to set out from what one might call "an economy of size", taking advantage, in other words, of its geographic and population potential. However, despite enormous social differences revolutionary forces, or the Left, if you like, have had difficulty making progress given that capitalism has developed slowly but constantly. The explanation for this situation is that since independence in 1947 India had relatively developed industry and a wealthy, powerful bourgeoisie very adept both at international politics (one should not forget India's importance in creating the Movement of Non-Aligned Countries) and national politics, integrating social measures-although without abolishing the caste system-with outright capitalist ones.

However, during the last 18 years, India has implemented neoliberal policies, gradually dismantling its centralized economy and privatizing its main sectors under the wing of a battery of laws to protect Direct Foreign Investments, especially those from the United States that have now increased from US$76m to US$4bn. At the moment, India's gross domestic product is about US$786bn, four times that of the rest of countries in South Asia.

This policy has led to an increase in the middle classes to around 300 million people, the Bollywood movie watchers and migrants to Europe or the United States and who are more and more isolated from disadvantaged classes not only along traditional caste divisions but in economic matters too. It is reckoned that more than 700 million Indians live in the most absolute poverty. Almost all of them are rural workers who live on small plots of land of less than one hectare and who depend on big private businesses for supplies of seed, fertiliser and other inputs. Furthermore they have to survive amidst impressive industrial projects (especially mining projects) and water projects that flood their land or else expropriate them at absurd prices. To that one has to add the traditional oppression that lower castes have suffered since time immemorial and the ever-increasing presence of paramilitaries in the service of big landowners.

So it is no wonder then that a Maoist insurrection is spreading across India like an oil stain across paper, already affecting 14 of India's 28 States (Chatisgarh, Jharkhand, Uttar Pradesh, Asma, Uttaranchal, Kerala, Tamil Nadu, West Bengal, Gujarat, Andhra Pradesh, Madhya Pradesh, Orissa, Maharashtra and Bihar). In figures, that means the Maoists are in control in 165 districts out of the total of 602 into which the country is divided. In fact in the last five states mentioned one can say that "popular new democratic power" is a reality, given that they are the ones who control the countryside, collect taxes from large businesses within their zones of influence, build dykes and irrigation systems, impart justice, decide land disputes among rural families and have suppressed, for example, child marriage. Prime Minister Singh recognised the Maoist advance on August 23rd 2006 when he declared solemnly to Parliament that the Maoists "have become the biggest internal challenge to security that India has."

To deal with the Maoist surge the New Delhi government put into practice the well known US strategy from Vietnam, later perfected in Central America during the revolutionary processes in El Salvador and, above all, in Guatemala : the creation of strategic hamlets and the formation of paramilitary patrols to defend them (in Guatemala, the Civilian Self-Defence Patrols). In India they are known as Slawa Judum (that translates as "Peace Hunters") and have the status of "special police agents" in rural communities. They are especially active in Chatisgarh and it is against them that the guerrilla offensive is currently aimed. An ambush on March 15th killed 50 out of a joint force of police and paramilitaries. The main activity of the paramilitaries is the forced displacement of rural families to "temporary camps" set up in the areas of Bhairamgarh, Gedam y Bijapur and in which 50,000 people are currently crowded.

Paid by landowners and by the Indian government itself, the paramilitaries earn about 1500 rupees a month (about €26 or US$35). The counter-insurgency war, as in the Central American countries mentioned or in Peru or Colombia, uses terror to try and cut off the guerrilla advance. It is estimated that Salwa Judum has 5000 members and the ideologue, just as with the Colombian paramilitaries protected by current President Alvaro Uribe during his time as governor of the

Antioquia province, was the main Congress Party leader in Chatisgarh. This is the party of Prime Minister Singh. To those 5000, one must add about 2000 "anti-terrorist" police who have undergone a similar training programme to that given to the Atlacatl battalion, in El Salvador, which committed countless mass murders, outrages, intimidation and forced displacements. In case this paramilitary force is insufficient to stop the guerrilla, the government also offers bounties of up to a million rupees (about €17,000 or US$23,000) for the betrayal of the main guerrilla leaders.

This strategy is favoured in the "red zone", a category applied by the Indian government to the states of Andhra Pradesh, Madhya Pradesh, Orissa, Maharashtra y Bihar, although in the last few months an impressive guerrilla military campaign has begun in Chatisgarh which has made the new Delhi government focus on this state leaving its plans for the other states in abeyance. The reason the guerrillas are prioritizing Chatisgarh is that this state, along with Jharkand, is turning into the spearhead of the government's neoliberal policies following the signing of juicy, million-dollar contracts with big national and multinational industrial corporations, on steel, iron, coal and electricity, which presuppose a new wave of rural families in exodus to wretched slums in the cities. In fact, the most recent guerrilla attack was on June 3rd against the electricity plant of Narayanpur, a district of Chatisgarh.

The Maoists say little when they carry out their actions. It is a fact that guerrilla control in this state is almost complete, with 10 of its 16 districts in their power and that their military actions are more and more daring, including attacks against officials, police, politicians and strategic economic and industrial targets.

The government's aim is to confine the Maoist presence to that "red zone" and avoid it spreading with equal force to the rest of the country. Once that objective is achieved, repression will centre on what can be called "support bases" or liberated zones. Nonetheless, it is the different States that have responsibility for security matters, not central government, which explains why police implement the repression rather than the army, and there are different opinions about the best way to confront the guerrilla. In Andra Pradesh the tendency is to negotiate directly, while in Chatisgarh the paramilitary phenomenon is used, to mention the most extreme examples. These positions are influenced by the role the moderate Left has in different State governments and even in the central government which would collapse without the Left's support, as was pointed out earlier. This is the reason why timid agrarian reform is being advanced throughout India and which has as a pilot experience the one implemented in 2005 in the mother State of the guerrillas, West Bengal.

For the moment the guerrillas are ignoring the cities to focus on total control of the countryside, following the old strategy of surrounding the cities from the countryside. The strategy is to penetrate rural areas, consolidate in them and, once the bases of support are deemed secure, to go on building up effective and efficient links with different cells in other states. It is the classic strategy that has given such good results in Nepal. As with their Nepalese comrades, the Indian Maoists respect local officials-including the police-if the people think they are honest and not compromised by cases of corruption or repression. They also respect businesses established in their zones of influence but they collect from them a "revolutionary tax", which varies between 15% and 20 % of their profits, to fund their operations.

History of the Naxalites

The Indian Maoists are known as Naxalites from the town of Naxalbari in West Bengal, where the first armed actions occurred of an organization called the People's War Group, the armed wing of the Communist Party of India (Marxist-Leninist) which, with the slogan of radical reform of land ownership, forced a stand-off through the 1960s with the Indian government. Although the rebellion they led-land occupations, burning of catastral property registers, forgiveness of rural families' mortgage debts and execution of the most important oppressors and usurers-only lasted three months, it ended with a very severe repression that caused more than 100,000 deaths and the virtual disappearance of the organization's members. But some groups carried on operating, although without mutual contact. This led to the fragmentation of the CPI-ML which lasted until 2003 when the Maoist Communist Centre and the Indian Revolutionary Communist Centre united to form the Maoist Communist Centre of India (CCMI) and, one year later in 2004, the integration of a tendency of the CPI-ML called "Popular War". That is how the Communist Party of India (Maoist) came into being with its main slogan as "the fight against feudalism and imperialism".

If one can believe reports of the Indian intelligence services, the country's Maoists have been tempered in the revolutionary popular war in Nepal where they have won greater political training and military experience. The intelligence services reckon that the People's Guerrilla Army (the Indian Maoists military wing) last year counted on 8000 combatants, 25,000 militia members-protecting support bases, carrying out intelligence work and logistic support for the combatants-and 50,000 political members. Small numbers if one considers that India is a country with 1bn inhabitants. But the rapid development of the Maoist movement has set off alarm bells among India's political elite. The immiseration of two thirds of India's people and their social oppression counteract elite desires to turn India into a regional power via nuclear weapons and an agreement with the United States. Today the Naxalites are a reality that has to be taken into account. Perhaps westerners looking to India have been able to learn that "naxa" in the Indian vocabulary now means "rebel rural worker" and that the current and past struggles of the naxalites are part of modern Indian culture, even of its cinema.

TACKLING MAOISTS: THE ANDHRA PARADIGM

Today the greatest danger to India's independence and flourishing democracy is the danger posed by the ever widening zones of Maoist influence. The Maoists want to turn back the clock of history by a hundred years and engulf India in flames, thereby ceding great advantages to our predatory adversaries who are playing a waiting game like the hungry wolves of the highlands. The Maoists are even prepared to split India in order to seize power over whatever parts they can effectively control. This danger will get magnified if ever the Indian Army gets involved in the political game to drag it into anti Maoist operations. We cannot let the same error committed by the

KMT regime in China during the last century be repeated in India. Since 'law and order' is normally a State subject, many of the States having large proportion of poor and tribal population have been turning a blind eye, and the *politicians-contractors-elites* have been desperately trying to work out temporary arrangements to buy peace.

Maoists and the Armed Forces

Today the Maoists dominated areas already cover the vast coal, iron ore, and alumina rich mining areas, as well as many vital hydroelectric and irrigation dam project areas of the country, thereby directly threatening swift national development and vital investments. As the Maoists can freely move from one State to another through the adjacent forested areas, they are able to concentrate their cadres and strike with dreadful effect even on very large targets like Jails, District HQs, large raw material factories, hijack trains, or disrupt national rail and road corridors with impunity.

These acts cause a further telling demoralizing effect on the affected State's Police Force, while the other neighbouring States watch and think themselves to be lucky this time. The Central Government has been busy keeping statistics and occasionally taking political mileage in opposition ruled States, while its Home Ministry's Paramilitary Forces remains divided as several separate entities without any central unified controlling, coordinating and internal security operations directing HQ.

Had this situation existed in say Iran, all the PMFs would have been merged into the Iranian Revolutionary Guards, and would have emerged as an elite force dreaded by their opponents even more than their country's Army. In this quagmire of political rivalries, bureaucratic inaction, police empires, and lack of support for imaginative, effective policing coupled with simultaneous government supported developmental schemes, the shining example of Andhra Pradesh stands out within the Indian Union - in tackling the Maoists' violence head on and winning the war hands down. The Andhra Pradesh Police have borrowed the motto of the famous *Selous Scouts* (of Rhodesia), "The Bush War has to be Fought in the Bushes" and lived up to it.

BACKGROUND TO THE MAOIST MOVEMENT IN INDIA

The first armed Communist movement in India took place in the Telengana region of present day Andhra Pradesh during the early fifties. It was brutally put down after great loss of life and unleashing of oppression against the poor peasants. The movement's leaders included several idealists, though they too committed heinous and unpardonable crimes. The Telengana region even today has produced the most dedicated and committed Maoist cadres and leaders in India.

During the late sixties and early seventies the Naxalite movement started and spread in many parts of India, most notably in West Bengal and Kerala. But within a matter of five to six years, this dangerous and anarchist ideology was effectively tackled by the State Police forces and many of those who had taken up arms were eliminated. Generally peace prevailed from the mid seventies onwards. Leftist ideologues continued their activities using democratic means and formed many regional splinter groups. However their mass influence and acceptance was minimal. From the mid nineties many armed radical Communist Dalams became active in the common underdeveloped and adjacent forested areas of Bihar, Jharkhand, West Bengal, Orissa, Chathisgarh, Madhya Pradesh, Maharashtra and Andhra Pradesh. However it was the leaders from Andhra Pradesh who took the lead to unify these groups, formulate their common dogma and policies, start centralized armed training of core cadres, ensure an efficient arms and explosives procurement network, coordinate the intelligence gathering by over ground workers and sympathizers, and develop operational capabilities based on hitting weak targets with overwhelming local superiority followed by quick dispersal. They worked amongst the poor and dispossessed and acted frequently against the exploiters thus gaining a strong local following and acceptability.

Maoist Threat and Politics

Their morale also got a tremendous boost when the Nepali Maoist movement became very strong and entrenched against the oppressive and corrupt Royal rule there. Thus a great swathe of Maoist dominated influence came into being by the first decade of this century. Funds flowed into their coffers from the mining interests, contractors, and from illegal octroi collections. The States abdicated their authority over vast regions, as long as the semblance of normalcy could be maintained and the electoral interests of the dominant political party could be taken care of. However this facade had to crack one day, as the doctrine of power dictates that the superior entity has to keep on expanding in order to ensure its very survival, until a balance of power and human failings combine to dictate the limits.

We have presently reached this stage in our country. The Maoists, respective State Governments, and the Central Government have all become aware of each other's strengths, but are not yet ready to raise the stakes any further and go all out for the required push which is essential to achieve total victory.

The Situation in Andhra Pradesh during the Nineties and Early Part of this Decade

The newly formed Telugu Desam had stormed to power in 1989 creating a world record for the shortest period after registration as a political party, for an entity to win an election. Many populist schemes were undertaken by NT Rama Rao during his first stint as CM, and he enjoyed vast mass support. During his next term in office after winning power again in the 1994 elections, many deviations and laxity of administration set in, besides family squabbles, which culminated in his being unseated and the reins of power going to N Chandrababu Naidu in 1995 who was an astute politician and a strong administrator. Simultaneously the Maoist organisations became strong all over Andhra Pradesh. Many youths flocked to this movement both as over-ground workers as well as in the ranks of the underground armed cadres. A parallel administration was created in many Mandals (Taluks). But Chandrababu Naidu also rose to the occasion and tackled the bull by the horns. Being not part of the Central Government, he did not expect much help from the Centre nor did he wish to be overly dependant. After several brainstorming sessions with his close advisers and noted security experts, he decided upon a two pronged approach of re-establishing the writ of the civil administration and ensuring that developmental works are pursued, and secondly strengthening and revitalizing the Police Force whatever be the costs. The Andhra Pradesh Police Force underwent a total transformation in its work culture and level of accountability and within a year's time started showing results against the Maoists. They gained the upper hand against the entrenched Maoists who then either laid low or migrated to neighbouring States, or got eliminated.

TERRORIST TENTACLES IN INDIA

This activist policy was continued by his successor YS Rajasekhara Reddy of the Congress who won the elections in 2004. YSR's entire focus was on the upliftment of the rural population. He spent the colossal sum of Rs 50,000 crores in setting up new irrigation schemes and improving the existing ones over a period of five years. Slowly the peasants became Kulaks and benefited from State sponsored subsidies like free power, land allotments, heavily subsidized housing schemes, scholarships, free emergency ambulance service, very low cost Group Health Insurance Scheme (Arogyasri) - where the costs of treatment in any private hospital for any serious ailment was fully reimbursed to the poor.

The oxygen of the Maoists got turned off, as here was a Government which was totally focused on rural development and upliftment of the poor classes, even though urban development and industrial sectors were gravely neglected compared to the previous Telugu Desam government. But at no time was security ever neglected. The Central funding components could be tapped to the fullest extent for various schemes, and this helped the State to usher in even larger budgets. Andhra Pradesh today has the largest state budget in India, even bigger than that of Bangladesh.

AP Government's Successful Methods Against the Maoists and Its Police Tactics

The State Police's Intelligence Wing has been separated from the Police HQs and made an independent establishment reporting directly to the CM's Office. It does not have any rigid territorial restrictions and can follow up any leads. The intelligence setup has been provided with competent officers, ample funds, and necessary technical backup. Next, most of the Armed Reserve Police Battalions have been converted into Commando Units and they come under the Greyhounds Grouping having a separate IG. All new Police inductees have to spend their first four years of service in these Greyhound Units before getting their transfer to the District Police Establishments. Meritorious service with the Greyhound Units has been made a mandatory requirement to get accelerated promotions, including for filling up of Grade I Officer Posts selection vacancies in the State Cadre.

The naked truth of Naxalism

All Greyhound personnel serving in Maoist affected areas were given 50 per cent additional Commando Pay as incentive. The Greyhounds Training School was revamped and new Training Courses and Methodologies introduced, which are conducted with strict devotion and supervision. Suitable training facilities have been built up at each Greyhounds Unit location for imparting refresher training.

The concept of keeping one Administrative and Security Duties Company and one Training Company at all times in the Battalion HQ has been strictly implemented. Most importantly the remaining six companies were deployed as three Joint Operational Bases (JOBs) consisting of two companies each. Experience proved that single company deployment was not giving optimum operational results nor providing the necessary nucleus for the civil administration to function safely and effectively in the Maoist affected regions. These JOBs in the heart of Maoist affected areas were located within mutually supporting distances.

It was normal for a complete Greyhounds Battalion to be deployed within 1-2 gravely Maoist affected Mandal (Taluk) areas, as then they could operate without fear of IEDs, ambushes etc. Each such Greyhound JOB also had two Home Guard Platoons who were recruited from amongst the locals. Over a period of time, they acted as guides, interpreters etc, besides performing most of the routine garrison functions, thus freeing the Greyhounds for 'area domination' and 'seek encounter' patrolling operations. Each Greyhound JOB could send out upto four platoon strength patrols out, at any given time. Hostel facilities were created within the JOB for the Government officials of various rural development departments as well as for contractors and their staff to stay and work in total safety. Each Greyhound JOB always had a Dy SP/Asst SP ranked Class I Gazetted Officer as In Charge. This created a sea change in the environment and ensured accountability for maintaining sustained operations. Within a few months itself, the Maoists started feeling asphyxiated as their domination ended.

Carrot and Stick!

Another important functional aspect was that the Greyhounds did not report to or work under the District Police set up. The Greyhound Units reported to the Special DIG HQ In Charge for that Maoist affected Region, overlapping- several adjacent districts. Their operations were supplemented by adequate Technical Intelligence Teams working under this Special DIG HQ, which could intercept any wireless transmission made by the Maoists and do the Direction Finding Fix. With the advent of cellular phones, they also specialized in tracking down Maoist locations using fixes made from two or more cell phone Towers.

This enhanced the accuracy of directed response, and reduced the time lag for the Greyhound patrol teams to make active contact with the Maoist Dalams. The credit for developing the Greyhounds' organization, selection, training and successful tactics primarily goes to their then IG Dr. Durga Prasad, who could out-think and outwit the well entrenched Maoists and also keep progressively adapting.

The sustained campaign carried out by the Andhra Pradesh State Police during 2005 to clear the Nallamalla Hills region in the heart of Andhra Pradesh encompassing the adjacent forested areas of Kurnool, Prakasam, and Kadapa districts is a classic success story in counter insurgency operations in India, worth being emulated by even the Indian Army in J&K. The Maoist Dalams were well embedded in this region for over 15 years and nobody from the Government dared to go into these areas. Four Greyhound Units working under a single

Special DIG HQ established 13 JOBs covering the mountainous and forested terrain of approximately 5000 sq km. This works out to an area coverage of approximately 400 sq km per JOB at the peak of operations.

The Maoists reacted very violently with great stealth, IED blasts, assassination of locals, and planned ambushes. But within a matter of six months, the weekly attrition rates started taking their toll and their cadres got demoralized, as they had to keep running in the jungles constantly without getting shelter and sufficient help from the habitated areas.

The Greyhounds went on improving in their tactics and morale. Their losses were few and were immediately replaced in both men and equipment. After a year's time there were no more Maoists left in this area and they were forced to give up this legendary bastion.

Thereafter the Greyhounds strength there was reduced to one half of the original deployment. After the period of active operations was over, the Greyhounds deployment in the JOBs was never brought down to below Company strength for very sound operational and functional reasons, and the Maoists have so far not ventured to come back into this erstwhile 'liberated' zone. The relieved Greyhound Units have been redeployed onto the other Maoist affected interstate border areas, where they have repeated their operational successes and driven the Maoists out of AP. The neighbouring States then started requesting the Greyhounds to operate across the border.

The Big Picture

The lesson learnt is that there is no armed insurgency in India which cannot be put down within two years, if the right proportion of forces differential is created and sustained locally for at least a period of six months. After wiping out the insurgents in a particular area, 50 per cent of the Security Forces can be redeployed to another area to create the right Forces differential there. The French treatise 'Pacification Operations in Algeria' written in 1963 by Col David Galuta clearly summarized counterinsurgency as "80 per cent protection of the civil population by cutting down 'unrisky access' to them by the insurgents, and the balance 20 per cent of the effort to be directed in maintaining a steady and sustained attrition rate - on weekly and monthly basis." At no cost should the first cleared target region be left totally denuded of Security Forces deployment, otherwise within a matter of a few months, insurgency conditions will be back to previous levels, and the hard won gains would have soon got frittered away.

The Economics and Good Governance Aspects of the Anti Maoist Offensive in AP

What Chandrababu Naidu perfected as the new Police methodology to tackle and root out the armed Maoist groupings, this has been exceeded in far greater measure and significance by his successor, the Late YS Rajasekhar Reddy (YSR) in his epochal shifting of the direction of State spending towards the Rural Sector, creation of additional irrigation potential (Jalayagnam Scheme), and several Poverty Alleviation Programmes never before seen in India since Independence. The total allocations for Rural Sector activities are double that of for all the Urban Sector - Infrastructure Development, and Industrial Promotion activities combined.

This approach had not only brought rich political dividends, but also has knocked the winds out of all Maoist and Naxalite 'ground level organizers' even in the most remote hamlets. The popular saying goes that though the roads in Andhra Pradesh may still be full of potholes, and the urban areas perhaps the dirtiest, but in the rural areas there is not a single member of a poor household who has not benefited from at least three of the following freebies - viz seven hours of assured and free electricity for agricultural activity, free low cost house, 25 kg of heavily subsidized rice for each household, Very Low Cost (and all encompassing) Health Insurance Scheme (Arogyasri), Reimbursement of Higher Education Fees for low income families, and anyone type of Social Welfare Pension for the Aged or Destitute.

YSR never gave the least opportunity or space to his political detractors to exploit any popular resentment, and he was always found touring and checking the progress of development activities in all the districts of this vast State.

Conclusion

Tackling the long-standing and burning issue of armed Maoist violence and unquestioned domination of the vital raw materials producing regions of the country has become an urgent national issue which can no longer be procrastinated or wished away.

The Maoists have cleverly played upon the sentiments and decades of developmental neglect experienced by the poor people in remote regions, to build up a strong base of sympathizers, dedicated over-ground workers, and most significantly - armed Dalams consisting of battle hardened cadres who have already tasted success and have no fear of the Security Forces. They can now converge into Battalion or Brigade sized groupings at their time and place of choosing. With each passing day the Police Forces of the affected States grow more limp and hold the Maoists in greater dread.

The Maoists are clearly winning the battle of the mind and they only have to wait to increase in strength. At this rate the Maoist problem will soon start pulling down the country's favourable GDP growth rate by at least one to two per cent. It is true that Law and Order is a State subject, but the Centre cannot wash its hand away, especially in areas where there is no law and order left and the affected States are asking for help. Anti-Maoist operations cannot be treated like the hurried and non-organic additional deployment of Paramilitary Forces during election time.

It is no point assigning some additional number of PMF Companies collected from different Units from many parts of the country, to be placed at the disposal of the district administration for short periods. The district police set up have neither the competence nor the required focus and skills to carry out full fledged anti-insurgency operations at their level. What is essentially required is to work out the 'CI Grid deployment' based on JOBs, and the State Police/Central PMF Special DIG HQs should be made in charge of operations, as had been done in Andhra Pradesh.

To ensure accountability, coordination, and willing cooperation of all the available Forces, there is the dire need to set up a single empowered DG level HQ of the Central PMF to coordinate with the respective State Police HQs. There should be a method worked out so that the deployment of the Central Home Ministry Forces should not last more than a period of two years, during which time the State Police Forces must get sufficiently built up and trained on the Greyhounds pattern, to relieve them permanently.

This implies that the deployment pattern of the Central PMFs has to change every year, so that the correct Forces differential can be created in the specified areas. The PMFs have the obvious disadvantage of not knowing the local language and customs, therefore adequate local State Police or Home Guards should be attached to them. The Maoist menace can surely be defeated by adopting a pan-India activist and sustained developmental approach, piecemeal and sporadic campaigns will surely fail miserably.

4

The Rise of the Maoists in Nepal

When the muddy seeds of the Maoist movement were dispersed in Nepal, in February 1996, no one expected the Maoists to rule the rooster of Nepalese politics in less than a decade. Informal attitude shown towards the Maoists by the Nepalese administration then was propelled furthermore by the widespread belief that radical communism had become a thing of the past except from a few cloudy facades of the world.

They argued that the Maoists couldn't hold their stake in Nepal, a country that shares its borders with India- the biggest democracy of the world. But nonetheless, eleven years later, it has become a major political force in Nepal. Although no one overlooks the Maoist's use of violent means and the way they came into power, solely riding on the barrels of gun, they do however on moral grounds, empathize the sentiments that ignited the revolution – a fight against the system that has overlooked the interests of the masses.

Origin of the Maoist's Conflict

Many observers see the strong correlation between the rise of Nepal's Maoists to the demise of the absolute monarchy (in 1990) and the introduction of parliamentary democracy in Nepal thereafter. According to this school of thought, Democracy failed to live up to the expectations of many Nepalese, especially the rural populations and the opportunity strived unemployed youths.

The fall of an age-old totalitarianism led to rampant corruption followed by social and political instability, and absolute abuse of authority and power. All of these activities fueled the frustration tanks of Nepalese. Their frustration level rose and exploded because even the restoration of democracy in Nepal deceived many as they watched in despair democracy turning into demo- crazy.

"Seventy percent of the country's wealth is in the hands of the top 12 percent households, and only 3.7% percent of the national income reaches the poorest 20 percent of the country's families, according to the report published by Nepal South Asia Centre, a Kathmandu – based think tank few years ago. Not only Nepalese researchers but also many foreign researchers saw Nepal 's enormous social disparity, rural poverty, and backwardness which acted as a catalyst for the outdated Maoists movement.

There was rampant poverty and it led to the emergence of Maoists movements. But many other scholars, though they find an iota of reality in the argument, don't agree completely. " If social and economic marginalization alone were responsible for the emergence of the communist revolt, the hill districts in the Karnali, Seti and Mahakali zones would be for a more likely candidates," wrote Saubhagya Shah in the book " Himalayan people's War: Nepal's Maoists rebellion."

He says the emergence of the Maoist's is "not only because of their grinding poverty and chronic food shortage but also because of the nature of the terrain and their remoteness from state centres." Both of these above arguments are right in their own place and vice versa. But, let us go a step further and relate the view of the expert, who has spent much of his life doing research on poverty and economic inequality.

"The relationship between inequality and rebellion is indeed a close one, and it runs both ways. That a perceived sense of inequity is a common ingredient of rebellion in societies is clear enough, but is also important to recognize that the perception of inequity, and indeed the content of that elusive concept, depends substantially on possibilities of actual rebellion." wrote Amartya Sen, a Nobel laureate of economics, in his book, "On economic inequality." He furthermore stated that the concepts of rebellion and inequality have changed remarkably over history. The very concept of inequality has gone through radical transformation. So considering this, Maoists movement in Nepal has not arisen only due to the inequality, poverty, and nature of terrain or the remoteness from state centres only. There are various factors behind the Maoists movement as their movement has gone through radical transformation and it is still transforming. What was termed as unequal by them during the initial days of their conflict may be equal today, and what was termed as equal by them may be unequal for them today. Why? Because the Nepalese society has been changing rapidly and so are its barometers such as equality, opportunity and poverty to name a few.

RIM factor

There are numerous reasons for the Maoists uprising in Nepal. And despite the argument about the domestic factors, all observers sensed an international connection that has exclusively contributed to the Maoists rebellion in Nepal. "Nepalese Maoists have openly talked about their RIM (The Revolutionary Internationalist Movement) connection and its influence in their movement. Likewise, RIM saw the Maoists movement in Nepal as one of the most significant developments for the worldwide revolutionary struggle," according to the media reports.

Meanwhile, now observers say that the Nepalese Maoists thundered the RIM's hope by locking their guns in the UN's cantonment and by joining the interim government. By doing so they sapped the blood out of the RIM. "Nepalese Maoists led entire RIM movements suffer a major setback," some experts are saying.

India, China and America factor

Maoist's transformation stunned the world, but what makes the Maoists transformation stunning are these details. Observers thought that India would never accept Maoists in Nepal as Indian government was deeply worried about the Maoists strong anti India dialects. And moreover, the linkage between the Nepal 's Maoists and Indian Maoists was also causing a headache for India. But contrary to all the popular beliefs, India changed its gear completely at the prime moment. Out of the blue, but probably with much homework, India changed its Nepal outlook. India, which was opting for the King and Seven Party alliance to alienate Maoists, upon scrutinizing the people's movement in Nepal, opted for the Seven Party – Maoists alliance instead.

New Delhi hinted that that the monarchy has derailed the democratic governance and that it has divided the political parties and endorsed bickering. Why India felt that way? Most probably because of the pressure implemented to the government by its own intellectual diplomatic communities who felt that Indian policy toward Nepal has become obsolete. India 's Nepal observers like S.D. Muni, sensed that the Nepalese traditional monarchy in itself is a problem and that it cannot be expected to solve the grave crisis engulfing Nepal. " India should therefore work with Nepal towards redefining its political order so as to help the rebels shed their arms and violent methods for a respectable and democratic place in the mainstream of Nepali national politics, "he wrote in the Sahara Times in September 2004, before then Prime Minister Deuba's visit to New Delhi.

Thereafter also, observers gave a slim chance for Maoists rise to fame in Nepal because even China, the land of Mao was against them. China was worried by the Maoists uprising in Nepal. The Chinese administration saw the Maoists movement as an indirect security threat to their own territorial integrity. " China feared that it the movement spills across Nepal 's southern border, it could provoke Indian intervention. That would be unacceptable to China, which still sees India as its rival and a security threat," according to the analysts.

Hence, alike India, China too accepted the Maoists peaceful transformation into the Nepalese political mainstream. Analyst cited the following reasons apart from the ones discussed above. Indian administration sensed that Nepal was slowly inching towards a failed state status. They feared that a failed Nepal poses a serious threat for India, which is affected by Maoist movements of her own, than a stable Nepal with Maoists in the mainstream of Nepalese politics.

And china sensed the similar prospect. "Rather than facing the possible Indian intervention in Nepal, it supported the Maoists transformation," analysts said. Meanwhile, the support of India and China to the transformation of the Maoists from rebels to the Nepalese political mainstream left no other option but to support the new political development in Nepal for the United States of America too. America also feared that if they do not support the new political development in Nepal, Nepal could end up as another failed state. And who more than America knows that in today's mutually dependent world threatened by terrorism, a failed state is alleged to be more precarious than even an aggressive but secure neighbor. That was the theory of the Europeans too.

Converging world's view of Maoists

Meanwhile, politics of Nepal has changed now. Maoists are no longer rebels. They have joined the Nepalese political mainstream and they are in the interim government too. Considering this, people and nation, are shifting their gears. With the exception of those with a conscientious partisan view, neutral observers are both critical and supportive of the Maoists joining the Nepalese political Everest. However, the success of Maoists in Nepal has opened up a broad range of issues for debates and discussions. The world's view of Maoists is converging but they are yet to reach a final ruling given the Maoists barbaric past history. Some points are clear. The world welcomes the transformation of Maoists from rebels into the mainstream of Nepali national politics but at the same time it is aware that the Maoists victory in Nepal may bolster revolutionaries all around the world. The world at this hour is scrutinizing Maoists movement. Let the Maoists keep this in mind and pave their political way forward with peace or else it is not too long before they will be diplomatically jettisoned, slowly but surely.

MAOISTS SEE RED IN NEPAL

There are rising doubts in Nepal that the country will have a new constitution by May 2010, and if it does, whether it will create a credible basis to cement the country as a democratic republic, as provided by the interim constitution enforced in early 2007. The party of Maoists which leads the incumbent coalition government continues to depict, by words and deeds, itself as a political force only capable of offering a revolutionary package. A striking instance of the Maoists' revolutionary zeal surfaced last week when the government enacted three ordinances - two of which pertained to fixing the reservation quotas for traditionally backward tribes and castes, and those whose names figure in the list of disappeared persons during the insurgency years (1996-2006). While the subjects taken up for action are not in dispute, the procedure adopted by Prime Minister Prachanda has attracted stiff opposition from the majority of the parties and their leaders, who see the Maoist move as a clear-cut case of evading the parliamentary process.

The 601-member Constituent Assembly (CA), elected last April, sits without interruption for the purpose of writing the statute; the same body, when required, can sit as a legislature any time of day or night. But Maoist ministers and their colleagues in the CA found it expedient to end the legislative session abruptly, on January 19, and about a week later took the course of ordinance to embark on a plan of action to show that their party has a progressive agenda. This rule by decree has made the Maoists unpopular as it was precisely the method the then-king, Gyanendra, adopted for 15 months after he staged a coup on February 1, 2005. He first lost power, then prestige, and eventually the institution of the monarchy itself.

Even the speaker of the CA could not help but comment on the Maoist's style of work. In an interview published in The Kathmandu Post on Monday, Subhas Nembang recalled the unpopular royal measures and made this observation, "Now the people in the movement [of April 2006] are in the government, it is their responsibility to analyze whether they have utilized the provision for ordinances in a proper manner." Members of civil society, too, are agitated by the Maoist defiance, and have urged President Ram Baran Yadav to use his discretion before giving the seal of approval to these new ordinances.

The content of some of the ordinances is not free from controversy either. For example, the ordinance for fixing reservation quotas for backward communities - Madhesi people residing in the southern region, called Terai, and men and women belonging to lower Hindu castes - have expressed anger and resentment. Rajkumar Lekhi, leader of the native Thaaru community in Terai, told a radio interviewer on Monday that his community would continue with its ongoing agitation until the provision to lump them together with rest of the so-called Madhesis is retracted. (Madhesis are recent Indian immigrants, mainly from Bihar and Uttar Pradesh).

Bin Kumar Biswakarma, who belongs to the community of blacksmiths, says it is ridiculous the way a “photocopy” of India’s reservation policy is being applied in Nepal. “How can I, even if a Dalit, support a scheme which seeks to revitalize caste hierarchy and institutionalize it?” countered Biswakarma, who is a budding youth leader in the country’s main democratic party, the Nepali Congress. Nepal could at least avoid the negative consequences of the reservation policy experienced in India. Other communities reject the entire idea of reservation, as it pushes qualification, competence and merits to the sidelines. They consider it anything but a progressive measure.

The bigger issue, however, is the task of writing a new constitution. Although the speaker has successfully set up a dozen odd thematic committees to assist the main drafter, the Constitutional Committee, there are subjects and areas where clarity of principle and objective are needed. The foremost among them is what kind of republic Nepal is to be: a democratic republic as has been promised in the interim statute, or a “people’s republic” as the governing Maoists often demand. The next question on the periphery is whether Nepal should have a presidential system like that of the United States and France, or a parliamentary democracy as in India and the United Kingdom.

“What is to be the game - boxing or chess?” asked Badri Bahadur Karki, a constitutional lawyer. The rules of the game have to be framed accordingly. The presidential system is believed to offer stability, whereas the parliamentary model is known for its accountability. Nepal has limped along the latter line for about six decades. The roots of the growing public concern are Maoist statements which appear at variance with the pledge they made in their election manifesto last year that they had entered the world of competitive politics and had joined the democratic process.

But once catapulted to power, the Maoists have changed their language. Public speeches of top leaders, including

Prachanda, indicate their loss of faith in the parliamentary tradition. As they approach yet another anniversary since the launch of the "People's War" on February 13, 1996, the Maoist leaders are sending a message to the masses that they are using the government and the CA as well as the street to "seize" the entire state apparatus as quickly as possible. This sounds incredible, but one has to be alert about Nepal, a "critically weak" state by some assessments. Prachanda usually talks about his party's ability to perform miracles. In a newspaper interview published on February 4, he blamed the Nepali people for giving the Maoists only a fractured mandate. "How can we bring about the hurricane they expect from us?", he asked in frustration. Still, Prachanda said, the Maoist leadership was trying to move ahead in a different way, hinting at the method applied to enact the three ordinances.

Finance Minister Baburam Bhattarai and Prachanda's senior colleague, is behind an apparent hair-raising plan to exacerbate the political uncertainty so that the Maoists can seize the state amid chaos and confusion. Bhattarai's elaborate scheme was printed in Nepali language daily Nayaa Patrikaa on January 30. Even if the Maoists allowed the CA to draw up the draft of the statute, they are unlikely to permit it to be democracy-oriented. "If it is written it will be tuned to our wish or else not a single letter will be written [in the name of the constitution]," Bhattarai said in the article. To add fuel to the fire, leaders of a left party in the ruling coalition, the Unified Marxist Leninist (UML), frequently make public utterances that if all the left-leaning parties came together they would make up a two-thirds majority in the assembly. To substantiate this, the Maoists made a gesture of supporting former UML general secretary, Madhav Kumar Nepal, to receive a seat in the assembly, despite the fact that he was badly defeated in the April polls last year, not from one constituency but in two places.

Working in tandem, they made a mockery of the elections by further "electing" him as the chairman of the main panel entrusted to work on the drafting of the constitution. It is already a disappointment to the political parties with democratic credentials. Whenever top Maoist leaders take questions from public platforms about their model of republic, they escape through ambivalent answers. "We have seen 26 types of republic in the existing world, ours will be the 27th variety," said Chandra Prakash Gajurel on February 3 in front of an audience which included outgoing United Nations envoy Ian Martin.

Bhattarai's claim that confusion and chaos work to the advantage of the Communist Party of Nepal (Maoist) seems to be a meaningful statement. The promise the Maoists made during the insurgency days for an ethnicity-based federal structure has intensified tensions between communities. Fatal onslaughts on media personnel and organizations using Maoist-affiliated trade unions as well as Young Communist League members have effectively worked to silence the critical voices. Prachanda's direct interference in the appointment of priests at a Hindu temple added another dimension to the state of confusion. More recently, a Maoist initiative reported in the media said that a panel of astrologers was working on a new annual calendar for Nepal which would have 11 months, instead of 12.

"The challenge in the midst of anarchy is a serious one," Surya Bahadur Thapa, a former prime minister, told Asia Times Online, alluding to Maoist excesses. In his opinion, political parties committed to liberal democracy needed to develop alliances and partnerships with the Nepali Congress as it is the most credible force with a nationwide reach. And despite his advanced age, leader Girija Prasad Koirala alone has the charisma to attract a large crowd of committed people who could offer a counterweight to the left-leaning force led by Maoists. One readymade alternative is to rely on assurances from India. Foreign Minister Pranab Mukherjee on January 28 gave an interview to the al-Jazeera television network in which he said India had "persuaded" the Nepali Maoists to give up violence and participate in mainstream political activities. "They agreed, listened to our advice and now... they are leading the government." If they indeed listened to New Delhi in the past, the Maoists might listen one more time and agree to promulgate a democratic constitution once the draft is finalized.

However, one section of the Maoists does not seem to have taken Mukherjee's remarks kindly, as they have diluted, if not nullified altogether, the Maoist claim that historical political change in Nepal was possible mainly because of their armed struggle for over a decade that took the lives of about 15,000 people. The Maoists have not issued any formal reaction to Mukherjee's statement, but sources in the party rejected it outright. Besides, there is also a perception that New Delhi is getting jittery over the Maoist initiatives to develop close contacts with Beijing. Efforts began in late August with Prachanda's first visit abroad as prime minister to China, during the closing ceremony of the Beijing Summer Olympic Games. In between, several senior Maoist leaders and ministers have frequented Lhasa, the capital of Tibet, among other mainland cities.

Knowledgeable politicians who appear alarmed at China's increasing interest in Nepal, largely due to Tibet, are of the view that India has to pay dearly for its earlier follies. A widely-shared perception is that the Indians went out of their way to assist the Maoists without anticipating that they could eventually be a liability in view of the fact that Nepal's border with India is both porous and unregulated.

Their fraternal relationship with Indian Maoists can add a dimension to the challenge India is already confronting. New Delhi's excessive involvement was bound to project India as the meddlesome South Asian neighbor. On December 13, 2008, the Economist newspaper noted, "As a neighbor, India is itself far from ideal. It has a long history of meddling in other country's politics, including Pakistan's. Nepal witnessed an embarrassing example of this in April, when India had its paw-prints all over the country's first proper election in a decade. Seeking to secure a pliable new government, its agents bribed and divided the field; this almost certainly helped a party of Maoist guerrillas, whom India disliked most, to a stunning victory."

CAN DEMOCRACY THRIVE IN NEPAL AMIDST THE MAOISTS?

It was a sigh of relief when Maoists withdrew their indefinite general strike. To General public who participated in peace rallies nationwide it was worth their effort. But to the incumbent government and to the political parties in the coalition, it has given another form of political game. It was a big mistake of the Maoists to call their general strike in the wrong place at the wrong time. It was not absolutely necessary nor propriety. Rather to general public it was a threat to peace and stability.

People have mandated through historic Constituent Assembly election the democratic means to achieve peace and stability through consensus politics and the Parliament proceeding. The day the Maoists led the government in coalition by keeping Nepali Congress party in opposition, the Maoists did kill the spirit of consensus politics. The Maoist leaderships failed to form a unity government to begin with the new political situation, which is diverse in every aspect. Knowing that without the consensus among political parties Constituent Assembly cannot succeed to draft the new constitution. Therefore, to place NC in opposition without forming a unity government was the big mistake the Maoists made to overrule consensus politics.

Veteran democrat GP Koirala, who played the most effective role to bring the Maoists to mainstream politics, had on several occasions warned the Maoist chairman "Prachand" not to overrule consensus among political parties. Frankly, Mr. Dahal did not respect the consensus politics from the bottom of his heart. In my opinion, Mr. Dahal made another gigantic mistake as a chairman of the Maoists party by not agreeing with NC's proposal to elect GP Koirala as the first president of Nepal. Mr. Dahal and the Maoist party had to pay the price for by arrogantly giving up the government leadership. The price again for not honoring GP Koirala, has not yet paid off politically. It might hound for a long period of time.

We believe that if GP Koirala had been elected the first president of Nepal, (which had put him above the politics with better health condition and chance for some longevity), the current political situation could have been completely different. NC perhaps could be playing different political role for the coalition and could have had avoided the role of opposition in the Maoist led coalition government. At the moment, Nepal needs desperately the foundation for peace and the rule of law. Unless the United Maoist party becomes completely a citizen-party and comply to the peace accord to abandon its ties with combatant politics and mechanism, the foundation for peace and the rule of law will not be there soon in Nepal.

The Maoists have been making mistakes after mistakes, and how much mistake they will be making in near future is capricious. This is due to their lack reliance in consensus politics and the Parliamentary proceeding. For example, if they had gone to the Parliament regarding the conflict with "NA-Chief" and the president instead of resigning from the government, they could have learned not to repeat same mistake.

Again, if they had once tried "the motion of no confidence vote" against sitting PM MK Nepal in the Parliament before going to general strike, the Maoists´ reliance in the Parliamentary proceeding could have been demonstrated. It seems the Maoists at this point have been less serious about the nation and people but more ambitious about their own ideology and worship to their chairmanship. But, Democracy does not care leaders like demagogues, who do little for the rule of law and justice to protect freedom and liberty of people, but die hard for their ideology and self-centered leadership.

The United Maoist party has to make a new choice of a leader, if it wants to lead a fresh national unity government. The Maoist chairman Mr. Dahal has failed to lead a consensus politics for the nation. He did not care about drafting the new constitution on time and nor secured permanent peace process when he had the opportunity. India supports Dr. Baburam Bhattrai, so the world community, just as for the United States the Maoist led national unity government is acceptable as long as the United Maoist party comply with the norms of citizen-party.

The United Maoist party must find the way out to meet these conditions as NC and UML have demanded – "Complete the integration and rehabilitation of Maoist combatants", "Return of properties seized during conflict", "Dissolution of the paramilitary structure of the Maoist with YCL", "Drafting of new constitution on time", and "Amendment of the interim constitution for extending the term of Constituent Assembly, if needed." The PM has already consulted the president for the amendment of the interim constitution to extend the term of CA. This means that the incumbent government has realized the fact that it can not possibly draft the constitution in the stipulated timeframe.

However, the amendment to extend the term of CA cannot pass the House without the support of the Maoist legislators, because it needs two-third of majority. The Hindu royalist party leaders, on the other hand, are saying such an extension is unconstitutional and demanding fresh election of the Constituent Assembly. At this point, if the Maoists could act responsibly for the sake of people and the nation then they have the chance to gain credibility of a citizen-party. Whether the national unity government is formed under the leadership of the United Maoist party or not the Maoist leaders must cooperate with CA first to complete the drafting of the new constitution or must support the amendment to extend the term of CA. If not the establishment of the secular federal democratic republic of Nepal will soon be too thorny to walk through. Unless the Maoist Chairman "Prachand" thinks he is the iron-man to put all who do not agree with him in "Gherau" - the YCL-Ring.

MAOIST INSURGENCY IN NEPAL: INTERNAL DIMENSIONS

It is no secret that Nepal, a country sandwiched between two Asian giants – India and China, is suffering from the worst political crisis in its history. A constitutional democracy that was established following the 1990 People's Movement appears to be on the verge of collapse due to continued success of Maoist guerrilla insurgency or "People's War" that was launched in February of 1996 by the Communist Party of Nepal-Maoist (CPN-Maoist). The Maoist People's War has become a direct threat and a death-knell to the government of Nepal.

The CPN-Maoist first fired its salvo of "People's War" on February 12, 1996 seeking to destroy constitutional monarchy and aiming to establish a Maoist people's democracy. By the end of December of 2000, the insurgency has taken the life of an estimated 1600 persons (unofficially the figure goes as high as 4,000 dead.) There are four categories of people killed in the process: Maoist guerrillas, police, alleged informers of police, and innocent civilians. Independent observers say that police has killed more innocent civilians in fake "encounters" than the Maoist guerrillas. The police administration is also accused of extra-judicial killings in captivity and disappearance of persons under custody.

Geopolitics of Insurgency and Government Policy: The insurgency that began from 3 mid-western mountain districts of Rolpa, Rukum, and Jajarkot, western district of Gorkha and an eastern district of Sindhuli has now spread to 68 of Nepal's 75 districts. According to government's own admission 32 districts are believed to be the hardest hit where guerrillas roam freely and organize open mass meetings. By mid-January 2001, the Maoists have declared the formation of a provisional revolutionary district governments in Rukum, Jajarkot, Sallyan and Rolpa districts.

A close study of insurgent activities in the country show that the most affected area is contiguous and concentrated in the mid-western region. This is one of the most backward and least accessible districts of Nepal. The affected areas are all too close to Kathmandu. Many of the affected areas are spread out along Terai districts close to India. Nepal government officials have reportedly filed a complaint with New Delhi that the Maoists are seeking shelter in India.

The most disturbing situation for the counter-insurgency planners is that many of the Maoist affected areas are inhabited by a large number of well trained retired Indian and British Army Gurkha soldiers. Authorities suspect that some of these retirees are providing training to Maoist guerrillas.

The Maoist insurgency-hit areas cover 165 of the 205 parliamentary electoral constituencies of Nepal. The insurgency has directly affected the lives of roughly two-thirds of the 24 million people of Nepal. The state is on the verge of defeat. The police operations have failed to control guerrillas. There is a widespread realization that if the guerrillas continue to expand their zone of influence at the current speed, they will be able to beat the Nepali State within a short span of time. Such realization is reflected in the government's recent activation of the National Security Council and its decision to create a para-military force comprising 15,000 men (to be increased to 25,000-men gradually) with modern sophisticated weapons. Although the royal army has not been officially ordered against the guerrillas, the government has decided to establish six new military bases at battalion level around insurgency hit districts. Twenty-five district headquarters are now under Royal Nepali Army (RNA) protection. Another twenty-five district administrators have reportedly sought RNA protection.

Since the start of insurgency in 1996, different governments of Nepal have treated the Maoist war as a 'law and order' problem. The government has sought to contain Maoists by means of police operations code named "Operation Romeo," "Kilo Shera Two," "Jungle Search Operation," and "Search and Destroy." The state has justified authoritarian policies in the name of suppressing the insurgency, but without addressing the basic inequalities that plague Nepali society. These police operations have applied the policy of "encircle and kill", a policy similar to China's Chiang Kai-shek's "extermination" of communists campaign in 1930s. In the process of this "encircle and kill" policy the police operation has in many places actually killed more innocent civilians than the guerrillas, a fact noted by several human rights organizations including the Amnesty International.

Insurgents' Strength: Despite the killings of hundreds of Maoists, real or imagined, under the policy of "search and destroy," Maoist insurgency does not appear to be dying. The insurgency, in fact, has appeared in districts which otherwise had been considered an area of influence of constitutional ruling parties. While no one knows exactly how many guerrillas are there in the jungles of Nepal, yet some experts believe that number of full-time guerrillas under arms is around 2000 and another 10,000 irregulars or militias armed with homemade guns. In almost all battles between the police and the Maoist guerrillas, the insurgents have proved their military superiority. These incidents have shaken the whole country and has established the fact that Maoist insurgency is a living reality and that the Communist Party of Nepal (Maoist) is an undeniable political force.

In view of the present day political uncertainties characterized by competition for office between and among parties of all shades and sizes, continuing split between and among parliamentary royal communists, and Nepali Congress's undeclared divorce with socialism, the chances for Maoist politics to reign Nepal appears pretty high. If history is any guide, Nepali communists, no matter how much divided they may be, have never been totally rejected by the electorate. In 1994, Unified Marxist & Leninist (UML) got an opportunity to form the government. The inexperience in ruling the country, on the one hand, and greed for power, on the other led to not only the exit from the government but also the vertical division of the UML party. The vertical split of UML has brought about qualitative as well as quantitative changes in the political balance of the country. The split has also helped in raising the centrality of Maoist movement. In fact, the communist movement has now polarized into Maoist and non-Maoist blocs. This process of polarization is a good source of power to Maoists. The failure of other left groups in forming and maintaining unity has certainly helped Maoists.

Popular Support

The successive failures of government's police operations in Maoist insurgency clearly shows that the insurgency is taking momentum with substantial popular support. This is no longer simply a law and order problem. Why are the people in rebel areas providing sanctuaries to insurgents? Why are insurgents finding sanctuaries in areas, which in the past had been strongholds of constitutional parties? Independent observers argue that the government suffers from political instability and rampant corruption.

The money allocated for development of interior areas never reaches there. A large number of villages are totally ignored by economic planners. There are no schools, no roads, no electricity, and no medical facilities. At the national level, the educated unemployment is increasing at geometrical proportions. Close to 100,000 rural youths failing high school examination every year have neither a job nor a school to go where they could be kept busy. These unemployed youths, 15 to 18 years in age, are joining the ranks of armed guerrillas. The Maoists, however, have problems of providing arms to these willing recruits.

Background of Communist Movement: Maoist insurgency must be viewed in the light of Nepal's history of communist movement. The communist movement in Nepal that first appeared in 1949 after the formation of Communist Party of Nepal under the leadership of late Pushpa Lal Shrestha emerged as an intellectual opposition to Nepali Congress's policy of compromise. Even during the days of king's absolutism Communist movement was unclear in its goals.

A few communist leaders then argued that their main enemy was domestic feudalism led by the king while others insisted that Nepali Congress with its support from expansionist India and imperialist America was the main enemy. As a result, Nepal saw at one moment as many as 19 communist parties!

The Maoist movement has emerged in the background of this history of Nepal's communist movement. The Naxallite movement of Jhapa in early 1970s, too, had the same background. The Jhapa movement evaporated in a few years due mainly to the suppression of Naxaliites in India, youthful inexperience of leaders expressed in term of middle class extremism, decline of Maoism in China after Mao's death in 1976, and lack of Jhapa-type militancy in other districts of Nepal. The leaders of Jhapa movement gradually took to the constitutional path and even participated in Panchayat elections as "pro-people Panchas."

New Realities: The present day Maoist movement, however, must not be viewed in light of Naxaliite movement of the early 1970s for several reasons: first, Maoists unlike Jhapali Naxaliites do not have the advantage of geographical continuity from India. Second, Maoists do not enjoy the ideological support from Radio Beijing.

So the charges of foreign inspiration is a moot point here. Third, Maoists have learnt many lessons from the mistakes of Jhapa uprising. Fourth, the communists of all shades and sizes are now available in every village of Nepal. Many of them are disillusioned with the inability of their leaders who have participated in parliamentary system telling the cadres that there is an alternative to armed revolution.

That the Maoist insurgency has survived five-year period and continues to enter into news phases is in itself a clear indication that the movement is no longer a temporary phenomenon without social bases. The official approach of viewing Maoist movement as an activity of individual killing and pure terrorism has not helped to solve the problem. While it is true that there is middle-class extremism inside the Maoist movement but it is not the extremism directed by indiscriminate terrorism.

The terrorist acts perpetuated by insurgents are carefully selective and are limited to the killings of alleged police spies and informers who are also notorious in the villages. In the past such extremism used to evaporate within a short span of time but there is no indication of such evaporation this time around anywhere near the sight. In fact, it is on the march towards new stages with each day passing.

New Characteristics: Broadly speaking, communist movement in Nepal in the past has been left-intellectual movement. The participating intellectuals in this movement had comprised of upper caste (Brahmin-Chhetri-Newar-BCN). In other words, past movements were basically the movements against BCN ruling elite by the BCN non-ruling elite.

That scenario, however, has changed now in view of the broader participation of persons from other castes particularly the untouchable castes such as Kami, Sarki, Damai, etc. In the past when non-ruling BCNs were fighting the ruling BCNs there was always scope for mediation and compromise due to the network of family relations. No such network of family relations exists now between BCN elite and guerrillas coming from untouchable lower castes, which narrows the chances of mediation and compromise.

Another notable characteristic of Maoist movement is the degree of women's participation in guerrilla ranks. Women's political participation in the past had been limited to electoral areas, especially, in voting and occasional candidacy in elections. It is a big surprise that Nepali women now have joined guerrilla organization under arms. More than a dozen women have already given their lives while fighting the police operations.

According to an estimate about 30% of Maoist guerrillas comprise of women. This is totally a new phenomenon in Nepal, which must not be taken lightly.

Furthermore, more and more persons from Janajati people (Rai, Limbu, Gurung, Magar, Tamang, etc) are joining the ranks of Maoist insurgency in the hope that they will be "emancipated" from the "clutches" of BCN. Although it is not quite clear whether these Janajatis will remain loyal to Maoist cause in the aftermath of the success of Maoist people's war, suffice it to say here that a peaceful settlement of the problem is no where near the sight.

Summary and Conclusion: Fighting a guerrilla war is an expensive proposition for any state. Guerrilla war has no front lines. Guerrillas operate in the midst of, and often hidden or protected by, civilian populations.

The purpose of guerrilla war is not to engage an enemy army in direct confrontation, but rather to harass and punish it so as to gradually limit its operation and effectively liberate territory from its control.

Efforts to combat such a guerrilla army- counterinsurgency- often include programs to "win the hearts and minds" of rural populations so that they stop sheltering the guerrillas. In guerrilla war, there is much territory that neither side controls; both sides exert military leverage over the same place at the same time. This makes guerrilla wars extremely painful for civilian population because the government armed forces fighting against guerrillas often do not distinguish them from civilians, and so strike both together.

Nepali strategic planners have failed to find a way in which people would stop giving sanctuaries to guerrillas. This could have been done by means of massive economic development package to people in the early period of insurgency. The relief package that the government has allocated after so much of killings has become irrelevant.

Counter-insurgency measures require civil-military coordination in which clean civil administrators are expected to disburse economic development package. Here lies the problem. Nepal's problem is not the Maoist war but an entrenched coalition of corrupt politicians and bureaucrats that profits from Maoist war. It is very much likely that the economic relief package announced to combat insurgency could be yet another opportunity to corrupt civilian as well as military authorities for embezzlement.

Counter-insurgency measure, if applied and executed by clean hands, will help minimize the distribution crisis, which in turn, will help to neutralize popular support to guerrillas. Otherwise, it remains a protracted problem and there is no way to obstruct Maoist revolution. The government forces, under the present policies, could win couple of battles here and there but will never win the war. The best they could expect is a negotiation for the safe passage with the victorious Maoist People's Guerrilla Army in years to come.

5

Nepal's Maoists: Their Aims, Structure and Strategy

BACKGROUND: MAOISM AND NEPAL

When Nepal's Maoists — the Communist Party of Nepal (Maoist), the CPN(M) — launched their "people's war" in February 1996, they were easily dismissed as a small communist splinter group that could do no more than stir up trouble in a handful of remote regions. They had almost no weapons, a tiny organisational base and a strategy that seemed outdated and unrealistic. But their movement has grown to the point where the state has relinquished control over most of Nepal's territory. They have proved capable of outmanoeuvring mainstream parties politically and, when conditions are in their favour, of successfully attacking the well-armed Royal Nepalese Army (RNA). In the face of concerted efforts to defeat them, their insurgency has proved resilient. Despite the Maoists' rise to prominence and the growing international concern at their threat to Nepal's established polity, surprisingly little is known about them. This is partly because of their own secretiveness: as an underground movement the Maoists are cautious about their security and keen to control their public image by restricting negative news. But it is also because most observers have been reluctant to grapple with the politics of the movement.

Like most communists, Nepal's Maoists are prolific writers and theorists and have produced a large body of work which sheds light on their goals and strategy. They have also been skilled propagandists, producing their own publications, running FM radio stations and using the domestic and international media to promote their point of view. In many key respects, the Maoists have done what they said they would do. Understanding their plans is not only crucial to tackling the insurgency militarily — a task which has proved beyond the state so far — but also to dealing with it pragmatically and plotting possible routes to a negotiated settlement. This background report draws on many of the Maoists' own writings and statements, as well as much other material, to examine three basic questions:

- Who are Nepal's Maoists and what do they want to achieve? Are they really Maoist at all? Politics lie at the heart of the insurgency and understanding Maoist goals and political culture is essential to understanding the rationale for their armed struggle. It can also help efforts to bring them into the framework of parliamentary politics by addressing reasonable elements of their program.
- How is the movement organised and led? On paper, the structure is simple: party, army and united front. But the differences between theory and practice are revealing, as are the ways in which the Maoists have departed from historical precedents. Questions of resources, support base and command and control also give clues to Maoist strengths and weaknesses.
- What are the Maoists' strategy and tactics? Are there signs that they will settle for a negotiated peace? The overall strategy of protracted people's war is well known in name but needs to be understood in context. The Maoists' public announcement that they have entered the final stage of strategic offensive implies confidence of a military victory. But in fact, there are more signs that the Maoists' internal politics are putting the party in a good position to compromise.

The Maoists themselves have fed the confusion over their true aims with a plethora of seemingly contradictory statements. Still proud to lay claim to the legacy of China's turbulent Cultural Revolution of the 1960s, they have also repeatedly insisted that they do not have a totalitarian vision for a future state. Calls for the rapid establishment of a "dictatorship of the proletariat" have been supplanted by emphasis on the need first to complete Nepal's "bourgeois democratic revolution" and establish a true multiparty democracy.

The Maoists have also welcomed the establishment of a United Nations human rights monitoring mission and vowed to abide by international humanitarian law. Which of the many faces presented to the outside world is the true one? What does the speed with which the Maoists have often shifted positions say about their ultimate intentions? There are no definitive answers to these questions. Indeed, as the ongoing debates within the CPN(M) indicate, it may well be that the Maoists themselves have yet to settle on final answers. But this report attempts to lay out the evidence on which at least a better informed estimate of Maoist intentions and capacity can be made.

The scope of this report is limited. It is analytical rather than judgmental, drawing on dozens of published and private sources, including Crisis Group interviews that allow the Maoists to explain what they stand for in their own words. In doing this it seeks not to endorse any position but rather to test assertions against available evidence, though these sources in many instances are inevitably inadequate and self-interested.

Nevertheless, published Maoist writings, if read carefully, do tend to provide a reasonable guide to the movement's political culture and strategic aims, though statements on topics such as military clashes and political achievements tend to be designed as propaganda and must be approached with some scepticism. The Maoists are understandably keen to portray themselves in a good light and are, therefore, hardly forthcoming about indiscipline within their ranks or violations of international law. Maoist strategy has been fairly consistent since the early 1990s but since they adapt tactics to changing circumstances, observers are often confused. This report concentrates on providing a background guide to underlying politics and structural factors as a basis for more detailed reporting on specific issues in future.

MAOIST POLITICS

Political Program

New democracy: The basic aim of the CPN(M) armed struggle is to capture state power and establish "new people's democracy" (*naulo janbad*). The concept of "new democracy" is inherited from the thoughts of Mao Zedong, which in turn built on the views of Lenin, Trotsky and Stalin. The "new democratic revolution" marks the transition from the classical Marxist stages of bourgeois hegemony ("old democracy") to proletarian hegemony ("new democracy"). For a society in which even the bourgeois democratic revolution has not reached completion, however — such as China in the 1930s or Nepal in the current Maoist analysis — the new democratic revolution can telescope the stages of bourgeois and proletarian hegemony. Combined with the Leninist theory of "continuous revolution", this forms the basis of the Nepali Maoists' vision of their struggle:

> This plan would be based on the aim of completing the new democratic revolution after the destruction of feudalism and imperialism, then immediately moving towards socialism, and, by way of cultural revolutions based on the theory of continuous revolution under the dictatorship of the proletariat, marching to communism — the golden future of the whole humanity.

When the Maoists launched the people's war, they used their appeal to citizens to declare their resolve "to initiate the process of forcibly smashing this reactionary state and establishing a New Democratic state", in accordance with "the almighty ideology of Marxism-Leninism-Maoism to free humanity forever from the yoke of class exploitation". The question of what kind of "dictatorship" would be required to oversee this process has been answered in different ways, with the traditional Marxist "dictatorship of the proletariat" generally being supplanted by the Maoist concept of a mixed-class "people's democratic dictatorship": "The fundamental character of New Democratic or People's Democratic republican state shall be the people's democratic dictatorship with the participation of all the progressive classes including the national bourgeoisie and oppressed nations/nationalities based on worker-peasant alliance under the leadership of the proletariat".

The concept of *naulo janbad* is far from exclusive to the Maoists. At the start of the 1990s almost all of Nepal's communist factions shared this goal. Most of them believed that multiparty democracy could be one of the stages in reaching this goal: "The disagreement was over how to travel along the road and on how pluralist the political institutions of *naulo janbad* would be". While the moderate Communist Party of Nepal (Unified Marxist- Leninist), the UML, opted for *bahudaliya janbad* (multiparty people's democracy), the Maoists hardened their opposition to the multiparty system that Nepal was moving towards. Interviewed in September 1990, Baburam Bhattarai, who became the chief Maoist ideologue, explained the reasons for his criticism of parliamentary democracy and plans for a reformed system:

> In a parliamentary democracy you don't redistribute the property, you just advocate free competition. Free competition among unequals is naturally in favour of the more powerful ones. When we perform this new democratic revolution, we will immediately redistribute property. We will confiscate all landed property and redistribute the wealth among the poor. The political institutions may be the same. We believe in political freedom. We will have elections, but the elections so far have been dominated by money.

Maoist thinking has veered between more radical and moderate versions of this basic line. But they have been flexible in their approach, eschewing hardline demands if the circumstances require. For example, in the second peace talks with the government in 2003, they were willing to compromise on fundamental economic policy measures, such as accommodating foreign capital, which they have otherwise characterised as imperialist and "comprador". The Maoists believe nationalism provides an emotional rallying point for violent struggle: "The Nepalese people are very conscious and sensitive about the question of nationalism, and...they feel proud to lay down their lives while fighting rather than submit to the pressures of the foreigners". Nepal's Maoists have also drawn heavily on caste and ethnic grievances to mobilise popular support. They have likewise selected targets for political activism— such as high private school fees — designed to win middle class support. Their relative openness to foreignaided development projects and ambivalence on key economic questions also points to a more pragmatic approach.

Immediate demands: Just before the launch of their people's war, the Maoists had submitted a 40-point demand to then Prime Minister Sher Bahadur Deuba. The headline points were related directly to nationalism. Four were targeted specifically at India, demanding the removal of "unequal stipulations and agreements" in the 1950 Treaty of Peace and Friendship (although not cancellation of the treaty itself); nullification of the 1996 Mahakali Treaty on water resources; control of the Nepal-India border and banning of Indian-registered cars from driving in the country; and lastly, a moralistic demand to stop the "cultural pollution of imperialists and expansionists", which primarily meant that "import and distribution of vulgar Hindi films, video cassettes and magazines should be stopped".

None of these demands can be described as particularly Maoist: many of them have been raised repeatedly across the political spectrum. Other nationalistic demands were primarily economic: that foreign (British and Indian) recruitment of Gurkha troops should cease and "decent jobs" be arranged for recruits; that foreign technicians should not be given preference over Nepalis; that the "monopoly of foreign capital" should be stopped; that customs duties should provide "sufficient income...for the country's economic development"; and that "bribing by imperialists and expansionists in the name of NGOs and INGOs should be stopped".

The primary Maoist demands have remained largely consistent since the earlier rounds of failed negotiation: a roundtable conference, interim government and elections to a constituent assembly. Since the royal coup of February 2005, however, their willingness to include the king in talks has decreased, and they have pushed the mainstream parties to accept the idea of a rapid transition to an interim government (in which they would hope to play a major role). They have already won considerable mainstream support for the concept of a constituent assembly, although their model has not been elaborated, and there are many potential pitfalls.

Attitudes towards the monarchy: One of the Maoists' ultimate goals is a republic. However, the initial 40 points they demanded did not tackle this question head on but rather called for a new constitution "drafted by the people's elected representatives" and for the army, police and administration to be "under the people's control". The only direct statement on the monarchy was that "all the special rights and privileges of the King and his family should be ended". The CPN (Unity Centre), the immediate predecessor to the CPN(M), had opposed the "the monarchical parliamentary multi-party system" and viewed the real aim of the 1990 people's movement as having been "to end the monarchical system". After two years of armed insurgency, the CPN(M) reiterated that "the analysis of the reactionaries that the king and monarchy are deep-rooted in the Nepalese society is not true....It was only after the emergence of the centralised feudal state in a certain stage of development of class division that attempts had been made to unnaturally impose the king and monarchism through the practices of the system of reward-and-punishment and divine theory".

Nevertheless, when it came to negotiations in 2003, the Maoists said they supported a freely elected constituent assembly and would, therefore, not impose their policy by force: "Different political forces can go to the people with their own views on monarchy and other progressive issues, and the final verdict of the people would be acceptable to everybody concerned". During peace talks in both 2001 and 2003, the Maoists signalled that they would likely accept a continuing role for the monarchy if it were purely ceremonial. The royal coup of February 2005 and the growing rift between the palace and the mainstream parties have led to a hardening of rhetoric. But the emergence of strong republican sentiment in student politics and within parts of the Congress and UML leadership has helped the Maoists pursue their preferred tactics.

While the CPN(M) wants a republic, it realises that it will be much more effective to encourage the pursuit of this demand by mainstream politicians than to push it unilaterally. Party chairman and overall leader Prachanda claims to be confident: "The Party wants to institutionalise a republican form of state through the Constituent Assembly and believes that in a free and fair election the mandate of the Nepalese people would be in favour of a republic". At the same time, senior mainstream politicians still believe the Maoists might accept a ceremonial monarchy, with no powers, especially over the military.

Economic Program

For the Maoists, changes in Nepal's political institutions are only the means to a much more far-reaching transformation of its social and economic structure. The concentration on headline demands such as republicanism and a new constitution has often distracted attention from their economic and social goals, many of which have been elaborated in some detail. Maoist attitudes on these illustrate the nature of their movement and hint at their likely program if they were ever to gain power.

Their economic plans offer a hybrid model incorporating capitalist elements on a strongly nationalist frame. This reflects the post-colonial "mixed economy" applied in countries such as India, Sri Lanka and Egypt rather than a Stalinist command economy. The basic idea is that the "commanding heights" of the economy should be controlled by the state, while the rest is left to private capital.

Plans for social and cultural reform, not least the ambitious goal of eliminating caste, ethnic, gender and regional disparities and discrimination, are both a central plank of Maoist policy and a major selling point to many marginalised communities. The Maoists have tried to put some policies into practice in areas under their control and have brought about limited change. But the questions of how genuinely they believe in their stated policy and how closely they would insist on it if they gained any share of national power remain unanswered.

The starting point for Maoist analysis is their conviction that Nepal is "semi-feudal", "semi-colonial", and at the mercy of imperialism and Indian expansionism. Its people suffer economic exploitation and discrimination on many grounds. For Baburam Bhattarai, the people's war is a means to solve the economic problems of underdevelopment induced by imperialism, semifeudalism and international capitalism. In this view, Nepal lost its economic self-sufficiency and independence with British colonial dominance of South Asia. Trade imbalances with post-independence India, Indian investors' control of much of the economy and exploitation of its resources, along with ready access to cheap Nepali labour, have exacerbated this loss of economic autonomy.

The Maoists claim that Nepal's dependence on agriculture is primarily due to the distorting effects of the Indian economy and trade. On top of this, Nepal's "semi-feudal" society has contributed to stunted economic development and extreme regional imbalances. Nepali capitalism is based on import-dependent merchant capital concentrated in the hands of a few magnates, usury-driven finance capital and aid-financed bureaucratic capital. This has retarded the development of production-oriented national capital: "Thus, to develop national industrial capital by destroying the [foreign-origin] and bureaucratic capital and to pave the path of self-reliant development by breaking away...[from] dependency, a revolutionary transformation of society and the process of People's War have become inevitable".

In this sense, the people's war is not only a political but also an economic program. Bhattarai proposes the following broad prescriptive measures for economic development policy:

- changing production relations: confiscating land from the feudals and capital from the comprador- bureaucratic classes;
- mixed ownership: land to be owned individually by peasants; major industries and financial companies to be state-owned, with joint-ventures between state and productive private capital; small and medium businesses and trade to be owned by private individuals;
- a protected and regulated economy: to ensure independent and self-reliant development; planned development: not a Soviet-style command economy but "a genuine mass-oriented and efficient economy functioning under a centralised leadership and guidance and decentralised initiative and management, which to a large extent was practiced in China during Mao's time"; and

- balanced development: economic and geographic balance between country and town, hill and plains, agriculture and industry, etc., but with industry as the leading sector and agriculture the foundation, the overall aim being "the urbanisation of the countryside and not the ruralisation of the cities".

ORGANISATIONAL STRUCTURE

Nepal's Maoists have attempted to emulate the classic Chinese communist structure of "three magic weapons": party, army and united front. The policy of the immediate predecessor to the CPN(M), the CPN (Unity Centre), explicitly endorsed the threefold revolutionary organisation. Significantly, it made clear that the united front would get only subsidiary attention, while the major effort went into the party and the army. This early indication of priorities may go some way towards explaining the shape the Maoist movement has subsequently taken: For the success of the New Democratic revolution, it is a must, as taught by Comrade Mao, to develop the three instruments of "revolutionary Communist Party, revolutionary United Front and People's Army". It is evident that in such a revolution the role of the Communist Party and the people's war would be primary and that of the mass and class organisations and the people's movement be secondary. It is of primary importance to move ahead with a concrete program for the development of these instruments.

The Maoists do not publicise their command structure, and they protect the identities of many people in leadership positions. The means by which they maintain a system of command and control is kept deliberately obscure, and most of their leaders remain underground. But they have definitely followed the Chinese threefold system, within which they have generally emphasised the development of the party over the army and both of these over the united front.

The party has overall responsibility for all activities related to the "people's war" and for the development of policy. The army (PLA), which is under the full control of the party, is responsible for both offensive operations against the "enemy side" and defensive arrangements. Prachanda retains the top positions in both organisations, as chairman of the party and supreme commander of the PLA. The central body of the "united front" is the United People's Revolutionary Council Nepal, which the Maoists have fashioned partly as a revolutionary tool and partly as a central people's government in waiting.

The Party

The CPN(M) is in many respects similar to mainstream political parties within Nepal and beyond. Its organisation follows communist principles but the resulting model is not dissimilar to that of the Nepali Congress or other moderate groups. Overall control of the party and military remains firmly with the "party headquarters", which in practice means Prachanda. He has the authority to take all immediate decisions, though these can subsequently be discussed by party committees which have the power to endorse, revise or — occasionally — reject them.

Political leadership. The organisational hierarchy under the chairman consists respectively of the standing committee, politburo, central committee, divisional commands, regional bureaus, sub-regional bureaus, district, area and cell committees. The politburo contains at least 27 members, of whom ten are alternates. Prachanda is chairman of the politburo's seven-member standing committee, whose other members are Mohan Vaidya (Kiran), Baburam Bhattarai, Ram Bahadur Thapa (Badal), Post Bahadur Bogati (Diwakar), Krishna Bahadur Mahara and Dev Gurung. The central committee has nearly 100 members and has grown as the movement itself has expanded: at the second national conference in February 2001, there were only 55 members. But the increase in numbers has not been accompanied by any increase in authority: the majority of political and military-strategic plans are still formulated by the politburo and the standing committee. There is also a central advisory committee of senior, experienced political leaders and activists. Regional and district commanders underwent a major reshuffle during July-August 2005.

Divisional commands. Beyond the central political bodies, the three divisional commands have been granted broad authority. The three divisions — western, special central and eastern — were defined during the June 2002 central committee plenary's wide-reaching review of organisational structure. The special central command (the Kathmandu valley, surrounding hill areas and the Tarai areas of Bara, Parsa, Rautahat and others) was dissolved by the August 2004 plenum to form a new mid-central command. Certain areas which had fallen under the special command were transferred to the eastern command but most remained with the mid-central division. The leader of each command – Maoists use the English term "In-Charge" — is an ex officio member of the standing committee. The radical redrawing of command borders was a particular feature of the August 2004 plenum: as well as shifting the Kathmandu valley into the eastern command, it also moved the Rapti area, encompassing the Maoist heartland of Rolpa and Rukum, into the central command. The geographical scope of the three commands is now: western central command — Mahakali, Seti, Karnali and Bheri zones; mid central command — Gandaki, Lumbini, Rapti and Dhaulagiri zones; eastern central command — Janakpur, Sagarmatha, Bagmati, Narayani, Koshi and Mechi zones.

International department. All units of the CPN(M) outside Nepal's borders fall under the international department, formerly headed by C.P. Gajurel (Gaurav) and now by Baburam Bhattarai. The latter, accompanied by other senior leaders, held meetings in New Delhi in late May 2005 with Nepali and Indian political party representatives. He has also been the main point of contact for other international dealings. The international department's responsibilities include expanding party organisation — recruiting expatriate Nepalis, establishing international contacts and relations, fundraising, purchase of ammunition and explosives and arranging training. It initially concentrated on trying to build a base among Nepalis in India, both permanent residents and temporary migrants. This type of work has now been expanded to Europe and North America.

Other departments. On paper, there are a number of further central departments, including policy and direction, broadcasting, publishing, schools, human rights, health, ethnic, legal and cultural. These structures are designed partly to shadow existing state entities and give the impression that the

Maoists are building a full alternative structure. Apart from the sporadically prolific publishing department, however, there is little evidence that these nominal structures embody the type of full-fledged administration that their enumeration is meant to imply. Indeed, because of the capture of central leaders — some fifteen are in prison in Nepal and India — and the killing of others, the Maoists' central command is if anything understaffed, with gaps in various positions.

The People's Liberation Army

The main base of the Maoists' military strength is the People's Liberation Army Nepal (PLA). Its strength is hard to estimate. At the lower end, some analysts suggest that the Maoists have only a few thousand hardcore fighters. One military expert and retired RNA lieutenantgeneral put their strength at 4,000 armed guerrillas, 5,000 militia who have received guerrilla training and 20,000 armed militia. The Maoists themselves claim they have more than 10,000 armed guerrillas in their nine brigades, a figure that many close observers tend to accept. Indeed, the RNA has offered a similar estimate: some 9,500 guerrillas and 25,000 militia. Other experts are more cautious, suggesting a range of core fighters anywhere from 5,000 to 8,000 or so.

Of course, the Maoists and the RNA both have reasons to give higher estimates. The Maoists obviously want to create the impression that they have a mass support base and a considerable fighting force. The RNA is faced with the problem that earlier state estimates of a small Maoist guerrilla cadre simply do not tally with their depiction of the current situation. The RNA says that over 8,000 Maoists have been killed in the conflict so far, more than half since the breakdown of the 2003 ceasefire alone. If both this claim and earlier estimates were correct, the entire Maoist army should have been killed by now. As one analyst commented on similar figures presented by the RNA in December 2003:

Wherever the numbers may lie, the fatalities inflicted on the Maoists would tend to suggest that the Maoists are now in flight, and the forces of the establishment are consolidating their domination over the country's hinterland that had, for some time, passed into the control of the insurgents. A closer analysis of developments, however, reveals the spectacle, rather, of a country hurtling towards chaos, with the state and its agencies in headlong flight.

The general headquarters of the PLA is under the leadership of Supreme Commander Prachanda. The "general staff" consists of the members of the party standing committee. The organisational hierarchy under the general headquarters is: division, brigade, battalion, company, platoon, squad and then militias, poorly armed fighters who have not received full guerrilla training. For certain areas such as Kathmandu, "special taskforces" have been established. These are raised from selected guerrillas either to serve in areas where there are no established regular units or to carry out more specialised actions from time to time. This elaborate structure is a relatively recent development. At the start of their military campaign, the Maoists were very limited in number and lacked weaponry and uniforms. The first units, which had minimal equipment, were organised into "fighting units" *(ladaku dal),* "security units" *(suraksha dal)* and "volunteer units" *(svayamsevak dal).* According to the then military commander of the Maoists' central region, Sandip, the real development of the "people's army" only took place after the start of the government's Operation Kilo Sierra 2 of May 1998-April 1999.

In August 1998, the Maoists' fourth expanded central committee meeting (plenum) adopted the slogan of building "base areas" and building up military strength in order to challenge government repression. The Maoist guerrillas became increasingly well organised and well trained, until by the start of 2001 they had effectively defeated the police. They knew they were not capable of fighting with the RNA, however, so, in July 2001, they – reciprocated the government's ceasefire offer and used it to strengthen their military capacity, running advanced training camps in many locations. In September 2001, the formation of the "People's Liberation Army Nepal" was announced at a gathering of guerrillas from across the country in Kureli, Rolpa district. With their forces now better organised and trained, they attacked the army barracks at Ghorahi, Dang, in November and brought the RNA into the war.

As the guerrilla army grew in size, the central committee plenary of June 2002 decided to form brigade-level military groupings. In August 2004, these were incorporated into three divisions of three brigades each: the eastern division under Barshaman Pun (Ananta), the central division under Nanda Kishor Pun (Pasang) and the western division under Janardan Sharma (Prabhakar).

The leadership of every fighting unit from company to division level is shared between a military commander and a political commissar, which the Maoists claim ensures political control over the army. The commissar ranks higher and is in charge of the party committee formed within each military unit. All units above section level, including special taskforces, are under orders to work within the central plan defined by party policy. From late summer 2005, however, there have been credible reports that military and political workers at lower levels will be deliberately separated, not least to avoid the demonstrated risk of captured Maoists betraying the identities of too many comrades.

Beyond this, Prachanda announced in August 2004 the aim of forming a 100,000-strong people's militia up to the company level, under the command of district and regional headquarters. In practice, militias take their orders from different bodies, from local party committees to people's governments. Militia members are not generally expected to carry out the same guerrilla duties as mainstream fighters but can be called upon as reinforcements. They are poorly armed and do not wear uniforms.

There have been credible allegations that the Maoists carry out forced recruitment and use child soldiers. That they do indeed carry out coercive recruitment is not in doubt. Two of their campaigns in particular — "one house, one guerrilla" and "shoes" — have been widely publicised. The Maoists also make no secret of the fact that they give military training to children and have militarised the school curriculum in areas under their control. Cases of Maoist student cadets have been well documented but evidence that child soldiers are used in combat is still patchy. Similarly plausible allegations that civilians are used as human shields surface after most large-scale attacks on security bases; again, however, the truth is hard to ascertain amid claim and counter-claim.

The United Front

The concept of the united front was central to Mao's thinking and to the communist victory in China. The idea is simple in essence but broad, and potentially difficult, in application. It means to "*unite with all forces that can be united with* in order to fight a common struggle against the enemy and to win in revolution and construction". The key is that the type of forces that can or should be united with may vary entirely according to circumstance. From the period of the anti-Japanese struggle, Mao formulated and continually emphasised the "unity-struggleautonomy" policy: "develop the progressive force, win over the in-between force, and combat the obstinate force". The categorisation of such forces depended on objectives and interests; the Chinese Communist Party went through at least five quite different united front experiments.

From the start of the 1990s, the Nepali Maoists planned the creation of a particular type of united front. It would be the least important of the three revolutionary "weapons", and it would be a hybrid of the various Chinese models: the "revolutionary United Front" would be "an instrument of struggle and an embryo of the new power". In other words, it would not only be a broad coalition of organisations assisting in the revolutionary struggle but would also function as an embryonic government. Despite the existence of a plethora of fraternal organisations created alongside the CPN(M) and repeated efforts to build bridges with mainstream parties, it is the latter role of the united front that has come to predominate in Nepali Maoist discourse.

Nepal's Maoists bitterly criticised existing "reformist trends" within the communist movement that "focus on the legal movement and put emphasis only on forging unity-in-action with the various reactionary and Right revisionist political groups and of sectarian and mechanistic trends that only create noises by mechanistically forging [a] 'united front' of their Party cadres alone". A true revolutionary united front should bring together "antifeudal and anti-imperialist patriotic, democratic and leftist forces as an instrument of developing class struggles....The principle function of such a front should be to develop struggles on the basis of people's problems that would gradually break the [limits of] law and the system. At the initial stages, the effective form of such a front would be confined to rural areas and at the local level".

As the Maoists approached the launch of the people's war, they defined a narrow role for the united front, with its component elements strictly subordinated to the party: "Armed struggle will be carried out by uniting all strata and categories of anti-feudal and anti-imperialist masses of the people under the leadership of the Party". Within three years the armed insurgency had expanded significantly, prompting consideration of formalising the united front under the rubric of the "Central Organizing Committee of the People's Republic of Nepal". Its role would still be to mobilise "various left, progressive, patriotic and democratic forces" but it would be explicitly transitional: "[S]uch a central formation will principally work as a means of struggle for the time being and will work secondarily as a means of power". In this, it partially reflects the "people's democratic front" of the early People's Republic of China, which was meant to help fulfil fundamental state tasks and oppose internal and external enemies. In September 2001, during the first ceasefire, the Maoists created a 37-member United Revolutionary People's Council (URPC) as such a front. It was headed by Baburam Bhattarai, with Krishna Bahadur Mahara as assistant convenor and Dev Gurung as secretary.

The Maoists have established a range of fraternal organisations to boost their popularity by carrying out above-ground political activities and mobilisation on their behalf. By 2000, there were more than twenty such organisations. Before the declaration of a state of emergency in November 2001, they carried out open or semi-underground activities. The most influential has been the All-Nepal National Free Students Union (Revolutionary) led by Lekhnath Neupane. Other active organisations include the Nepal Trade Union Federation (Revolutionary) led by Salikram Jamarkattel; the All- Nepal Women's Association (Revolutionary) led by Jayapuri Gharti; the All-Nepal Janajati Federation led by Suresh Ale Magar; the

All Nepal Peasants Association (Revolutionary); the All-Nepal Teacher's Organisation (Revolutionary) led by Gunaraj Lohani; the Nepal National Intellectuals Organisation and the All-Nepal People's Cultural Union led by Mani Thapa; and the All Nepal Peasants Association led by Shivaraj Gautam. These organisations, termed "people's class organisations" *(janvargiya sangathan)* by the Maoists, are not strictly speaking part of a united front but ancillary wings of the party structure. They follow its direction and act as subsidiaries with specialised tasks or support bases. They are also useful as a way of drawing recruits into underground activities via semi-open groups that operate at a slight distance from the central party. New members of the CPN(M) tend to have been inducted from such groups, especially if they have earned a reputation for good work in them.

Apart from the students union — the ANNFSU(R) — all these organisations were formed after the start of the insurgency, and their contributions have been patchy. The ANNFSU(R) demonstrated the Maoists' reach in urban areas for the first time with a strike which shut down more than 30,000 schools across the country in November 2000. It further expanded its activities from the period of the first ceasefire in 2001, targeting the inefficiencies and inequities of the education system, in particular the fee-paying private schools which had mushroomed after 1990. Its campaigns to reduce private school fees were a clever tactical move that won support from a large lower middle class struggling to educate its children. The ANNFSU(R) claims a large membership but does not have an established structure in urban schools and colleges. Nevertheless, it continues to make political interventions, often school shutdowns.

The other organisation that has recently gained an active profile is the Nepal Trade Union Federation (Revolutionary), which brings together some dozen nominal unions. Its main task is to advance Maoist aims through industrial action and to mobilise a support base by organising labourers in various sectors of the formal economy. Its leaders and members have also reportedly played an important role in collecting "donations" from industrialists and businessmen in Kathmandu, Biratnagar and Birgunj. It was initially said to be behind scattered incidents of extortion, vandalism and bomb explosions but it gained a wider reputation in September 2004 when it forced the shutdown of twelve major businesses over labour conditions and complaints about the foreign capital and exploitive multinational corporations. It enforced its strike with a minor bomb attack on the grounds of the five-star Soaltee Hotel, which hurt the tourism sector and also served as a symbolic attack against the royal family, which is closely linked to the hotel.

However, the Maoists have yet to attempt the type of united front politics that was decisive in the Chinese revolution. Creating their own support organisations is not the same as persuading forces with different aims to join them in a shared task for limited common objectives. The main reason for this has probably been the Maoists' compulsion to eliminate political rivalry across the countryside by targeting other parties' activists. This has not created fertile ground for the kind of understanding that would be necessary to build a viable working alliance with other political groups. Nor, until the royal coup in February 2005, was there sufficient feeling within the mainstream parties that any collaboration with the Maoists could be safe or profitable. The Maoists' subsequent efforts to work with the mainstream parties will be the first, and probably most crucial, test of whether they can build a true united front.

LEADERSHIP, SUPPORT BASE AND RESOURCES

Leadership, Command and Control

The Maoists are in general disciplined and united but still face problems in controlling their large movement. Since the CPN(M) was formed in 1995 it has not suffered a single split; in contrast, each of the major mainstream parties has been fractured at least once. Prachanda is unlikely to face a serious challenge to his monopoly on power within the party. Apart from Baburam Bhattarai, there are no other leaders of a stature sufficient to present a threat to his authority; Bhattarai himself has repeatedly insisted he has no designs on the leadership and may have been chastened by the disciplinary action he underwent in early 2005. But maintaining such discipline requires constant effort. Senior leaders spend significant time dealing with policy debates and trying to prevent disagreements from becoming damaging. According to the RNA, this has had a direct effect on operational effectiveness by distracting attention from the implementation of plans and strategy.

There are other tensions within the party but none at the moment pose a grave threat to its unity or operational capacity. The most obvious area of current and potential divisions is the relationship between the party and the various ethnic front organisations. In 2004 there were notable splits in Saptari, where Maoist leader Jay Krishna Goit separated from the Madhesi National Liberation Front, and in the eastern hills, where there were several defections from the Kirat National Liberation Front. These received significant press attention but the Maoists insist they are unlikely to cause serious damage to the movement. However, the fact that similar disputes have flared up again in the months following the royal coup suggests they do indeed represent a serious challenge. The arrest of many senior leaders has caused the Maoists more serious problems. Among the fifteen central level cadres in prison in India are Mohan Vaidya (Kiran), a senior ideologue and respected figure who has in the past helped smooth over differences between Prachanda and Bhattarai, and C.P. Gajurel (Gaurav), who was working on the international front before being caught in Chennai trying to fly to London on a fake British passport. Other imprisoned colleagues were also carrying out significant tasks, and their loss has affected Maoist capacity. Two important leaders were arrested in India and handed over to Nepal: Matrika Yadav, whose role was central in the Maoist expansion and mobilisation in the Tarai, and Suresh Ale Magar, a figurehead for ethnic activists within the movement. Since the Maoist unilateral ceasefire declaration of 3 September 2005, a number of mid-level commanders have been arrested, some apparently through their carelessness.

Many of the most capable Maoist leaders have been killed. Alternate politburo member Suresh Wagle (Basu) was killed by police in Gorkha on 8 September 1999; central leader Dandapani Neupane (Dipendra Sharma) disappeared from Kathmandu on 21 May 1999 and is assumed to have been killed; regional level leader and pro-Maoist journalist Krishna

Sen was killed in police custody during the first emergency in 2001; central committee member Rit Bahadur Khadka (Pratap), of Dolakha district, was killed in Rautahat in July 2002; central committee members Mohan Chandra Gautam (Kumar) and Sherman Kunwar (Vishal) were killed in Siraha in 5 September 2004. On 13 May 2004, central committee member and brigade commander Nep Bahadur K.C. (Parivartan) died in an accident, and in March 2005 central committee member and Satbariya Second Brigade commander Jit was killed in a military clash in Bardiya.

There have also been surrenders, in particular after the RNA was deployed, such as of brigade commander Hom Prakash Shrestha (Himal), battalion commanders Jaya Bahadur Gharti (Prabhat) and Man Bahadur Malla (Sangharsh) and company commander Janu Chhantyal (Pratap). Political workers who have surrendered include regional bureau members Khop Bahadur Kandel, Ravi Karki and Mandavraj Karki.

Surrenders and defections have taken place from most lower party levels but they do not seem to have extended to the central level. However, central committee members Rabindra Shrestha, Rekha Sharma, Mumaram Khanal, Krishnadhvaj Khadka and Bamdev Chhetri were accused by the party of "weakness" while in state custody in 2001; Sharma, Khadka and Khanal have not been rehabilitated, and Khanal has publicly declared that he is no longer associated with the CPN(M).

The writ of Prachanda still runs throughout the Maoist movement, and central-level decisions are fed down to the regional, district and village levels. There have been no major disruptions to this chain of command, so to this extent the movement remains united and disciplined. The reason is a well organised national command structure firmly in the grip of the central leadership. Numerous accounts of strong central management illustrate this, such as the cautionary tale of local Maoists who tried to make money out of the medicinal *yarcha gumba* trade: "At one point several years ago, local Maoists inserted themselves as intermediary dealers and profited from the larger transactions. When the Maoist leadership learned of this practice, they stopped it, returned the trade to its traditional private dealers, and confiscated and remitted the ill-gotten gains to the Maoist central treasury". But many observers question the firmness of central control, pointing to incidents where local commanders appear to be working against higher-level policies or simply in ignorance of them. The party has also taken action against cadres for carelessness or mistakes but such disciplinary measures are normally only publicised if there is particular pressure.

This was the case with the killing of Dailekh journalist Dekendra Raj Thapa on 11 August 2004. It was only after intense national and international criticism that the then Maoist western central commander Diwakar was compelled to explain the murder. He claimed that Thapa was not just a journalist but also an informer, who had caused the deaths of a number of people. But there had been a mistake: according to Maoist central policy "any journalist guilty of such serious crimes could be arrested but capital punishment should not be carried out". He announced that the party had ordered an inquiry but no results have been published other than a short statement on their website.

One reason for cases of indiscipline is the degree of autonomy granted to lower levels of the party. A certain amount of decision-making power is devolved to committees and other regional bodies according to their status. In particular, the three divisional commands theoretically have significant freedom to decide their own programs and plans of action in line with overall policy. But as their leadership is drawn from the standing committee, there is little likelihood of them taking a line that has not been agreed upon at the top level.

Local and district committees are granted the authority to decide on military targets and assassinations but the misuse of this authority has been a recurring feature. The most sensitive part of the Maoist movement, the military, has so far not known significant internal indiscipline or anarchy. This is partly due to the system of dual military/political leadership: while commanders lead guerrillas in action, the commissars' party rank is higher. The requirement for significant decisions to be taken by commander and commissar jointly reduces the likelihood of indiscipline.

Frequent claims that the Maoists have descended into anarchy or are "running amok" seem to be exaggerated and are denied by their military command. However, the Maoists suffer from a widespread problem of individual indiscipline. This is partly due to their rapid expansion. In the early years their cadres would be carefully selected, screened and educated in Marxist and Maoist doctrine before being given responsibilities. This created a small but politically focused and disciplined group.

But as the movement grew rapidly, especially with the need for increased recruitment once the RNA was mobilised, the process of careful selection was more or less abandoned. The average age of party cadres, whether on the political or military front, was also lowered. As a result, indiscipline and related problems have greatly increased. The Maoist dictum used to be "it is ideas that control the gun, not the gun that controls ideas" but for many cadres the gun seems to have grown more powerful. In recognition of the problem, internal corrective measures have been taken from time to time.

It does not appear that the Maoists have reached a command and control crisis but they clearly face difficulties. A large and diffuse movement which has doubtless attracted a fair share of criminal elements poses inherent management challenges. The loss of senior leaders through death, arrest or internal disputes has hampered theirr capacity. Internal tensions have a particularly damaging effect on general morale as well as operational effectiveness. It is surely no coincidence that the Maoists suffered several significant military defeats during the period of intense speculation over the possible breakdown of the Prachanda-Baburam partnership in early 2005.

Membership and Support Base

The Maoist movement could not have grown to the extent it has without mobilising a significant support base, even if it remains only a small percentage of Nepal's population. The RNA, for example, estimates that beyond their armed cadres and 14,000 political workers, the Maoists may have some 100,000 supporters. The Maoists, obviously, would claim a far greater number, and there is certainly a larger category of latent sympathisers as well as committed supporters. Retired RNA Lieutenant-General Sadip Bahadur Shah estimates 24,000 active supporters and 200,000 sympathisers.

A number of surveys have indicated that while the Maoists might only win a low percentage of votes in a free and fair election, a much wider constituency agrees with their aims but not their means. Overall, there are three categories of supporters: committed "whole-timers", who have gone underground and take part in either military or political work; supporters, who provide assistance in a number of ways but are not declared Maoists and operate above ground; and sympathisers, who offer little if any practical help and may include those who are dissatisfied with Maoist violence but nevertheless back their political agenda.

Class: Before launching their armed struggle the Maoists made a class analysis of the motivating forces on which they could hope to draw. They identified six broad classes from whom they could expect some support: the proletariat, poor peasants, middle peasants, rich peasants, petty bourgeoisie and national bourgeoisie. The latter three were expected to be only "vacillating allies", although the Maoists saw the petty bourgeoisie as playing a potentially "important auxiliary role". They also noted that "imperialists" and "reactionary forces" were concentrating on co-opting intellectuals.

Like traditional Marxists, the Maoists believe that although the Nepali proletariat is small, it remains "the most revolutionary class" and still bears the "historical responsibility of identifying and giving leadership to other allied classes". They concluded that the main motivating force, however, would be a mix of rural and urban workers: "farm workers, bonded labourers, landless peasants, porters, and poor peasants, and in our case in the cities the cart pullers, rickshaw pullers, drivers of tempos, taxis, and transport and hotel workers, etc." Interestingly, the middle peasants were also singled out both for the fact that they survive with difficulty despite owning land and because they outnumber other classes in the hills. While these were the primary class categories for the Maoists to work with, they were assisted by the fact that other communist groups had built up a base of cadres schooled in

Marxism. The Maoists were able to benefit through defections from the discontent of some members of mainstream communist parties. According to one Maoist leader, this was particularly the case with disaffected UML cadres in the east of the country. This ideologically sophisticated core was instrumental in helping the Maoists in their early expansion.

Many of the Maoists' early campaigns also helped them win broader sympathy. For people long ignored by central government and conscious of the unequal development of the country, the Maoists seemed to offer new hope. The first experiments in "people's court" justice won support when exploitive moneylenders and landowners were punished, while campaigns against alcohol abuse and domestic violence painted the Maoists in a bold, reformist light. However, the novelty of these campaigns wore off, and their doubtful efficacy has limited their ability to boost Maoist strength.

Ethnicity and caste: The wide participation of otherwise excluded ethnic and caste groups is a notable feature of the Maoist movement. But participation has not translated into control at the top levels. The concentration in Rolpa and Rukum of independent-minded Magars, well aware of their historic exclusion from the Nepali state, was one of the factors that made this a suitable crucible for Maoist mobilisation. But there have been repeated accusations that young people from minority communities have been cynically manipulated by the leadership and used as little more than cannon-fodder.

There are only two members of ethnic minority communities — Ram Bahadur Thapa and newly appointed Dev Gurung — in the seven-member Maoist standing committee. Other bodies are more representative. Of the URPC's 37 members, twenty are from ethnic and *dalit* (outcast) communities, while there were eleven members of ethnic and *dalit* communities in the sixteen-member United People's Front, dissolved in 2000. There is also a significant presence of ethnic, *dalit* and Tarai leaders in the central committee. Whatever the composition of the leadership, the fact that the Maoists have made an apparently serious commitment to minority rights — something neither the palace nor the mainstream parties have ever been able to bring themselves to do — means that they offer an alternative that many in such communities, especially the radicalised and disillusioned youth, find attractive.

Women: The Maoists have made a particular effort to appeal to women and to recruit them as active participants in their movement. Gender equality has always been a feature of their political program. In the appeal that marked the start of the insurgency, the CPN(M) complained that "whereas this state has been treating women as secondclass citizens for long, now it has intensified rape, trafficking and the process of commoditisation through advertisements, against them". The URPC devoted a separate section to women and family in its policy manifesto, promising that under Maoist rule, "all forms of patriarchal exploitation of women shall be ended, and women shall be given all rights equal to men. Like son, daughter shall enjoy equal rights to parental property. Women shall be provided with special rights for participating in all organs of the state". They also vowed to eradicate commercial sex work, take harsh action against traffickers, permit only marriage by mutual consent, permit abortion and give special consideration to women in divorce proceedings.

Women have been inducted into all areas of the party, army and front organisations. It has been estimated that they constitute anywhere between 30 and 40 per cent of the Maoist guerrilla force". The Maoist women's organisation, the All-Nepal Women's Union (Revolutionary), has led campaigns against alcohol and domestic violence. It was particularly active around the time of the 2001 ceasefire but the arrest of its then leader, Rekha Sharma, and other senior figures caused severe disruption. In 2003 Jayapuri Gharti, a central committee member from Rolpa, was appointed the new chair of the organisation, and it has started to work more in rural areas. The Maoists have a stated policy of including as many women as possible in each military unit. According to their leaders, by 2000 there were many female squad commanders and deputy commanders, and in some areas there were all-women guerrilla units. According to Hisila Yami (Parvati), by early 2004 women formed a third of the PLA and were represented up to the levels of vice-commander and commissar at the battalion level". However, women still have a long way to go if they are to approach equality even within the Maoist movement itself. There are very few women in the central committee and politburo and not one on the powerful standing committee. The only politburo members are Pampha Bhusal and Hisila Yami, who faces disciplinary action. On the central committee, the remaining women members are Jayapuri Gharti, Uma Bhujel, Kumari Moktan and Rekha Sharma (who is also apparently under disciplinary action). As many observers commented at the time, the lack of women on the Maoist negotiating team during talks with the government in 2003 seemed to belie the movement's rhetorical commitments.

While the Maoists certainly have brought about a degree of change in the role of women and attitudes towards them, it has not all been positive. The most significant result of conflict-induced rural depopulation has been that as men have left, women have been burdened with an even larger share of work than before. And the durability of other reform is yet to be tested. As one report, which details many Maoist-led improvements, cautions, "...change seems to have taken place due to Maoist action or threat of action. Only through continuous reinforcement of these positive practices by local people will they become sustainable social norms and values".

Prospects: The Maoists' early gains in public image and sympathy have not been sustained; most observers believe they have been significantly eroded during a period when the public has come to view all the actors in the conflict — the monarchy, the Maoists and the political parties — in an increasingly harsh light. When asked what popular support the Maoists might enjoy, a veteran communist activist said, "four or five years back they might even have won 50 per cent in a vote, two years ago maybe 20 or 30 per cent, but now I don't think they'd even get 10 per cent". Such assessments are based on the perception that the innocent idealism which encouraged passive support for the Maoists in the earlier stages of the conflict has worn off as the movement has shown continued brutality without delivering on its seemingly progressive agenda. The Maoists have been more successful at mobilising support in rural areas than in the towns. The urban revolt called for by the "Prachandapath" strategy adopted in 2001 has proved a damp squib. Even radical students in the towns and cities still prefer to work within the mainstream parties, and the Maoists have not made any major breakthrough in general backing. The relative ease with which the royal government since February 2005 has broken the power of the Maoist *bandh* (general strike) in Kathmandu indicates the lack of committed support in the capital.

Meanwhile, the increased resort to coercive recruitment seems to indicate the hollowness of the Maoist support base. This does not necessarily affect their ability to continue fighting — for that they only need to sustain their core cadre of guerrillas and political workers — but it may affect their strategy and their calculations on the benefits or drawbacks of entering electoral politics.

Resources

The Maoists have managed to find sufficient resources to maintain the various facets of their movement. Fighters have been provided with weapons and ammunition, and the political campaign has been sustained with significant funding. It is not possible to give a full picture of Maoist resource mobilisation but the following sections outline their pattern of operation.

Finances: The CPN(M) is Nepal's richest political party. Accurately estimating Maoist income and expenditure is difficult, primarily because of the nature of the movement itself but also because much of their support, such as forced donations for food or accommodation, comes in kind rather than cash. What figures are available on Maoist finances tend to be scattered and not always reliable. Most income is dedicated to running the party and military activities, of which supporting thousands of full-time workers forms a large proportion. Little money seems to be allotted to building administrative capacities or carrying out development work.

According to a study based on direct interviews with Maoist fighters, it costs Rs. 17,000 (approximately $250) annually to provide one armed guerrilla with clothes and other basic necessities. This excludes the cost of food, accommodation, weapons and ammunition and medical treatment which, whether in cash or kind, add up to many times this amount.

Other sources agree that guerrillas are not paid a salary but are given a monthly allowance of Rs. 150 per month (just over $2) for basic items such as soap and toothpaste.

Given the scale of the Maoist movement, the resources needed to sustain its political and military operations are on a scale far beyond that of any other party. Even in early 2002, a former Maoist district commander estimated that "the Maoists need to spend about Rs. 10 million (almost $150,000) every month to keep the war going: for the upkeep of their own guerrilla force, logistics and hardware". This did not include political and administrative expenses, and the movement has grown significantly in the past three years.

The Maoists' main sources of funds are bank robbery, donations and extortion. Of these, the former has become more difficult as banks have increased security, and in most rural districts all deposits are moved to army bases at night for safekeeping. Nevertheless, raids continue, with the Maoists claiming to have netted almost $6,000 in one bank robbery in June 2005 in Bardiya district. Despite a crackdown on Maoist fundraising since February 2005, extortion continues. Secret contributors to the Maoists include not only businessmen, industrialists and traders but also senior politicians and civil servants. In the rural areas under their sway, the Maoists collect "taxes" from individuals with a cash income, such as teachers, and seasonal donations in kind, such as portions of the harvest, from farmers. Rates of "tax" on incomes vary from 5 to 25 per cent. Tourism has also become a source of cash for the Maoists, who levy compulsory contributions on trekkers of most popular mountain routes.

As the insurgency has progressed, Maoist networks in India and overseas have tried to build up their own fundraising capacity. It is impossible to estimate the significance of these, and most funds channelled into the country would, like the vast majority of regular remittances, follow unofficial routes. But Maoists based in Western Europe say they have been able to raise funds individually or through support organisations. In comparison to external sources, the amounts raised from among Maoist cadres themselves are minimal. Apart from centralised efforts, the Maoist regional autonomous governments have been instructed to seek financial self-sufficiency by raising their own levies. This has led to the identification of natural resources as potential revenue opportunities. As the head of the Seti- Mahakali government explains, "the resources for running our government come from taxes on the natural resources available in our region (such as herbs and timber), trade duties and voluntary contributions from various professionals and the ordinary working population". Medicinal herbs are a particularly lucrative option in the Rapti, Bheri and Karnali regions, where one people's government official claimed that the then "special district people's government" brought in more than $7,300 annually.

The seasonal trade in valueble *yarcha gumba* is especially profitable. In 2003, a Maoist cadre claimed that tax had been collected in Dolpa on 1,300 kilograms of *yarcha gumba* at a rate of $74 per kilogram. One international official reported Maoist earnings on *yarcha gumba* exported to India from Darchula district in the summer of 2004 to be in the range of $600,000. The Maoists have also been accused of profiting from trade in marijuana. The U.S. has stated that "Maoist guerrillas are involved in drug smuggling to finance their insurgency.... [Nepal's] Narcotic Drug Control Law Enforcement Unit reports that the Maoists levy a 40 per cent tax on cannabis production in certain areas". However, any income from narcotics is likely to be minimal and, given that Nepal is not a producer of hard drugs, unlikely to develop into a major source. Fears that Nepal will follow a Latin American or Afghan model of narco-insurgency are unfounded. The Maoists have proved more than proficient in marshalling sufficient resources to sustain their campaign to date, primarily by illegal and coercive means. The fact that they do not, as far as can be ascertained, rely on significant inputs from overseas makes them more resilient as there is no simple cash pipeline that can be cut off. But it also affects their strategy: as long as they depend on living off a percentage of Nepal's overall economic turnover, they have no incentive to undermine the economy dramatically. A total collapse, or the destruction of particular industries such as tourism, would have serious knock-on effects for the Maoists' own income. Ironically, therefore, the Maoists have an important stake in ensuring that the economy continues to function. As national dependence on income from migrant workers in other Asian countries and the Middle East increases, the Maoists appear to be concentrating on claiming a proportion of remittances. Meanwhile, the Nepali government unintentionally helps to sustain the Maoists, with proportions of education, health and rural development budgets regularly finding their way into the CPN(M)'s coffers. And the Maoists' generally conciliatory attitude towards international aid is likely to continue: not only do internationally funded development projects deliver some services to rural areas that the Maoists are incapable of managing themselves, but they also disburse large cash budgets that the Maoists are adept at tapping into. Funding a movement of the size and geographical extent that the Maoists have created is not easy but there is no sign that a lack of income alone will prove a decisive factor in weakening the insurgency.

Weaponry: When the Maoists started their armed struggle, they had no organised military force to speak of and no real weaponry. According to Maoist leader Rabindra Shrestha, at the outset they had only two rifles, one of which was broken. But as the Maoists stepped up their campaign, they started making their own muskets, taking licensed shotguns and other weapons from local residents and capturing the .303 rifles of the police. More recently they have enhanced their arsenal, primarily by capturing weapons from the security forces, to include sophisticated automatic weapons, explosives and mortars. Prachanda states that, "in the process of waging war we managed to snatch [a] few rifles from the armed police. It is these rifles that are now capturing automatic weapons from the royal army. Thus weapons sent by George Bush to suppress Nepalese people will soon be reaching the hands of Nepalese people, which will be directed against imperialism". Estimates of the exact number of weapons they hold vary significantly.

The Maoists have also purchased arms, in particular from the black market in the neighbouring Indian states of Bihar and Uttar Pradesh, where there is a flourishing trade in illegal weapons. They had concentrated on buying detonators, explosives and bullets rather than guns but there is some evidence that they have also brought in AK- 47 assault rifles, which some analysts suspect are from north east India. A large arms seizure in the Bangladeshi port of Chittagong in April 2004 caused various observers to speculate that Nepal's Maoists were the intended endusers.

The Maoists have skilled bomb-makers who initially devoted their efforts to refining various types of homemade explosives— socket bombs, pipe bombs, pressure cooker bombs — and gradually became more skilled in electronically detonated landmines. They have also used Indian army grenades, which may have been obtained on the black market. While their main source of weapons has tended to be the state security forces themselves, there are indications that their needs for fresh ammunition and explosives are met primarily from smuggling across the border with India. According to the Maoists, they have brought equipment from abroad in order to set up factories to produce high quality weaponry inside Nepal.

Their general approach, however, has been to avoid unnecessary escalation in armaments. While they were only fighting with the police, they were happy to rely primarily on weapons looted from police posts. It is since engaging with the RNA that they have sought to increase their stock of semi-automatic and automatic weapons and resorted to foreign purchases. The basic personal weapons of most guerrillas are SLRs,.303 rifles and muskets, while political commissars, senior officers and leaders opt for Chinese pistols, mostly looted from the police. The government's published policy on Maoist surrender from 2003, which offers rewards for handing over weapons, indicates the range of armaments it believes the Maoists possess. One crucial difference that gives the Maoists an edge over the RNA in certain situations is that their weapons come from a variety of flexible sources. The RNA's highly specialised hardware requirements make it dependent on a few official sources and so vulnerable to supply constraints. While the Maoists have developed their own training methods they were initially reliant on guidance from Indian insurgent groups. They are still far from reaching the standards of professionalism that a regular army would expect. "They seem to know what they're doing with their basic tactics when it comes to ambushes", observed a British military expert, "but they're still a rag-tag bunch that should be no match for a decent army".

The Maoists have benefited from increasingly sophisticated communications technology, from radios and satellite phones to email and internet. It is estimated that they are the largest users of satellite phones in the country. They have also exploited the growth in mobile phone connectivity: suspicions that they had purchased many pre-paid mobile SIM cards was the main justification cited for the continued suspension of this service following the royal coup of February 2005. However, in the period immediately following the coup the Maoist communications network appeared to be functioning better than that of the government. While some Nepali diplomatic missions were cut off from all home news, Maoists in Europe were receiving regular updates by satellite phone. They also use radio sets and cordless telephones adapted to function as walkie-talkies. The turn to e-mail and internet started in November 2001. Following the breakdown of the ceasefire, the Maoists' unofficial mouthpiece, the weekly newspaper *Janadesh,* was shut down and its journalists went underground.

6

Thoughts on the Maoist Problem in Nepal

Nepal's Maoist insurgency is often seen simply as a reaction to poverty and exploitation. Such an analysis is at once profoundly true and also profoundly inadequate because the pressures generated by poverty manifest themselves in many ways, including temporary or permanent migration and 'normal' (i.e., non-politicised) criminal activity. Other factors are needed to explain why an insurgency of the present type has appeared at this time in Nepal.

The list of contributing causes is a very long one. Nepal has always possessed both ethnic cleavages and mountainous terrain, a combination which is itself quite a good predictor of insurgency (Ramirez 2004). To this has been added in recent years the spread of Communist ideology (of which the Maoists themselves are one among many vehicles) and the tactical and organisational skills of the leaders of the Communist Party of Nepal (Maoist) which built upon the earlier work of Mohan Bikram Singh in the same region of the western hills. The Maoist leadership's decision to abandon constitutional methods was partly dictated by their ideology but also probably influenced by electoral arrangements which made it more difficult for small parties to gain a stake in the system.

The growth of the rebellion was greatly aided by the general political environment. Externally the Indian authorities failed to prevent the rebels making use of Indian territory as a source of supplies and as a refuge. Internally, a political culture of no-holds-barred struggle for power led governments to misuse the police force and administration for partisan advantage and political parties (including the Maoists themselves in the pre-'People's War' stage) to use their activists to over-awe or intimidate opponents.

Because so many people were already disregarding legal restraints in practice, the Maoists' explicit rejection of the whole legal order did not trigger as much public outrage as it might otherwise have done. However, perhaps most crucial as a factor in the rapid spread of the insurgency was the inability of the Nepalese state to respond fully at the outset because of tension between the palace, which was in *de facto* control of the army, and elected governments. The police campaigns, on which the government was almost solely reliant until the Maoists attacked the Royal Nepal Army (RNA) in 2002, was both brutal enough to antagonise local populations and too ill-focused and spasmodic to seriously hamper the insurgents' activities.

In the present circumstances, it is extremely difficult to assess the true extent of the Maoists' support base. Election results suggest that there is widespread backing for the general aims of the Nepalese Left, which, were it united, would be the single largest political force in the country.

However the Maoists' own claim to enjoy the enthusiastic backing of the bulk of the population is not accepted by any non-Maoist analyst. Gersony (2003: 79) suggests that, while they do have solid popular backing in the area of the western hills where they were electorally successful in 1991 and 1992, their influence elsewhere depends principally on an effective network of coercion. He believes that, given a free choice, most voters in the districts he surveyed would still back the United Marxist-Leninist (UML), leaving the Maoists with at most 15% of the vote nationwide.

Gersony's analysis (relying considerably on interviews with UML activists in district headquarters during 2003) is probably over-schematic and it should be remembered that, at grassroots level, activists can move readily between Leftist factions and even maintain links with more than one group simultaneously. Nevertheless, his findings are generally plausible, tallying with de Sales' depiction of both Maoists and the security forces as unwelcome intruders into village life or with the International Crisis Group's assessment of most ordinary Nepalese owing little allegiance to either side in the conflict army itself was unwilling to co-operate (which was certainly the case in 2001).

Where public opinion was concerned, the Maoists' advantage has been a negative one. They are not particularly popular but an opening was created for them because the police and the state apparatus in general could not expect the kind of automatic public support they would receive if subject to armed attack in stable democratic societies.

Most ordinary citizens of Nepal are trying to survive by following the orders of whoever appears more powerful at a particular time and place. One hundred and fifty years ago, Jang Bahadur Rana told a British officer that in Nepal 'although revolutions (i.e., violent transfers of power) often occurred, ... the country as a whole did not suffer more from such disturbances than England would from a change of ministry; neither the army nor the peasantry taking any part in the disputes, and submitting without a murmur to the dictates of whichever party might emerge the victors.' (Cavenagh 1884: 132). The struggle for power unfortunately now has much greater effect on ordinary people's lives but the old tradition of acquiescence survives and was encapsulated in a remark made by one Jumla resident in 2003: "We obeyed the Ranas and during the Panchayat we did what we were told. Democracy came and we followed. Tomorrow there may be another system and we will have to listen to them too. We can never say we won't obey" (Mainali 2003).

Amongst those who do voluntarily and enthusiastically support the insurgents, the most marginalized groups, including Kham Magars, the Tharus of the western *Tarai* and *dalits,* appear especially well represented, even though the top leadership of the Maoists, as of almost all political organizations in Nepal, is high *Peace and Democracy in South Asia*, Volume 1, Issue 2, 2005. caste. If and when the western hills are able to vote for a government of their choice free of intimidation, it is conceivable that substantial *dalit* support for the Maoists could cause more members of other castes to swing behind the

Maoists' opponents. There could well be a split of votes along caste lines as seen in recent years in Bhaktapur, where the highest castes have generally backed Congress, the Maharjan agriculturalist caste provided the power-base for Rohit's Nepal Workers and Peasants Party, and the lowest castes aligned with the UML. In the Far West, where the *janajati* presence is relatively low, the Thakuris might rally to Congress and the *dalits* to the Maoists whilst Khas/Chhetri cultivators either follow their traditional patronage links to the Thakuri elite or back the UML.

At the moment, the actual fighters on the Maoist side of the 'People's war' clearly have a wide variety of motivations. There are the 'true believers' who have thoroughly imbibed the CPN (Maoist)'s ideology but, particularly among the 'volunteers' supporting the better trained and equipped People's Liberation Army 'PLA' units, there are many who have simply been conscripted. In western Myagdi in May 2004, for example, one journalist was told by villagers: 'Those who have money have to give them cash, those who have food have to give them rice, those who have clothes have to give them clothes, and those who have nothing have to give them one member of the family' (Ogura 2004: 123-24). Then there are others for whom joining the Maoists was, like enlisting in the Indian or British army, simply a job opportunity. The analogy with Gorkha/Gurkha recruitment into foreign armies has been frequently drawn. Saubhagya Shah (2004: 193) actually cites the existence of this tradition in the hills as a major factor in the rise of the insurgency and Prachanda's own comments about 'brave and honest' hillmen echoes the language of many British officers' memoirs (Shah 2004: 219). There is now some concern in Indian official circles because in many cases one member of a Nepalese hill family may be serving in an Indian army unit whilst another is with the Maoists. In some cases, families may be divided on issues of political principle, in many others the brother (or sister) with the Maoists was either given no choice but to join them or saw them as just another prospective employer.

MAOISTS' OBJECTIVES

Whatever the personal motivation of those carrying guns on their behalf, the Maoist leadership's own objective is to use military force either as a direct means to wield political power and/or as a bargaining card to leverage themselves into an advantageous position in the post-conflict political order. They have for some time been claiming that, whatever the eventual institutional set-up in Nepal, they would in the interim be prepared to work within a multi-party system.

However, participation would be restricted to parties 'opposed to feudalism and imperialism." A restriction of this sort has in fact been advocated by a large section of the Nepalese Left including (at least in the early 1990s) some members of the largest parliamentary Communist party in Nepal, the UML. What they then envisaged and what the Maoists would probably prefer now is a system something on the lines of the present Chinese one, where other political parties do exist but operate under broad control of the Communist Party.

As a matter of short-term tactics the Maoists would probably be willing to operate in a more genuinely pluralist system but they hope that their own organizational strength, including in particular the framework of coercion they have established at village level, would let them gain control of the levers of power. There are precedents for Communist revolutionaries abandoning pluralism if it proved inconvenient.

Mao himself, when still trying to obtain power, advocated a considerably more liberal system than the one he actually eventually established, while Lenin dissolved the Russian constituent assembly when his opponents won a majority, and the Communist regimes installed in Eastern Europe after World War II often started as coalitions with other parties and only afterwards established rigid control.

Apart from the question of the Nepalese Maoists' intentions for their own country, there is also the question of the effect across South Asia and beyond. Although the Maoist insurgents in Northeast India do not pose an existential threat to India, they are a major headache, which would worsen if 'People's War' tactics are perceived to have succeeded in Nepal. This assessment is shared by the Indian security establishment, the US government and also (whatever they may say at particular moments for tactical purposes) by the Maoists themselves. Li Onesto, the leading western apologist for the Maoists, told an

Association for Nepal and Himalayan Studies conference in 2002 that '[the Maoists] know that when they take control of Nepal, it will upset the stability of the whole region' (ANHS 2003: 68). The choice which the Maoists faced in the mid-1990s, between operating in alliance with a larger, more moderate Left-wing party, or opting for insurrection is also one faced by similar groups in many parts of the developing world. Since such groups devote so much of their time to analyzing and debating the experience of their counterparts elsewhere, a Maoist success in leveraging themselves into a controlling position in Nepal would strengthen those advocating the option of insurrection in many different countries.

These international implications are the reason why major Western countries still see the Maoists as the greater danger, even though Gyanendra's clamp down on party politics and basic freedoms has prompted some in the parties to consider an alliance with the Maoists as the lesser of two evils. Gyanendra's penchant for authoritarianism does indeed mirror that of the Maoists: just as the latter want dominance for their own Communist Party with a pluralist fig leaf, the King envisages some kind of multi-party façade with himself pulling the strings. However, neither in South Asia nor anywhere else are there groups whom Gyanendra's example would encourage to use violence to establish active monarchies. Within Nepal itself, even if Gyanendra managed to stabilise some kind of neo-Panchayat system it would not last long before succumbing to the kinds of pressures that brought the old one down. In contrast, Maoist-style authoritarianism could be considerably more difficult to shift.

RECOMMENDED ACTION

None of this means that the Nepalese Maoists could not eventually come to function as just one party in a genuine multi-party system but this is only likely to happen if the non-Maoist forces are sufficiently strong to block any other path. At the moment, those forces are in disarray, largely because of Gyanendra's attempt to use the present crisis as a pretext for curbing the constitutional parties and of his disregard for the advice which India, the US and the UK had all been giving him in the run-up to February 2005. As a first step, he clearly needs to be induced to reverse course through a combination of persuasion and pressure. It is unlikely that pressure from the political parties themselves will be sufficient to achieve this, so the role of external power here remains crucial. The three countries mentioned above remain in a good position to exercise decisive influence even if the royal regime is able to obtain a small amount of military supplies from other sources. There are presently signs of disagreement within both the Indian and U.S. administrations on how strong a line to take against the King. The Indian Defence and Home ministries, worried about giving any encouragement to India's own Maoists, would perhaps prefer to resume military assistance to the King whilst the Foreign Ministry seems more willing to back the constitutional parties in their current agitation against the royal regime and also to countenance their current (October 2005) overtures towards the Maoists. 9 Similarly, the American ambassador in Kathmandu has appeared more understanding of Gyanendra's position than some others in Washington. However, since February 2005, the embargo on 'lethal' military aid maintained by both countries as well as the U.K. and also their repeated public criticism of the King's actions suggest that they are, at present, willing to make use of the leverage they possess. Another measure that could be considered is the blocking of Nepal's participation in international peace-keeping operations (recommended by Amnesty International recently as a sanction for use in connection with human rights abuses). This would deprive the Royal Nepal Army (RNA) of a valued source of both funds and prestige without altering the military balance within the country in favour of the insurgents.

The next step, as has now been agreed by the main parties, would be the reconvening of the 1999 parliament with a mandate to establish an all-party government and an agreed position for negotiation with the Maoists. The parties would need to reach consensus amongst themselves and the King to be willing to follow their lead. No one should underestimate the difficulties in achieving such an agreement, given the poor track record of both the parties and the palace in maintaining trust and co-operation. During summer 2005 the obstacles mounted with the growth of republican sentiment amongst the mainstream political parties. Many of their rank-and-file, who frequently clashed with the police in demonstrations against the royal regime, have become more attracted to an agreement with the Maoists rather than with the king. Even with considerable prompting and support from the international community, the process would thus be fractious and time-consuming but, as argued in a recent ICG report (2005b), retuning to the constitutional path remains the best of the various bad options available to Nepal at the moment.

The third step, namely bringing the Maoists into the settlement process after an understanding has been reached between the countries' other political forces, will be even harder despite the apparent flexibility suggested by the insurgents' declaration of a unilateral three months' ceasefire in September 2005. Their public bottom-line remains the summoning of a constituent assembly but this would be unacceptable to the palace unless some kind of agreement was reached informally on the position of the monarchy, an agreement which, given the sensitivity of the issue for Maoist cadres (and increasingly for cadres of other parties), would have to be reached secretly and probably also kept secret. There could, though, be public agreement on some kind of compromise on the procedural issue – for example, the election of a legislature which would be specifically empowered to amend any provision of the 1990 constitution or possibly to submit proposed amendments to the electorate in a referendum. This would have the advantage of appearing open to all arrangements, including the monarchy itself, to debate but at the same time not granting the Maoists precisely what they have for so long been demanding. Again, though, reaching agreement would surely be a lengthy process, particularly because even when formal principles have been established, the Maoists own role in the interim administration would still have to be decided.

Such negotiations will be particularly important because of the likelihood that people without strong, pre-existing loyalties would 'follow the victor' and vote for whichever side appeared the stronger. In one of my last conversations with the late Rishikesh Shaha, a one-time advisor to King Mahendra turned political dissident and writer, he confidently predicted that the tendency to side with the winner would deliver victory to

Baburam Bhattarai (whom he knew well personally) if the negotiations then (summer 2001) underway led to elections. Other observers would be less categorical than Shaha, but there is something to what he said. Voters will be anxious to make sure that they themselves are not excluded from any benefits to be distributed by the winning side, but may also feel that backing the stronger faction will help guarantee that the conflict does not start again later. Everyone involved in the negotiation will be aware of this reality and will therefore be determined not to let the other side appear to be in a stronger position.

The fourth step would be the holding of elections to whatever kind of body was decided upon. Here the first difficulty would be ensuring that the campaign and voting could take place free of intimidation. While it will be relatively straightforward to require the RNA to return to its barracks and to require the Maoists to stop overt military operations (which they themselves in any case unilaterally suspended in September 2005), covert intimidation by the Maoists will be much more difficult to detect and prevent.

The scale of the problem is clearly illustrated by the upsurge in Maoist demands for 'donations' that occurred during the 2001 ceasefire. very large monitoring effort will be required – not just a few more 'Aidocrats ...in their air-conditioned SUVs', to borrow C.K. Lal's dismissive characterisation of the Office of the United Nations High Commissioner for Human Rights (UNOHCHR) inspection effort (Lal 2005). Ideally there ought also to be some kind of peacekeeping force from outside South Asia with Maoist fighters required either to surrender their weapons to the peacekeepers or to move to 'holding areas' under international supervision. It will also help if a start has already been made on the rehabilitation of the Maoists' full-time fighters. The Maoist leadership's own preferred plan is their amalgamation into a new national army but a large standing army for post-conflict Nepal would be a financial burden and also politically dangerous, whilst any merger proposal will be a sticking point for the RNA and the palace, so the former insurgents will have to be found civilian roles (Kumar 2003).

The key point for steps three and four is that unless they are put under very strong pressure, the King and the Maoists are unlikely to yield what they presently possess: in Gyanendra's case, open border into India. effective control of the urban areas, and in the insurgents', their status as the strongest force at village level. Above all, if genuine supporters of the Maoists are a minority outside their original mid-western stronghold, the Maoist leadership will be even more anxious for a dominant role in interim arrangements and Maoists at village level will have every incentive to continue covert intimidation.

As already argued, continuing international pressure on the palace is essential to start the whole process but once a government of all the main parliamentary parties is established, pressure on the Maoists will also be necessary. This is why the Indians were previously urging the King not only to mend fences with the political parties but also to make more effective use of the RNA. The army has been rightly and heavily criticized for human right abuses but there are also grounds for worry about its professional competence. Failure to disclose information about persons in military custody is in some cases a deliberate intimidatory tactic but in other cases may reflect organisational failure in transferring and acting on information. The latter may well be the reason why some of the Maoists' attacks on district headquarters have been so costly, even when it has later transpired that there were prior indications that an attack would take place. Military action on its own will not end the insurgency but a negotiated settlement acceptable to other parties will result in Maoists holding considerably less power at the village level than they do at present and the Maoists can only be expected to accept this if the alternative is the slow erosion of their present position. Bringing the army and police themselves under the rule of law and then gradually extending the areas of the country where they can maintain a basic level of security will be one important way of ensuring this. As with insurgencies in India, the 'time-honoured combination of coercive and accommodative measures' (Manor 1998: 28) will be needed to restore peace in Nepal.

7

Revolution in India: Lalgarh's Hopeful Spark

BACKGROUND OF THE MOVEMENT

Although one could accurately say the point of eruption of this rebellion occurred early in November of 2008, it is necessary to step back further in order to appreciate the context within which these events have unfolded. Lalgarh is an incredibly impoverished area of West Bengal. It contains one well-developed road— built to accommodate police—that is of little use to its indigenous inhabitants to whom even a motorbike is a rarity. Neither clean water nor electricity is avail- able. Police brutality was a regular occurrence where villagers were detained and tortured for little or no reason—some singled out for repeated horrific abuse. For many years the State promised development in the area, yet little to none was seen.

In 2007, the Jindal Steel Group was given rights to set up a Special Economic Zone (SEZ) for steel production and was awarded a huge portion of land (different reports claim figures somewhere between 4,500 and 5,000 acres). Large sections of these lands were tribal lands, supposedly protected by law for allocation to the indigenous people through a land-reform program. When the development began, adivasi people were displaced, and due to the specter environmental damage, many of their livelihoods were threatened. For years the system had abandoned these people, leaving them under the boot of petty bureaucrats to live as paupers and subjected to every imaginable abuse. Then, in a final act of force, it sought to drive them off of the only land they knew. This callous act was no less than applauded by the ruling powers of the area. After word spread of the land rights being granted to Jindal Steel Group, the region shook choking with outrage.

On November 2, 2008, a landmine detonated in Shalbani in the West Midnapore district when a pro- cession of business and governmental leaders—including the chief minister of West Bengal—returned from the inauguration of the Jindal Steel Works SEZ, having been planted by Maoist guerrillas to target their convoy in opposition to the shameful industrial project. The high-profile attack spurred a massive campaign of police terror in local villages where many of the indigenous population were targeted as suspects or Maoist sympathizers [support for the Communist Party of India (Maoist) is widespread in many areas of the region]. Men, women, and children were targeted without regard and were subjected to physical abuse, torture, and rape. Particularly polarizing moments were when one woman was struck in the face with a rifle butt resulting in a permanent loss of sight in one eye, eleven women were severely abused, and three students were arrested and detained (in a manner more resembling a kidnapping than arrest) on suspicion of being Maoists. However, the inhuman treatment of villagers by police extended far beyond these few vicious incidents and was rooted in a long history of such acts. Several days later thousands of villagers mobilized. Armed with only traditional weapons such as bows and arrows, and an iron resolve forged on decades of suffering, they dug trenches and laid tree trunks across roads to prevent security personnel from entering. In retribution they descended on police stations, damaged their cars, cut off electricity to the buildings, and demanded that police explain why so many of the adivasi people had been hurt.

Huge mobilizations of this nature went on with- out pause for more than a month, drawing widespread attention. Police officers became subject to a social boycott, making it difficult for them to acquire the basic necessities of food and sanitary items required to stay in the area. Coupled with a strong Maoist presence, the social boycott made the Lalgarh area almost impassable for governmental authority figures. Since these events, the uprising has spread like a wildfire influencing hundreds of villages in the West Midnapore district and has drawn immense support not just in West Bengal, but also from many areas in India. It has assumed a definite political character.

On November 8, 2008, the People's Committee Against Police Atrocities (Pulishi Atyacharer Biruddhe Janaganer Committee, or PCPA) was formed in Dalilpur Chowk. It was composed upon formation of elected representatives from 95 villages. These numbers have vastly grown its foundation. Its inception bypassed previous organizations of tribal elders and mainstream political parties which had utterly failed in providing relief to the people of the area, and gave an organized and democratic voice to those from oppressed groups. The committee now makes all major decisions at large public meetings which are often attended by more than 10,000 people from hundreds of villages. The committee also put forth a 13-point set of demands—as well as the police and administrative boycott—to make clear the adivasi people's grievances.

Many demonstrations, blockades, and strikes have been called by the PCPA, and relatively peaceful as- saults on police camps and mainstream party offices were organized, initially by adivasi people. In many cases, police have been forced to withdraw entirely according to their demands. Another significant gain was to win the majority of their 13-point list demands as well as large monetary concessions for development, although these monetary gains were viewed as hoaxes that would never, in the end, benefit the adivasi people. However, their most important demand—that police go to each village and apologize—had yet to be won.

The months after the initial uprising have been characterized by constant forays and negotiations between police, government officials, their respective party cadre, and the people of West Bengal. These conflicts have often taken the form of liberating and losing village territory to government factions. A particularly interesting moment occurred during the weeks prior to the April 2009 Lok Sabha elections. The PCPA put forth a popular demand that no police be allowed into villages during the elections. Although the residents of the areas supported the idea of allowing the polls to occur, they refused to allow them to happen if any police personnel were going to be present. After a long stand- off, the villages finally allowed the polls to occur with police presence, but only far outside the villages where the police boycott existed. Any villagers interested in voting were given rides to the designated polling place on buses chartered by the Election Commission. An important feature of the uprising has been the oppressive role played by the Communist Party of India (Marxist), known as the CPM—the dominant party in West Bengal's Left Front government.

This "communist" party has been deeply involved with West Bengal's capitalists for decades and has brutally exploited West Bengal's large tribal population. In the Lalgarh area, CPM leaders routinely pocket development funds meant for the villagers, and their police forces arrest and torture adivasis suspected of working with the Maoists in the area.

Recent Developments

On June 14, 2009, the PCPA and Maoists conducted a large campaign where they liberated 48 villages and took control of CPI (Marxist) party buildings in Dharampur. They were met with fierce opposition and were involved in furious gun battles for days preceding these events, but, in the end, succeeded in freeing these villages.

On June 16, 2009, there was another significant uprising in Lalgarh in which a large number of adivasis set numerous police camps on fire, drove security forces and CPI (Marxist) cadre and leaders out of Lalgarh, retaking control of the area. An especially important moment was the destruction of the palatial building of CPI (Marxist) leader Anuj Pandey, one of the most hated government officials of the region. The destruction of this building was of great symbolic meaning. It had stood as a tower of oppression keeping the adivasi people under its heavy shadow for many years. Its destruction has finally allowed the sunshine to pour in, lifting the spirits of flowers once so heavily choked by weeds. Unfortunately, since this uprising security forces have descended into the area and have carried out murderous repression campaigns of the same nature that sparked the initial movement. We can only hope those facing these campaigns can effectively defend their new-found freedom in significant ways.

During at least the past few weeks the United States has been providing technical assistance to the Indian government to quell the rebellion, which has allowed them to monitor the areas of Baroperlia, Kantapahari, Ramgarh, Mahultal, Kadashol, Pingboni, Goaltore, Dhrampur and Jhitka as well as plan assaults. The CPI (Maoist) was officially "banned" throughout India as well in June. Soon after, a spokesperson of the Maoist party, Gour Chakravarthy, was arrested in Kolkata while giving an interview. The government has even gone so far as to arrest outsiders who have arrived as neutral observers. A team of intellectuals from Kolkata, including filmmaker Aparna Sen, and a ten-per- son team of social activists, were arrested and assaulted by police.

Despite the huge mobilization of military units and support from foreign imperialist countries, the people of West Bengal and the Maoists have been able to hold their own against the Indian paramilitary forces by conducting guerrilla-style battles and by driving police back out of newly-seized areas.

The tribal people have often mobilized blockades while the PCPA and Maoists have conducted more military-based struggles. Since July 4, 2009, paramilitary forces and the West Bengal State police have been sent to capture Pingboni and Birbhanpur. They also have been combing the forests of the Lalgarh area of Kadashole, Salboni, Godamouli, Jhitka, Kantapahari, and Ronja as part of an assault on Maoist forces and tribal people. Some leaders of the PCPA are also being explicitly targeted for allegedly supporting the Maoists. Sixteen paramilitary groups are operating in the area including COBRA.

According to some press reports, the military groups plan to stay in full force until at least the end of July. As of July 8th, mainstream news agencies have reported that Lalgarh was recaptured. However, the Maoists forces stationed there were able to escape relatively unscathed to the jungles of Ayodhya hills in Purulia via Belpahari and still a number of villages remain liberated (up to date numbers are difficult to ascertain).

Notable Characteristics of the Lalgarh Uprising

From the beginning the Lalgarh uprising has been a progressive force. Since its birth, this movement has had an undeniably organic character, and at its height, drew tens of thousands of villagers out to fight against the corrupt establishment. The movement, clearly born out of the struggles of the noble adivasi peasants, has transcended rural tribal lines in important ways by drawing solidarity and defense from broader sections of the populace including students, human rights organizations, small store owners, and adivasi migrant workers.

Since its birth, the movement has quickly taken shape and developed leadership along democratic lines. The first leading mass organization rising out of the struggle was the PCPA. After its formation, committees quickly appeared in multiple villages, often being led by women. All the major decisions of this organization were decided at mass meetings consisting of up to 10,000 adivasis from hundreds of villages.

Aside from the mass democratic organization the PCPA, embryonic parallel governing structures have begun to emerge as well. These are known as Gram Committees, which were formed in January of 2009 as an alternative to the panchayat system, a tool of the ruling factions of India. Each committee consists of a 10-member elected body—five men and five women—with each body having two delegates for larger area meetings (10 villages).

Above those committees are a total of 35 representatives for central committee meetings—at this level the male/female ratio is not required to be equal (with females occupying a minimum of 12 seats)—who play governing roles. Each decision these committees make must be ratified by a general assembly of people and at least 150 of these committees have been formed (although these numbers are rapidly changing). Along with Gram Committees, the villagers also have set up village defense committees—a form of militia—to protect the people from hermad, police, and CPI (Marxist) attacks. (Bhattacharyya, 2009) These committees are quite radical and novel departures from the traditionally patriarchal and authoritarian institutions of the area.

Whenever these organizations meet with representatives from the official government, they demand that the officials sit on woven mats alongside them. This occurs in direct contradiction to the traditional practice of governing officials sitting in a chair while the people sit on the ground around them. (Ray, 2009) These practices have served to shatter the chains wrapped around the inhabitants of the area, elevating them from a subservient childlike position, to one of equality, one of a people no longer subject to the rule of a small elite.

Over the course of the struggle, new developmental initiatives have taken place. In Kantapahari, a hospital set up two years ago, but never utilized by the government, was seized by the PCPA and renamed the "People's Hospital." The hospital opened its doors staffed with one physician and six health workers. (Bhattacharyya, 2009) The PCPA has also taken steps to deal with agriculture and water scarcity problems with the instillation of tubewells in multiple villages and irrigation projects such as canal dredging. These initiatives have all taken place solely on the basis of monetary contributions and voluntary labor.

The Maoists have been playing an important role in developmental projects by encouraging a model of self-sufficiency and sustainability as opposed to projects dominated by foreign capital and a wealthy elite. These projects have included health centres, drinking water and irrigation projects, and road development. Along with the establishment of parallel governing structures, the Maoists and villagers have built at least 50 kilometers of gravel paths, set up tube wells and water tanks, set up irrigation initiatives, and are running health centres. These projects—coupled with the defense by the Maoist army and their ongoing people's war—create the potential basis for developing revolutionary power structures independent of the Indian state.

Exciting developments have occurred explicitly within the women's movement—practices such as fair representation have been won and women's leadership in the general movement has served as an important offensive against traditional patriarchy. An all-women's branch of the PCPA has been formed, which is not only responsible for the fight against police repression and CPI (Marxist) attacks, but also against domestic oppression. One important initiative of this movement has been the seizure of businesses that distribute alcohol. Those who ignore the ban on consumption can be subject to social boycott.

Concluding Remarks

It is my belief that the facts overwhelmingly demonstrate that the battle occurring for Lalgarh's liberation is a just one. This movement is one of unprecedented size to the area, born from and led by the indigenous inhabitants of the region for an undeniably just cause. Revolutionary people should be watching this movement, learning what we can, and offering whatever support possible. No doubt this struggle will be a long and brutal one, with the people of West Bengal facing many trials and tribulations. This is a uniquely polarizing moment in recent political history, already being called the new Naxalbari, and will most likely prove to be a locus of revolutionary struggle for some time to come.

LALGARH BEYOND MAOISM, MAOISM BEYOND LALGARH

In politics, the truth is almost always counter-intuitive. In this realm – where the art of the possible intersects in strangely unexpected ways with the science of the impossible – ominous portents of anarchy often conceal messianic promises of deliverance. Lalgarh, today, is perhaps the starkest symbol of this confounding cocktail, which has come to characterise the polity of Left Front-ruled West Bengal. But the violent upheavals, which have been rocking this tribal-dominated village of West Midnapore over the past several months, are unlikely to yield any meaning as long as socio-political violence continues to be envisaged as a moral question. If anything, such a moral approach would only produce counter-productive programmes and practices that would inexorably push politics further down the hopeless pit of a degenerate status quo.

Whether the Lalgarh movement constitutes an unconscionable disruption of social peace, or is a legitimate popular upsurge cannot be conclusively determined unless the objective political condition and logic of that movement and its subjective ideological orientation, especially with regard to the adoption of violence as an instrumentality of politics, is accurately accounted for. What clearly distinguishes the Lalgarh uprising from other apparently similar violent incidents and agitations that have scarred West Bengal over the past few years, and which have registered a sudden spurt in the aftermath of the resounding victory of the Trinamool Congress-Congress alliance over the CPI(M)-led Left Front (LF) in the 15th Lok Sabha elections, is that the calculus of competitive electoral politics has had absolutely no bearing on the movement. The reason why electoral considerations have figured rather significantly in most other zones of unrest in the state is because the strife in those zones has been ignited mainly by the collapse of the CPI(M)-led LF's well-oiled and calibrated network to differentially distribute political patronage by way of governance. This has particularly been the case in areas such as Nandigram and Singur where the main battle has been against acquisition of farmland for industrial development.

The struggle for patronage is essentially a competitive struggle that has no concern loftier than that of conserving and progressively concentrating positions constitutive of a structurally inequitable and undemocratic status quo. That does not, however, mean the distress and disaffection caused by the collapse of such patronage, which is all that is there by way of governance in LF-ruled West Bengal, is not real. The trouble is the political idiom in which such genuine anxieties are being articulated is, in being shaped by the all-pervasive regime of patronage politics, thoroughly competitive. That has inevitably rendered such mass movements susceptible to all sorts of cynical manoeuvres and manipulations.

The popular eruption in Lalgarh, on the other hand, has been driven by no such competitive consideration precisely because the remote tribal belt of which it is a part has had little or no patronage network to begin with.

The insurgency of the Lalgarh population has been shaped by its experience of a state that has registered its presence in the area through the brutal effectiveness of its repressive security apparatuses but has been absent as an organic expression of the will of the people and an efficient purveyor of emancipatory social development and vital public goods. Clearly, the problem there is not, as many seem to believe, the absence of the state but its existence as a completely alienated and foreign entity. Those being the objective conditions for the emergence and expansion of the Lalgarh movement, it is highly unlikely that it is capable of positing, or even articulating, anything other than a transformative critique of the alienated and repressive state, and the intrinsically competitive and hierarchical socio-economic order that engenders it.

And that is precisely why the temptation to classify the Lalgarh uprising as a tribal identity movement, driven by the ideology of some organic notion of autonomous communitarianism, should be resisted. The majority population of Lalgarh is doubtless tribal but the anti-competitive orientation of their struggle, thanks to the objective politico-economic conditions that have shaped them, serves to completely invert the competitive logic of identitarian movements, which always articulate their politics in supremacist terms of ethno-cultural pride and domination. Put simply, the Lalgarh movement clearly manifests characteristic features of a working-class struggle.

The People's Committee against Police Atrocities-led revolt, which was sparked seven months ago by a repressive combing operation launched by the West Bengal police in Lalgarh and surrounding areas in response to a Maoist mine attack on the chief minister's cavalcade, has steadily morphed into a more proactive and comprehensive struggle for a fundamental transformation of the socio-political structure. That has yielded a two-pronged movement of resistance and reconstruction. It is, therefore, no accident that the PCPA, which has been leading the militant mass movement against the West Bengal government in Lalgarh, is now also at the forefront of an incipient social reconstruction programme for the enforcement of a cooperative and democratic management of resources and rudimentary public services such as healthcare developed by the local community itself.

That the CPI(M)-led West Bengal government, infamous for its autocratic ways, was extremely cagey until a few weeks ago to crack down on the movement was largely due to its mass insurrectionary character. In Lalgarh, violence against state apparatuses has not been launched by a clearly identified group acting on behalf of an oppressed but largely passive population. Instead, it has been an expression of disaffection and opposition by a population entirely insurgent against a repressive state and the oppressive socio-economic order it protects and perpetuates. Even the guerrilla operations carried out by Maoists in the area and its neighbourhood have become a seamless extension of this insurrection, which inevitably enjoys wide-ranging local legitimacy and has some serious moral standing, vis-à-vis the rest of the state. It is this legitimacy, which derives from an assertion of popular sovereignty, that had kept West Bengal's Stalinist dispensation away from open repressive manoeuvres for so long. That it had burnt its fingers in Nandigram, where its cadre together with the state police had attempted a scorched-earth operation a couple of years ago, has only compounded its diffidence on that score.

After all, a modern state formation, no matter how repressive, has to always act in the name of protecting popular sovereignty. But in an insurrectionary situation, like the one in Lalgarh, the sovereignty vested normatively in the state is clearly in conflict with actual sovereignty on the ground. In such circumstances, the state, if it cracks down on the movement, runs the grave risk of losing all formal legitimacy it enjoys as the keeper of people's sovereignty. In fact, it is the state or the government that, in such a situation, comes to be seen as an external threat to the sovereignty of the people and the violent insurrection of the latter against the state pushes it and its laws into a state of crisis. That renders the legal-illegal dichotomy problematic and consequently makes it difficult for the state to legitimately monopolise violence to crush popular movements in the name of combating anti-sovereign lawlessness and insurgency. That is a risk the CPI(M)-led LF could ill-afford at a moment when the electoral drubbing it has received in West Bengal signals significant erosion of its moral-political standing.

The Lalgarh movement could, nevertheless, hardly have gone on for ever without inviting the wrath of the ruling classes of West Bengal and India. The only way a movement like that could possibly evade state repression and keep itself alive and kicking is through continuous political growth accomplished through a relentless process of engagement and integration with concerns, anxieties and disaffections in other areas and sectors of the state. Yet, an unpardonable tactical blunder on the part of the Maoists, who indisputably have a sizeable numerical presence in the PCPA, has cleared the way for the West Bengal government to unleash repression on the Lalgarh movement sooner rather than later.

The recent claims by various senior Maoist leaders and activists that the PCPA was a front of the underground outfit, which was controlling and running the show in Lalgarh, has given the repressive arms of both the LF government of West Bengal and, to a lesser extent, the Centre the alibi they had been waiting for. The West Bengal government has, over the past few days, turned proactive and has been dispatching contingents of heavily armed police and central paramilitary forces to Lalgarh to crush the popular uprising. That the LF dispensation has suddenly regained its usual repressive element is because it knows the police operation in Lalgarh would now be widely perceived as a legitimate measure taken by the state to protect popular sovereignty from Maoists and some sections of the local community they have bamboozled.

The Maoists, thanks to their doctrinaire programmatic commitment to agrarian revolution and the concomitant tactical emphasis on guerilla struggles exclusively in tribal and rural areas of the country, have failed to focus on developing large-scale popular movements in the semi-urban and urban areas. Their time-worn approach of encirclement of cities by people's army raised from the countryside has, willy-nilly, militarised their politics, what with their roving guerrilla squads carrying out dramatic raids on behalf of a rural population they have barely organised. That, among other things, has ensured their politics enjoys little concrete ideological-political support among working people in Indian cities. As a result, it has been rather easy for the state at all levels and the ruling classes it represents to paint the Maoist movement into an illegal corner and successfully delegitimise it as an external threat to popular sovereignty.

The Maoists doubtless have a significant numerical and ideological presence within the PCPA and the wider Lalgarh movement. But the committee, which is much more diverse in its broad Left ideological composition, is far from being a front of the Maoist group. And that, as far as the Maoist commitment to a militant working-class movement is concerned, would have spelt no harm.

If anything, the Maoists and their sympathisers in Lalgarh ought to have envisaged such a situation as an opportunity for them to continue to work quietly within the PCPA and provide the insurrectionary movement with requisite logistical support and ideological orientation to expand politically to engage with and integrate a multitude of other disenfranchised and exploited sections of West Bengal's society and economy such as the embattled peasants of Nandigram, Rajbongshi separatists of north Bengal plains, the Gorkhas of Darjeeling and the large masses of workers rendered unemployed by the sharp decline in the fortunes of the state's tea and jute industries.

This process of integration through continuous engagement would have had to address the specific concerns of each of those sections even as it transformed their mutually competitive idioms of political articulation into a coherent but multitudinous critique of the logic of the larger political economy responsible for all their various miseries. That would not only lead to an aggregative programme of social change but would also make Maoism into an ideological current that is always internal to an ever-growing variety of popular movements.

In such circumstances, the modality of political violence would always be that of popular insurrection. And even guerrilla tactics, as and when they are deployed, would necessarily be envisaged as an integral part of this insurrectionary paradigm. That would not only make it hard for the state to delegitimise such violence as illegal or the movements that generate them as anti-sovereign, it would also ensure that Maoism is rescued from the excesses of its current sectarian militarism that have, often enough, ended up replicating the same configurations of superordinate state power, which the movement has sought to unravel. Clearly, the Maoists can avoid tactical blunders like the one they have committed in Lalgarh only when they reframe their political-organisational vision. Their obsession with territorial expansion, which has spelt no real political-ideological breakthrough for Maoism, essentially stems from the Maoists' insistence on envisaging the party as an a priori state-form, which seeks to subordinate the singularity of various experiences of disaffection and registers of struggle to its doctrinaire conception of politics, which is no more than the generalisation of one particular experience of social oppression and resistance. What they need to do, instead, is to imagine the organisation as a movement-form, wherein Maoism is a dynamic organisational impulse and the party is always in a state of bottom-up formation through a perpetual process of politicisation at the grassroots.

West Bengal, ironically enough, provides the most conducive political climate for the Maoists to effect such a reorientation. Their struggles against a repressive state, controlled for over three decades by a coalition of Left forces helmed by the largest Communist Party, ought to compel them to reflect on how communist-left forces, which were once the undisputed principal representatives of a genuine working-class movement, have come to distort it beyond recognition.

The degeneration of the CPI(M)-led LF, contrary to the popular belief shaped by the neo-liberal consensus, is not because of its failure to turn fully social democratic but precisely because it has abandoned the tortuous dirt-path of working-class struggle for the comfortable highway of social democracy. Social democracy, which envisages social progress and the well-being of the working people and the poor essentially as a question of distributive justice, is a form of governance that seeks to equitably distribute a given basket of socio-economic entitlements. In such a 'Leftist' scheme, there is no place for interventionist and transformative politics because the state, which for social democracy is an instrument of efficient regulation and equitable redistribution, is treated as a passive and neutral entity that must be captured and then merely controlled.

The state, however, is in reality constitutive of an exploitative, oppressive and hierarchical social order. To that extent, a radical socialist programme must actively articulate the tendency to erode, not capture, it. For, it is only through such erosion that the structural reinforcement of a stratified society can be undermined. The preposterous contradiction the CPI(M)-led LF has created between industrial development that is inescapable, and universal democracy that is indispensable, is a symptom of its social-democratic degeneration. Its failure to imagine more democratic and participatory configurations of socio-political power, which could drive truly cooperative consolidation of land and other resources, and posit an alternative model of development, is because of its social-democratic fixation on the state.

That the Maoists too should call themselves the CPI(M) – Communist Party of India (Maoist) – is uncanny. But more eerie perhaps is the fact that their conception of the party as a state-form predisposes them to a social democratic approach to politics that virtually makes them a mirror-image of the original CPI(M). It's time the Maoists woke up and smelt the gunpowder.

8

The Maoist "Problem" and the Democratic Left in India

One key paradigmatic subtext of Naomi Klein's argument that runs in her *The Shock Doctrine* (London: Penguin, 2008) is how the supposed undemocratic, violent character of "totalitarian" Marxist movements serve to justify repressive measures by the neo-liberal state. In inviting such a repressive response from the state, "undemocratic" revolutionary left movements are presented as causing the erosion of democratic spaces and the right to dissent. But what if upholding so-called democratic spaces by shunning the undemocratic, revolutionary left is premised on blocking off emerging possibilities of radical transformation, thereby ideologically legitimising capitalist democracy?

Thus, today, even as dissident democratic leftists like Klein expose the repressive neo-liberal order and its double standards and hypocritical claims, they display a fundamental attachment to its basic premises, as they uphold and legitimise the norms of capitalist political democracy. They oppose their agonising attachment to democracy (and so-called democratic struggle, livelihood approach, rights-based discourse, subaltern approach and so on) to the "shock doctrine" and repression of the neo-liberal state in a way which excludes the revolutionary left from the field of acceptable, "legitimate" political struggle. However, as we see in India, in portraying the "undemocratic,""totalitarian" Maoist movement as a mirror-image of the repressive state, the democratic left objectively speaks from within and, therefore, for the so-called democratic space of this neo-liberal, repressive state.

This shows that the dissident left in India has accepted democracy or democratic struggle as the only game in town, a fidelity to formal democratic norms, thereby rejecting "undemocratic" political struggle as liable to be "shocked and awed." What is true is that in the face of a political threat to the very liberal democratic, or even radical democratic consensus, by a force which refuses to play the democratic game, the capitalist state invariably functions with the democratic left as its oppositional ally. Thus, as oppositional allies, both the state and the dissident left view the Maoist movement as a "problem": the difference lies only in the way they understand this problem.

The debate in India on the Maoist movement, thereby, centres on whether one views this movement as a "law and order" problem or a socio-economic problem. Since both viewpoints regard the movement as a problem, the two positions can be collapsed into one. But that is precisely what is not allowed: it is in somehow retaining the two positions as distinct that the dominant order constitutes the political field as one of struggle, opposition and hence "democracy" (akin, say, to the false political distinctiveness of and competition between the Republicans and Democrats in the USA). As we shall see, this political field is sustained by blocking off the Maoist alternative from the field of vision.

The Maoist movement, also called the Naxalite movement, after Naxalbari the name of a rural town where a 1967 peasant uprising ignited this tendency within the Indian Communist movement, has the New Democratic Revolution as its declared objective, the overthrow of the "semi-feudal, semi-colonial" state through protracted people's war. Because of this, it has always faced severe state repression. All along, the brutality with which the state sought to eliminate Maoists, in a seeming paradox, chimed well with the so-called socio-economic approach of the dissident left. In recent years, however, a good swathe of politicians and Home Ministry officials view the Maoists as a law and order problem and officially classify them as "terrorists." The prime minister recently singled out Maoists as the single largest internal security threat. This security-centric understanding of the Maoist "problem," is challenged by sections of the dissident left who see it as a socio-economic problem, arising from deprivation, loss of livelihood, lack of employment opportunities and abject poverty, given a neo-liberal state abdicating all welfare functions. They argue that the "Maoist threat" is used by the government as a ruse to justify the rise of the security-centric state, with its repressive laws infringing genuine democratic voices and dissent.

Within the dissident left, the old social democratic tendency, once invested in Nehruvian socialism and planned development, with concerns about reducing inequality, poverty amelioration and so on, advocates the socio-economic approach. The adoption of neo-liberal policies by the Indian state since 1991 weakened the hold of this section within the Indian state and bureaucracy and hence its "humane" socio-economic approach cannot be understood without reference to its specific elite interests. Thanks to the presence and efforts of this faction, the once-powerful welfarist Indian Planning Commission recently instituted a study of the Maoist movement, expounding the socio-economic approach. This commentary deals with Development Challenges in Extremist Affected Areas.

The Report

The Report captures the Naxalite/Maoist phenomenon at three moments of its relationship with this pre-defined political field fundamentally structured around the two approaches: the security-centric one and the socio-economic approach. Given that this political field is taken as given, the Maoists are simply made to traverse it in three instances. Since these instances are interrelated and one flows into the other, they form a simple dialectic. A triadic structure is formed where the Naxalites/Maoists are, in the first instance, shown in their alienation from the system. In the second instance they are shown in their "positive content" (fighting for the rights of adivasis, land rights, forest rights and so on), which is essentially shared with the socio-economic state and also has a positive content (employment guarantee for the poor, decentralisation, tribal rights and so on).

In the third instance, the Maoists are shown to be in a position to join the system if only both sides (Maoists and the security-centric state) could reform themselves. From the first to the third instance, the Naxalites/Maoists finish a journey from alienation from the system to having something positive to offer, to then absorption in the system. Meanwhile, the basic structure of the political field comprising the two tendencies within the state - the socio-economic approach and the security-centric approach - is not only maintained and reinforced but also purged of the Naxalite/Maoist threat; all this is achieved through the humane socio-economic approach!

The Report comprises three corresponding ideological moves. The first consists of treating the Naxalites/Maoists as the consequence of the "failure" of the state's "development model," so that they are then understood as simply a by-product, an epi-phenomenon within the given political field pre-defined to rule them out as a political alternative. There is then the second ideological move which seeks to identify their "positive" aspect as fighting for the rights of the marginalised. It is this benevolent activity and not their political and ideological goals that are regarded as primary: beneath the veneer of political objectives, they are just a bundle of benevolent acts. Once this is settled, can the Naxalites/Maoists be very different from the benign state if only this state implemented plans for local self-government, rural empowerment, adivasi rights, Dalit rights and so forth?

The third ideological moment of the humane socio-economic approach therefore consists of finding a common ground between the Maoists and state agencies. This is supposed to provide the basis for negotiations between the two parties. Interestingly, Indian politicians who brokered the entry of Maoists in neighbouring Nepal from a people's war into "democratic politics" were precisely those who uphold the socio-economic approach to Maoists in India. The ideologically reactionary role they played in Nepal should be a warning about their character to the Indian Maoists. It will be seen that the "humane" socio-economic approach to the Naxalites/Maoists advocated by the Report presupposes stripping them of their politics as a prelude to bringing them back into the "normal political process." In dissenting from and contesting the security-centric approach, the socio-economic approach, therefore, so constructs and structures the political field that the "humane approach" it advocates towards Naxalites/Maoists becomes a way of "including them out" as a political alternative. The socio-economic approach's contestation with the security-centric approach is premised on excluding the Naxalites/Maoists as an alternative political force.

Terms of Reference

The Report's terms of reference mean that it is not about the Naxalite movement as such but about how the state has failed to deliver in "extremist affected areas:" it is about "the elements of discontent of the people arising out of failure of the system" (p. vi). The Naxalites are said to capitalise on this discontent and win over marginalised sections of society for their political programme: "the failure, inadequacy or injustice of State mechanisms and institutions created space for the Naxalite activities". This is the basic thrust of the socio-economic viewpoint which, unlike the law and order approach, does not hold that the Naxalites are merely a terror group.

Instead of taking the Naxalite movement on its own terms, the socio-economic approach treats it as the by-product of the failed development policies of the present state. This approach, however, is contextualised in the larger need to defend the Nehruvian kind of developmental state against the neo-liberal, growth- and security-centric marauders who now control the state. Thus, before the "paradigm shift of economic policy from 1991," says the Report, the state policies "used to reiterate the commitment to reduction in inequality of income and wealth," but not any longer.

The Report approvingly recalls "positive state responses" to the Naxalite movement in the 1960s and 1970s. It points out such responses from the Communist Party of India (Marxist) or CPI(M), a "revisionist" party and sworn enemy of the Maoists. For example, due to the CPI(M)'s land redistribution policy, "when the peasantry found that large areas of land would be distributed amongst them, their loyalty shifted from the Naxalite militants to the normal political process". In the 1970s, the

Indira Gandhi government issued guidelines for land reform and to revise existing laws and rural unrest waned, thereby eroding the Naxalite's mass basis.

But now, rues the Report, under the neo-liberal security-centric state, "the responsibility of the state for providing equal social rights recedes in the sphere of policy-making," essentially abdicating its constitutional obligations to the rural poor. There is a "directional shift in Government policies towards modernisation and mechanisation, export orientation, diversification to produce for the market, withdrawal of various subsidy regimes ... hurting the poor in several ways". Thus, in trying to explain the rise of "rural discontent and unrest" and hence the increasing strength of the Naxalite movement, the Report locates itself in the larger critique of the state's neo-liberal policies. The increasing strength and belligerence of the Naxalite movement is taken as evidence of the "failure" of these policies.

Ideological Move One: Consequence of a "Failed" Development Model

For the Report, the Naxalites are just an instance of the "failure" of the state's present policies of development. In a political field marked by the contest between these two statist poles, the security-centric and the development-centric poles, the Naxalite movement serves only as "raw material" to validate the claims of the now-marginalised faction of the state against the neo-liberals who control it, a contestation indistinguishable from that among the different state factions (Planning Commission vs. Home Ministry). In denying the Naxalite/Maoist movement a constitutive space in the political field, it gets presented as an epiphenomenon: precisely at the moment when the socio-economic approach promises a more humane state response towards it.

The search for how the state can provide a humane response, appear caring and maintain the "democratic way," comes at the expense of diluting the politically radical character of the movement. In its contestation with the security-centric state, the socio-economic approach in the Report takes the bold step of counting the Naxalites in its own likeness! This is accomplished by showing how Naxalite struggle for the rights of the marginalised is also (incidentally?) the main concern of the welfarist state. It is as though the rise of the Naxalite movement allows the welfarist dissident left to shower further blows on the neo-liberalists who have dislodged them from state power. This explains the "softness" of the welfarist, dissident left to Maoists in India.

Ideological Move Two: Maoists as Service-providers

Distancing itself even more from the competing security-centric approach, the Report proposes that the Maoist movement is not just a consequence of the failed development policies of the present state but is itself trying to address this problem in its own way. Says the Report: except for "the ideological goal of capturing State power through violence, the basic programmes of the Extremists relate to elimination of poverty, deprivation and alienation of the poor and the landless". This shows that once the Naxalites are portrayed as an epiphenomenon, overlooking their "identity" as a political force, the "humane" approach can now treat the ideology, political programme and "their declared aim to overthrow the Indian state" as also epiphenomenonal to their "identity."

Thus, this humane approach to the Naxalites/Maoists is based on "excluding the ideological goal," the political content of the movement. In therefore paring off the Naxalites/Maoists to their welfarist best as a way to counter the security-centric aggressiveness of the Indian state, this approach, in the same move, takes the political steam out of the Naxalite/Maoist movement. In recognising what is empirically true about the "pro-people" activities of the Naxalites/Maoists, the socio-economic approach is "more progressive" than the security-centric approach. However, in working within the political field that presupposes the continued existence of this latter pole, this approach reinforces the given political configuration. In challenging the security-centric approach, the dissident left reasserts the existing political field, denying Maoist attempts at its reconfiguration. Contrary to what one would expect, therefore, not treating the Naxalites/Maoists as a political movement is not a "short-coming" naturally arising out of the constraints placed by the "terms of reference" on the Report.

Rather, it is the result of the workings of the very logic of the Report's socio-economic approach. Thus, this approach is at its ideological best precisely when it takes a progressive position against the security-centric approach by pointing out the benevolent activities of Naxalites/Maoists in solving livelihood problems. The Report works with an implicit assumption that the political objectives and ideology of the Maoists could very well be treated as just an outer garb beneath which the socio-economic approach discovers the Maoists' positive core: meeting the basic requirements and grievances of the people (aren't Naxalites the benevolent rebels, Robin Hood style?). The hidden ideological assumption of the Report is: are we not, after all, basically humanitarians at the end of the day, out to provide "goods and services" and livelihood entitlements to the people, so that questions of power, democracy, oppression are all secondary?

That is why, says the Report, even though it does not directly deal with the Maoists as a political force engaged in a violent struggle to overthrow the state, yet that issue is already covered: "the link between what the report deals with, and what it does not, lies in the fact that it is in the course of providing answers to the people's problems and needs that the Naxalite movement seeks to obtain their support from the masses". That is, even though "Naxalite activity is not confined to solving people's grievances," yet this is why people are with them (it is: you provide stuff to the poor so that they vote for you). One is led to think that the masses support the Naxalites/Maoists only since they happen to solve their livelihood issues and are better service-providers than the state agencies! It is in this vein that the Report lists instances of the benevolent deeds of Naxalites/Maoists, putting them alongside those of state development agencies, easily extendable to NGOs who are service-providers. More crucially, it is not only Maoists who are treated as service-providers but ordinary people (who join the Maoists) who are portrayed as service-seekers. People who could be political subjects, active agents of social change and willing to "suffer" its consequences are here depicted as mere seekers of humanitarian aid. This is what Alain Badiou calls treating "Man as a victim," a "being-for-death," so that human rights become "rights of survival against misery".

If the first ideological move, in portraying the Naxalites/ Maoists as an epiphenomenon - a consequence of the failed development policies of the state - laid the political field with the socio-economic approach and the security-centric approach as the two given poles, the second move (identifying their positive role in securing the means of livelihood to the people) reduces their politics to welfarist activities. This anticipates the third move, which is one of treating the Naxalites/Maoists, duly castrated, as some sort of an adjunct, a possible partner to the state's welfarist mission to ensure certain rights to the marginalised. It is on this basis that the Report recommends negotiations with the Naxalites/Maoists: which, in effect, is no less than a recipe for liquidating them, or, to put it humanely, bringing them into the "democratic process."

IDEOLOGICAL MOVE THREE: NEGOTIATIONS (OR LIQUIDATING MAOISTS)

The socio-economic approach involves treating the Naxalites as seriously engaged in efforts to provide goods and services to the rural poor, access to livelihood resources, forest rights and so on. In presenting the Maoists as plugging the increasingly large gaps left by the neo-liberal development model, the Report assumes a continuum between a socially responsible state, upholding social rights and its constitutional obligations to the marginalised, and the Naxalites/Maoists. The Report argues that a socially responsible decentralised state will wean people away from the Naxalites/Maoists and provide the basis for negotiations with the Maoists who engage in similar activities.

In laying out this meeting ground between the Maoists and the welfarist state, the socio-economic approach transforms the Naxalites/Maoists into potential allies. This approach, in its third instance, thus builds a case for the state to enter into negotiations with the Maoists.

To sum up, the socio-economic approach starts, in the first instance, by portraying the Naxalites/Maoists as an epiphenomenon, a by-product of the failure of the system; then, in the second instance, portrays them in their positive aspect as service-providers; and, finally, in the third instance, opens the possibility of viewing the Naxalites/Maoists as allies in providing the solution to the system's problems. As S. Banerjee points out, the message of the Report is clear:

> The Maoists may have to shelve their "maximalist" aim of seizure of power for the time being, and negotiate with the state in the humanitarian interest of the thousands of poor and innocent families who have been caught in the crossfire between the police and the Naxalites.

Implicit in this approach is that Maoists should enter into negotiations with the welfarist state and suspend their violent people's war. If they don't, they stand accused of being fixated on violence and killings rather than on solving the peoples' most basic problems. (Interestingly, in neighbouring Nepal recently, once Maoists bought into these ideas of the need to set aside "political differences" and work towards "reconciliation, development and peace" for "a new united modern Nepal," their liquidation as a radical political force inexorably followed.) Hence the question: is the socio-economic approach any less than a recipe for a "democratic," or "humanitarian" liquidation of Maoists?

Critique, Ideology

The dissident left recognises the split but does not dare traverse it and so remains wedded to the existing political field. The socio-economic approach and its critique of the neo-liberal state precludes the possibility of any radical transformation: in this sense, they are ideological. Ideological not in the sense of promoting false consciousness but in sustaining the given political field through a blocking off of the emergence of a new political field opened up by the possibility of Maoists traversing the split. In other words, it is misplaced for the dissident left to think that it is their humane subjectivity, their progressive critique of and challenge to the security-centric position that confers "recognition" on Maoists as a socio-economic problem. Instead, it might be the other way round: that it is the "totalitarian," and "undemocratic" Maoist intervention from outside the political field, out to overthrow the existing state order, which provides the dissident left the democratic space in it to expound the socio-economic approach. Indeed one of the recurring themes of the dissident left is how the poor and the marginalised are being forced to take up arms and become Maoists since the neo-liberal state has abdicated its welfare functions. Arundhati Roy writes

But now more and more are reaching for guns. Will the violence grow? If the "growth rate" and the Sensex are going to be the only barometers the government uses to measure progress and the well-being of people, then of course it will.

With people reaching for guns, the Maoist "totalitarian threat" is then instrumentally and opportunistically used by the dissident left to undermine the rule of the neoliberal security centric extabilishment by accusing the latter of undermining the 'democratic' legitimacy of the state, representative institutions and the government. It is thus from the shoulders of the Maoist movement that the left-learning Expert Group fired their volleys at the present 'neoliberal', 'anti-people' Indian state, claiming that 'the left' can better manage the existing state (the so-called 'democratic', 'people-oriented' state) - and of course 'democratically safeguard' it from challenges from revolutionary movements.

Thus, it is too superficial to say that the Maoist movement, because it is violent and "undemocratic," merely becomes a pretext for the state to stifle dissent and crush democratic voices. Such an opinion, depressingly ubiquitous, displays a deep attachment to a state-centric notion of democracy and liberty. Striving to remove the Maoist pretext so that the state does not err in its repression is too considerate an attitude towards the state, as though it is not repressive in itself. More crucially, any attempt at radical transformation is ideologically demonised by this accusation of providing the state a pretext to curtail democracy.

In the course of their critique of neo-liberal policies, some of the key positions taken by this dissident left have been supporting and working towards the National Rural Employment Guarantee Act, the Right to Information, opposing displacement of people by different projects like dams, mines, Special Economic Zones, forest rights for tribals and suchlike. The dissident left has also raised its voice in other cases, including opposing a situation of near civil war in Chattisgarh, where the state has been arming the Salwa Judum vigilante group against the Maoists and supporting the movements against displacement in Orissa.

One good instance of how the system, the political field, gets reinforced precisely by demanding and sometimes securing concessions from it has been the demand seeking human rights activist Binayak Sen's release since he is "the good doctor" and "a true humanist"- and since his continued detention would mean "bad press" for Indian democracy. While the refusal to frame this demand by taking cognisance of his "Maoist links" augurs well for the Maoists as it preserves their radical otherness, what it also does is displace the struggle against the state as such to one against its draconian laws, repressive measures and similar particular manifestations.

The point is that this critique and the movements and campaigns that it has inspired invariably remain either wedded to the dislodged or social democratic faction of the Indian state or even when it is the anti-totalitarian, neo-Gandhian, anti-modernist, "anti-state" left, a third position never emerges. The National Advisory Council formed under the present United Progressive Alliance government empirically demonstrated the character of this dissident left.

This Council was a convergence of the old Nehruvian "socialistic pattern" approach, the social democratic left of the CPI and CPI(M), the neo-Gandhian left and "non-party political formations"- pushed to unite both due to the neo-liberal onslaught as well as the Hindu right-wing upsurge. One major event which brought these different shades of left together was the 2004World Social Forum in Mumbai.

Resistance to the CPIM government's bid to set up Special Economic Zones in 2007-08 however marked a public disavowal of this alliance and it emerged that the major section of the old social democratic left, the CPI(M), with an always unsure CPI, would go ahead with neo-liberal policies. The CPI(M) is a seasoned practitioner at effortlessly shuffling between rhetorical attacks on World Bank and IMF policies, critiquing neo-liberal globalisation, and doing just the reverse with great single-mindedness. Its anti-imperialism increasingly appears as no more than a palate from which it draws in order to keep itself alive in the game of parliamentary politics. The dissident left has, of course, actively opposed the CPI(M)'s pro-imperialist, capitalist policies and repressive measures.

Rumblings and Shifts

However, the space for the dissident left's democratic critique of neo-liberalism and of draconian laws is increasingly narrowing as class polarisations sharpen and the response from the masses is increasingly desperate, sometimes violent and radical, in the face of an untrammelled and ruthless state allied with an increasingly powerful capitalist class. That is, the pre-1991 political field marked by the two poles of the social democratic socio-economic approach and the security-centric, free market state is undergoing significant shifts. The spectacular rise of the neo-liberal, security-centric state has seen the transformation of social democracy - particularly the CPI(M) - from being nominally on the "side of the masses," to being openly on the side of capital and the state. This change redefines the nature and scope of the protests and resistance, including the Maoist movement.

Events around the mass resistance in Nandigram to the proposed SEZ, the brain-child of the CPI(M) party and government, made it clear that social democracy has graduated from its role of containment of the masses in the service of capital and the state, to itself spearheading the neo-liberal onslaught. Social democracy, or rather the two main communist parties, the CPI and CPI(M), have for decades been at the forefront of channelling and subverting mass resistance. It seems though that social democracy is now no longer satisfied just managing mass threats to the system - having made too many "historic blunders" in not breaking out from this lesser role - it now wants a direct stake in managing capital and the state.

While this strengthens the ruling political classes by diversifying its composition (adding the colour red), the problem for the thinking members of the ruling elite today seems to be that there is no credible "left" force out there to contain the "social discontent" of the masses. NGOs, social movements, Hindu right-wing have all failed. Further, there has been a significant exhaustion of the energies of neo-Gandhian social movements (for example the Narmada Bachao Andolan), which were committed to militant but professedly non-violent, non-hierarchical struggles. Concomitantly, there has been the shift of the entire spectrum of parliamentary political parties, including communist parties and social democracy, openly to the right. With a security-centric and repressive neo-liberal state destroying the lives and livelihood of millions of people, the change in the role of social democracy means that there is no credible "left" political force that would contain and channel the resistance from these masses along "democratic" lines: a problem for the ruling classes but an advantage for revolutionary forces. The present conjuncture therefore opens up the possibility of a response from the masses unmanaged by one or the other faction of capital or the state. Nandigram showed how this change in the nature and role of social democracy and other left forces opens a possibility for a more radical resistance from the masses: the resistance was uncompromising and radical in a way that allowed for no negotiation and mediation. Thus, the role of middle class social activists, such as Medha Patkar, supporting the resistance was limited to being visitors to these "affected areas"- unlike earlier movements, such as the Narmada Bachao Andolan, where middle class activists actually provided leadership, albeit in a so-called non-hierarchical way.

In this situation, any left force which emerges can be expected to carry the seeds of radical change beyond the given "reality:" this is where the present expansion of the Maoist movement needs to be placed. In general, the Maoists apart, it seems that the resistance and responses from the masses are going to be less democratic and less constitutional and more violent, if not always radical. The presence of Maoists in large parts of the country enhances and deepens this process. The resistance in Nandigram derived at least some its energy and direction from the presence of Maoists; such developments carry the potential of restructuring the existing political configuration.

However, the dissident left still seems unwilling to take account of this possible turn in the political balance of forces In refusing to understand the strength of the state and the stridency of capital in relative terms, that is, by weighing and judging it in the face of this "undemocratic and unconstitutional" mass mobilisation and resistance, the dissident left treats it in its pure and abstract existence, hence all-powerful and something we can only go on critiquing no end.

Critique becomes self-referential and even self-indulgent as it is heavily invested in and fundamentally attached to the present political order. That is why, for the dissident left, the kind of resistance that falls outside of the dominant political field does not carry the seeds of any possible alternative.

It only qualifies as an example of the failure of the neo-liberal state to address the "grievances of the masses." Urgent concerns, as in the Report, about "social discontent", "democratic overload", "crisis of democratic governance" and the "need" to address these "genuine grievances" now reveal the fear of the dissident and parliamentary left of an emerging revolutionary armed struggle. It is here apt to recall Frantz Fanon's characterisation of the middle chasses in the struggle against colonialism: that in spite of the anti-colonial rhetoric they want the armed struggle to be stalled at all costs.

The not-so-secret wish that the system, after all, must "succeed" (in say containing "social discontent") blinds sections of the dissident left to the political alternatives that are being constantly generated in an incipient form. That is why its critique of the neo-liberal state seems more like an advance friendly warning to the state - crisis management for the state. With experience from the grassroots, the dissident left moreover knows better: it reveals its deep knowledge of the real interests of the state, the real dangers and would not want the state to float on superficial growth-centric ideas, and bloat on the arrogance and greed of those in power.

As the true voice of the state, the dissident left seems more interested in setting things right for it, so that it does not invite more trouble for itself and hence for democracy. It seems least interested in facilitating the emergence of a force that might restructure the political balance of forces in the country. Thus, when resistances, such as in Nandigram, throw up new forms of democracy and organs of power, outside of the given political system, the dissident left rushes back to revive moribund constitutional provisions of self-government and panchayats for "democratic decision-making," that is "involving communities." Amit Bhaduri (in Development With Dignity: A Case for Full Employment, New Delhi: National Book Trust, 2005), therefore, argues for "decentralisation through panchayats" and "development through participatory democracy" following Constitutional provisions.

Fear of the Fear

So it seems clear that it is precisely the kind of political mobilisation and response feared by the security-centric state, which the socio-economic approach of the dissident left too wants to keep out of the political field: the repressive, security-centric state complemented by the ideological, progressive approach. This state fears the masses, mass resistance and, worse, the masses becoming Maoists and, in its bid to secure itself, it imposes more and more repressive measures, trampling on human rights and so on. This erosion of democratic spaces and rights, the rise of the security-centric state is what the dissident left in turn fears. Alain Badiou ("The Communist Hypothesis,"New Left Review, 49, 2008, p. 30) calls this the "fear of the fear:" the dissident left fearing the undemocratic consequences of the state's repressive response to mass resistance. This "fear of the fear," is, however, "a secondary, derivative emotion whose content is barely detectable." Secondly, "it has no concept of any alliance with the large masses of people".

Fear of the state's response and the inability to join the political response of the masses: this is the dissident left's predicament in India. Let us take the jailbreak by the Maoists in November 2005 in Jehanabad town. The debilitating assault on state power, with townspeople pouring into the jail as prisoners happily roamed around, had one policeman on duty comment that the entire town's population are terrorists. This collapse of state order and increased confidence of the masses, however, only increases the dissident left's fear of the fear: what they see is "people [are] caught between the state and the Naxalites, with the democratic space for other forms of struggle having shrunk dramatically".

Isolated from the large masses of people, the dissident left seeks the "right to dissent" and "democratic spaces" to defend and uphold an empty neutral space. Its critique alternates between uniquely singular expressions of radical dissent to fanciful radical chic flights.

Thus, Roy, once fantastically declared herself "an independent, mobile republic," seceding from the country! To say the least, there is an unmistakeable element of middle-class self-indulgence in making the search for so-called democratic spaces the prime political task, when large masses of the people are mobilised in a collective revolutionary project way beyond these spaces.

9

The Marxist

'MAOISM': AN EXERCISE IN ANARCHISM

In recent times, some areas of West Bengal have witnessed activities of the 'Maoist' group. The group has tried to draw attention to itself through committing several grisly murders and by triggering some explosions. They are engaged in setting up 'bases' in the remote and relatively inaccessible locales of West Bengal that border Bihar-Jharkhand. They seek a foothold in some other districts of the state as well. A section of the corporate media has also been encouraging them, by legitimising the Maoists' killing of CPI (M) leaders and workers in districts like Bankura, Purulia, and Midnapore west.

The CPI (M-L)-People's War and the Maoist Communist Centre, two groups of the Naxalite persuasion, came together on 21 September 2004 to form a new party, the CPI (Maoist). As with the two erstwhile constituents, the Maoists are active in selected areas of Andhra Pradesh, Orissa, Chhattisgarh, Bihar, and Jharkhand. Because of the secretive style of their working, their political outlook and activities are largely unknown to the mass of the people. The name of the CPI (Maoist) has been associated with violent acts and spreading terror. Going by their programme and ideological stand, the party is a violent anarchist outfit. Anarchy can cause harm to the democratic struggle and Left movement. The CPI (M) will counter this party politically and ideologically.

The CPI (M) formed after a long ideological debate in 1964, and a new Party Programme was adopted. Sectarian and ultra-left adventurist trends arose in the ongoing struggle against revisionism and reformism. In those years, the entire country, especially Bengal, saw mass anger against the anti-people policies of the ruling party. In particular, Bengal witnessed a massive wave of mass movements.

Following the establishment of the United Front government in 1967, the land movement, along with the movements of the workers, employees, middle class, students, youth accelerated further. A peasants' movement was organised at Naxalbari based on the land movement and capture of state power through that movement. The CPI (M-L) formed in May 1969. In its attempts at creating 'liberated zones' and transforming the decade of the 1970s into the 'decade of liberation', the CPI (M-L) chose the CPI (M) as its target. The CPI (M) had to wage a tough political-ideological battle while under attack from the ruling Congress and the Naxalites.

The Naxalite movement splintered within the period of five years. The Naxalites split into innumerable small groups. The division and re-division went on for three decades thereafter. In the process of this disintegration, the People's War Group (PWG) was set up in Andhra Pradesh under the tutelage of Kondapally Seetaramaiah. The PWG looked to Naxalite leader Charu Majumdar as the 'pathfinder'. The Kanai Chatterjee-Amulya Sen-Chandrasekhar Das-led anti-Charu Majumdar group established the Maoist Communist Centre (MCC). The newly-formed CPI (Maoist) chooses to salute both Chatterjee and Majumdar as 'great leaders'. Current imperatives have brought them together, but their documents show how from the 1980s until 2000, both the groups were at each other's throats and the battle of attrition saw casualties pile up on both sides.

The draft programme of the CPI (Maoist) denigrates the glorious tradition of the Communist movement in India. In this, they are at one with the *pracharaks* of the RSS. They forget how it was the Communists who first raised the slogan of complete independence in India. The Communist movement had called for the inclusion of the socio-economic content to the call for *swaraj*. The Communists had also been deeply involved in building up a mass base among the people. The Communist movement was severely repressed, and the colonial rulers brought a series of conspiracy cases—Meerut, Kanpur, and Peshawar—against Communists. The Communist Party had also been in the vanguard of building up an anti-imperialist movement in India. The Maoists would have us believe that the 'betrayal' by the communists in British India had prevented a revolution although the 'revolutionary content was present then'. We may only note that the Maoists have declared that they do not form part of the Communist movement in India; this is a bit of unexpected self-revelation that shows them up in proper light.

What is being touted as 'Maoism'?

There is no doubt that Mao Zedong is one of greatest revolutionary leaders of the twentieth century. Under his leadership, the Communist Party of China (CPC) and the mass of the people organised a democratic revolution in that backward country and started the work of socialist construction. New democracy or people's democracy meant a link between the democratic and the socialist revolutions, the basis of which was the leadership of the working class and a worker-peasant unity. In advancing the various stages of the Chinese revolution, Mao had implemented the principles of Marxism-Leninism in the specific conditions prevailing in China. In particular, Mao had explained analytically the dialectical materialism of Marx, helping the CPC to take the correct stand in the different phases of the Chinese revolution. Despite the admitted errors of the Great Leap Forward, Mao had led from the front the task of socialist construction in China.

What is 'Maoism'? It is a totally incorrect concept and reeks of motivation. It is an attempt to separate the theory and implementation of Mao from the classical and developing stream of Marxism-Leninism. The term 'Maoism' is utilised by those who stand opposed to the CPC as well as by the bourgeois 'Marxologists' who use the term 'Stalinism' in an equally jeering fashion.

In the so-called Lin Biao Congress, or the 9th Congress of the CPC (April 1969), a touchstone for the Maoists, it was declared that the CPC believes Marxism-Leninism-Mao Zedong

Thought as the theoretical and directional basis. One should note that even by the adulating Lin, the word used was not 'Maoism' but Mao Zedong Thought. Mao Zedong Thought was defined at the CPC Congress as the theoretical coordination of the reality and practice of the Chinese Revolution with the universal principles of Marxism-Leninism.

The theoretical basis for this is erroneous. Characterising Mao Zedong Thought as the Marxism-Leninism of an era when imperialism has been 'destroyed' and when socialism 'has made worldwide progress', is not an objective evaluation.

It was, among other things, an attempt to impose on the world situation the specific experience of socialist reconstruction in China. In fact, this kind of an attempt ends up negating the most notable features of Mao's own thinking and his mode of functioning. Mao certainly enriched Marxism-Leninism through his thought and practice, but it would not be correct to say that he brought up Marxism-Leninism to a 'completely new stage'. It was under Lin's tenure as General Secretary of the CPC that Mao's theorising was turned into philosophical precepts and adored. Notably though, it was the CPC central committee under Mao which later criticised Lin for his activities.

A wide attack on the precepts of the 9th CPC Congress is found in the address delivered at the 30th anniversary of the formation of the People's Republic of China by CPC vice-president Marshall Jianying.

He said that the CPC and the people of China regarded the application and development of Marxism-Leninism in the Chinese revolution as Mao Zedong Thought. He went on to say that Mao Zedong Thought was not the product of Mao's personal wisdom; it represented the crystallisation of the experience of fifty years of the revolutionary struggle in China; it also represented the crystallisation of the common wisdom of the CPC. He pointed out that during the 'Cultural Revolution, they turned the relationship between the subjective and the objective, between the mind and the matter upside down'. Similarly, 'they passed off idealism and metaphysics as materialism and dialectics, historical idealism as historical materialism, and their utterly ridiculous pseudo-socialism as scientific socialism'.

The sixth plenary session of the eleventh central committee noted that Mao Zedong Thought which came into being through the collective struggle of the Party and the people, was the guiding ideology of the Party; 'Mao Zedong Thought is the integration of the universal principles of Marxism-Leninism with the concrete practice of the Chinese revolution'. The document militates against the attempt to universalise Mao Zedong Thought. The report mentions repeatedly the specificity of the Chinese situation and the Chinese experience.

Maoists, whether in Peru, Nepal, or India, never seem to get over this habit of gathering together sayings of Mao Zedong and treating them as universal principles. They also alienate the people with the slogan 'China's chairman is our chairman'. No Communist Party that recognises the term Mao Zedong Thought, and, like the CPI (M), recognises the need to draw the correct lessons from Mao's historic role, talks about 'Maoism'.

After 31 years of the formation of the MCC, the term 'Maoism' was adopted by the CPI (Maoist) 'amidst great debate and controversy', according to Kisan, a leader of the party (*People's March*, 7 November 2004). He believes Maoism to be the third and higher stage in the qualitative development of Marxism.

Let us now see what Pushpa Kumar Dahal (a k a Prachanda) has to say about 'Maoism' (*On Maoism*). According to him, Mao Zedong 'thought' is confusing: Maoism is 'scientific'. Inter alia, Prachanda talks about such inanities as Mao having identified (presumably as an original contribution) class struggle, struggle for production, and scientific experimentation. According to Prachanda, Mao Zedong brought philosophy out of the reading room of philosophers and spoke of necessity of making it a massive and real power. Is Prachanda not familiar with Marx's eleventh thesis on Feurbach? Does he consider Lenin to be a philosopher confined to reading rooms? Then again, Prachanda accredits Mao Zedong with having uniquely contributed to history through his destruction of Chinese feudalism by giving land to the peasant, and of nationalising foreign and Chinese monopoly financial institutions, and for his control over private capital. Prachanda cites Mao's slogans—'barrel of the rifle is the source of power', 'imperialism is a paper tiger'—plus his concept of the people's war as original contributions to the growth of scientific socialism. These are clearly comments of a person who understands neither the practice nor the breadth of Mao's thinking.

Indeed, the Maoists seem to be obsessed with armed activities that inevitably result in individual terror and annihilation. The slogan of 'people's war' generates a lot of verbosity, but ignores socio-economic analysis and political activities. 'Maoism' has been created to allow the selective use of Mao's sayings on military science and guerrilla warfare out of context and without a logical analytical framework.

A CONFUSED VIEW OF THE WORLD SITUATION

One of the principal issues before a Communist Party is its outlook on the world situation towards formation of its strategy. The Maoists fare extremely poorly in this regard. In the draft document of February 2005, they devote only a few lines in their confused and confusing analysis of the world situation. They denigrate the Soviet Union for its 'deterioration into a capitalist country', and deal with what they call 'proxy war with the USA' in which 'millions lost their lives'.

The CPI (M) has identified throughout the 1960s the 1970s and specifically in at the 14th Party Congress the lacunae in the socialist construction in the erstwhile Soviet Union. The CPI (M), however, does not believe that in the 1960s the Soviet Union had turned into a capitalist country. In its role in the world situation, the Soviet Union stood by the newly independent nations; its nuclear capabilities were used for the cause of peace, not war. It is US imperialism that had carried on 'proxy wars' in the Third World to clamp down its hegemony; the US used the debacle of socialism in the Soviet Union to build a new world order. Do the Maoists seek to shield US imperialism by lambasting the Soviet Union out of context? Interestingly enough, the Maoists do not consider the contra-diction between the forces of socialism and those of imperialism to be a core contradiction. By doing this, the Maoists ignore and deny the transition from capitalism to socialism. They also characterise, out of context, the People's Republic of China as a 'capitalist country after the death of Mao', and turn a blind eye to the process of socialist construction in Vietnam, Cuba, and Democratic Korea.

The puerile nature of the analysis of the world situation in the Maoists' document is glaringly apparent. Kisan writes simplistically that the world situation is replete with revolutionary possibilities in an unprecedented manner, because imperialism is in deep crisis and revolution is the principal trend in the world. Imperialism is always shadowed by crisis, and it is true that anti-imperialist movements have grown around the world. However, to deny the need for conducting anti-imperialist struggles with greater fervour reeks of the anarchism of the 1970s, when the Naxalites used to speak in the same vein as do their Maoist successors today.

Character of the Indian State Incorrectly Posited

The Maoists would characterise the Indian state, which it sees as having gained sham independence in 1947, as semi-colonial and semi-feudal, and controlled by the forces of imperialism. They characterise the big bourgeoisie as 'comprador bureaucratic bourgeoisie' who have an understanding with the big landlord class who dominate the rural areas. According to the Maoists, the Indian revolution can be characterised as 'new democratic revolution' although they also talk of the Indian revolution as 'nationalist revolution'. Their aim is to make India independent, self-reliant, and democratic.

This is confusion of the worst order. The 6th Congress of the Comintern defined comprador bourgeoisie those who subserve imperialism by exporting raw materials and importing finished products from imperialist countries. It is not possible to characterise the Indian big bourgeoisie as comprador as per this definition. The process of capitalist accumulation in India and the foundation of the industrial base of the country are conveniently ignored by the Maoists in their hurry to prove that India continues to be a dependent country.

Mao Zedong himself defined the Chinese comprador bourgeoisie as the class, which directly subserve imperialism and which is nurtured by imperialism. By this definition, the Indian big bourgeoisie cannot be defined as comprador. The CPI (M) believes that the big Indian bourgeoisie goes in for dual relationship of struggle and entente with imperialism as per the dictates of their class interests. The state sector, devoid of socialist content, has nevertheless been a factor in laying the technical-industrial base and helped in lessening dependence on imperialism. Later, especially from the 1980s, the big bourgeoisie took advantage of the commencement of liberalisation and started to eat into the state sector, even in core areas.

It is wrong to claim that the policy of liberalisation was put in place because the Indian big bourgeoisie were comprador. The big bourgeoisie have joined hands with imperialism and international finance capital based on their strength, not weakness. The big bourgeoisie, who lead the Indian ruling classes, form the principal target of the democratic revolution. The Maoists stand that seeks to weaken the position of the big bourgeoisie would *hinder* and not help the struggle against the big bourgeoisie.

The Maoists think that India is yet to gain independence and that we have a semi-colonial state in a neo-colonial set up. They carefully avoid the term 'Indian state' while indulging in their theorising. The CPI (M) does not believe that in practice, as of now, the forces of imperialism control the Indian economy and the administration. While such an attempt may be going on, the Indian big bourgeoisie is far from comprador. If the Maoists are to be believed, however, everyone in India has turned into lackeys of imperialism—the only exception, as ever, are the Maoists themselves!

This is of a piece with the other erroneous understanding—that India is not independent. The forces of imperialism have continued with their efforts to interfere with the policy making of Third World countries. Nevertheless, it would be simplistic and downright incorrect to conclude that the post-Second World War newly independent countries remain devoid of independence. The political indepen-dence in these countries has not been transformed into comprehensive sovereignty of the people because of the domination of the bourgeoisie. However, it would not do to hold the simplistic view that the Third World countries remain devoid of independence. It is a wrong formulation on the part of the Maoists.

'THE CHINESE PATH': AN ARTIFICIAL CONSTRUCT

Ignoring Mao Zedong's postulate that the Chinese Revolution was a combination of the principle of Marxism-Leninism with the evolving reality of China, the Maoists talk of the Indian revolution following the Chinese path. They insist on aping the model followed in pre-Revolution China. The Maoists need to learn not just the history of pre-Revolution China but also the Indian reality. Revolution can hardly be cloned from country to country. Stalin had pointed out how theory becomes useless, devoid of practice. Mao himself called such a deviation 'seeking to catch the sparrow with the eyes closed'. There are differences between the Chinese situation and the Indian reality. Apart from the differences existing in the unfolding of the colonial heritage of the two countries, differences exist in the realm of economy, political structure, and growth. The Maoists, by invoking pre-Revolution China as India's model patently ignore history. The Maoists would do worse than paying heed to the dictum of Mao Zedong during the height of the Sino-Soviet debate in 1960.

Mao had argued, in effect, that the party which was not able to analyse the situation evolving in its own country and would rather emulate experiences of another country without analysis was a hotchpotch of revisionism and sectarianism, and would never be regarded as a party driven by the principles of Marxism-Leninism. The CPI (M) believes that it would not do to mechanically follow the revolutionary experience of other countries without a scientific analysis, something that the Maoists revel in doing. One recalls that during the 1970s, the CPC had criticised the Naxalites for raising the slogan of 'China's Chairman in our Chairman', and thoughtlessly using such terms as 'liberated zones' in the Indian context. The Maoists do not learn from history, even from the party of Mao!

Ignorance about the Element of Class Struggle in the Parliamentary System

Lenin had long ago characterised the parliamentary system as a scene of class struggle. Entangled in the web of what Lenin called 'left-wing communism', the Maoists deny India bourgeois democracy and dub as illusions institutions such as the parliament, assemblies, panchayats, and the entire electoral procedure. Their view is erroneous, lop-sided, and self-contradictory. Marxists know that the character of class domination defines a State and its political character. The CPI (M) has the programmatic understanding that the Indian State represents a class rule of the big bourgeoisie and the big landlords, led by the former who indulge in cooperation with international finance capital. In India, the bourgeois democratic revolution remains unfinished and the task is to establish real democracy. Yet, the fact can never be ignored that the parliamentary system has been a sign of progress for the masses in the sense that it has acted as a weapon for the extension of the democratic rights of the people. The democratic rights won have been the result of ceaseless struggle and do not represent gifts from above. Waves of popular struggles have overcome authorita-rianism of the 1970s, the ousting of democratic governments, the clamping down of internal emergency, and the inroads of communal forces in government.

In countering the false claim of the Maoists that the parliamentary system is a complete illusion, one needs to point out that in a capitalist society, as Lenin had pointed, the parliamentary forum affords the communists opportunities to expose the system of capitalism. In addition, it would be downright foolhardy not to take full advantage of the opportunities afforded by the parliamentary structure and to further the struggle in and out of parliament. Elections are called electoral struggle because in the process, millions of people take part and the opportunity is created to expose the role played by the State, bourgeois politics, and the bourgeois parties. An opportunity is created to pull the people out of the fold of the bourgeois parties. However, as the CPI (M) has maintained consistently, the extra-parliamentary struggle cannot be supplanted by the parliamentary struggle, but has to be supplemented by it. Why do the Maoists think, and on what objective basis, that the masses remain inert witnesses in the arena of parliamentary struggle? Why cannot the Maoists recall Lenin's saying that participation in the bourgeois democratic parliamentary system would go a long way in exposing the system before the masses and convincing them of the necessity for its removal. Will the Maoists learn from history?

Staying Away from the Daily Struggles of the People

Declaring that there remained no alternative before a revolutionary party other than conduct of long-standing and armed people's war towards an armed peasant revolution, the Maoists talk only of guerrilla warfare, liberated zones, headquarters, capturing cities and identify these tasks as the only worthwhile revolutionary tasks. They aim, through performing these tasks, to capture state power.

The Maoists give great attention to military strategy and military tactics. They have, however, no time to spare for the task of enhancing the political consciousness of the people and of uniting them on the questions concerning politics, economy, and society. They ignore the importance of the trade union movement and the role the movement plays in enhancing the class-consciousness of the workers. Would they also turn their faces away from the land movement on the plea that without the completion of the democratic revolution, such movements would not lead to comprehensive land reforms? How then do they propose to make the teeming million of India conscious, *sans* movements that stand opposed to the bourgeois-landlord policies, of the need for fundamental changes? Reliance on the armed might of a minuscule part of the people is Blanquism of the worst kind.

Mao Zedong wrote that the Communists must never be isolated from the majority of the people and must take cognisance of the total situation. The Maoists would fulminate against international finance capital but would not take part in the actual struggle taking place against it across the country, a struggle in which the CPI (M), other Left parties, and the TUs have played a stellar role. The Maoists have stayed away from the struggle—to what purpose? In *People's March*, Kisan has confessed that the Maoists have not been able to build up struggle against the forces of imperialism, neither in the rural areas not in the cities and towns.

The confession reminds us of another confession by Charu Majumdar when he had lamented back in 1972 in a letter written to his wife that the involvement with the policy of annihilation, the anti-imperialist struggle had suffered. Kisan has also regretted the fact that the Maoists could not organise adequate response to the onslaught of the forces of communalism, in the struggle in which the CPI (M) and the Left parties play a commendable role.

Distorted Exposition of Guerrilla Warfare

In the worldview of the Maoists, democratic struggle and mass-political programmes have no place. They believe that the entire struggle of the new democratic revolution would be armed struggle with the guerrilla forces building up red bastions in the villages. They have devoted the bulk of the space in their document on the strategy and tactics of the Indian revolution to such guerrilla actions. It was the subsequently discredited CPC leader, Lin Biao, who had first propounded the theory that the Maoists have embraced. Lin had spoken of encircling the cities (i.e., the developed countries) by the villages (i.e., the developing world). Lin had also spoken of Mao's annihilation theory against the Japanese occupation army to mean that such action was necessary for the armed peasant revolution to succeed in the Third World. The Naxalites had lapped the theory up and were later being cautioned by the CPC about misinterpreting the annihilation theory and taking it out of context (and this was admitted by several Naxalite leaders of the 1970s in a published document). The revolutionary path can never be one of conspiracy minus the objective and subjective conditions; there is no alchemy (as Marx noted in 1850) to bring about revolution. Making conspiracy the chief implement to bring about revolution is a sectarian and self-defeating notion. The Maoists are verily prey to this idea and in an obsessive manner.

It devolves on the Party of the working class to bring within its capabilities the entire range of complexities existing in the country where the revolutionary struggle is to be launched. It must also bring together as many allies as possible. The notions of united front and coalition rise out of this consideration. Lenin points out that there is need for a revolutionary party to bring into the fold mass allies out of the fold of the bourgeoisie even if such allies are politically restless and are unfaithful, and offer only conditional support. To deny this is, according to Lenin, a form of crass failure to grasp the basic principles of scientific socialism. The Maoists are certainly victims to this folly. They are not able to understand the tiniest iota of the revolutionary path.

The Maoists appear obsessed with guerrilla warfare. We point out for their edification the conceptual framework on the same theme by Lenin. Lenin wrote that no party of the proletariat could consider guerrilla warfare the only path to adhere to. The guerrilla warfare must subserve the other modes of struggle and it must be enriched through a drive to advance the Socialist perception and organisation. The point to note is that Lenin had underlined this thesis in the case of every form of struggle, whether through strikes, through parliamentary form, or through newspapers.

Lenin explains that in a departure from the old forms of 'socialism', Marxism recognises the variegated forms of struggle, but the Maoists comprehensively reject this thesis. Their doings have inevitably created alienation from the mass of the people. The own initiative of the masses has suffered. This is the result of not attaching due importance to mass-political initiative.

Lenin is uncompromising in insisting that Marxism demands historical consideration while pondering the form of struggle. Any aberration here, Lenin pointed out, was a deviation from the fundamental principles of Marxism-Leninism. Lenin said that 'to attempt to answer yes or no to the question whether any particular means of struggle should be used, without making a detailed examination of the concrete situation of the given movement at the given stage of its development, means completely to abandon the Marxist position'. This is something the Maoists are squarely guilty of all the way. Marxism does not approve of the 'thesis' that guerrilla warfare is the only viable path during the period of revolution, and that all other paths are unimportant and irrelevant.

Mao had identified the conditions and conditionalities in China for the unleashing of armed peasant revolution and of armed revolutionary zones. These are:

- In capitalist countries, the workers build up their strength through overt and 'legal' struggles while educating themselves; they advance through utilisation of such fora as legal struggles, parliament, and political and economic strike actions. In China, there was no parliament, and no scope for utilising a legal forum.

- The peasant economy of China was 'localised'.
- With a low degree of capitalist development, China did not experience a unified, countrywide capitalist economy.
- Warlords remained isolated and engaged in warfare with other warlords.
- With the imperialist forces slicing up China for control, there was frequent inter-imperialist clashes in China.
- There was lack of central political command in China and thus there was a lack of concomitant control in the administration and the army.

Considering the reality prevailing in India, the attempt to build up 'bases' in remote villages, to set up 'liberated zones', and to encircle cities is pure fantasy. How to deal with the central political authority and the powerful army in the course of striving for a revolutionary social transformation does not concern the maoists. They do not see whether there are any circumstances which are compatible with the concept of armed struggle based on guerrilla warfare. None of the features like the capitalist development in India, the connectivity with the world economy, the experience of parliamentary democracy, socio-economic changes, the social position of the classes, the consciousness and lifestyle of the Indian people, the development of ideological instruments and media—are suited to guerrilla warfare on the basis of liberated zones.

Despite the weaknesses of mass struggles, advances have been registered in the case of both the urban and rural working classes and their organisations. Marxists regard momentum as the life force of matter. Considering the changes wrought in the Indian economy, society, politics, and politics, it would not be difficult to understand that the so-called 'guerrilla tactics' can create not permanent but transient flashes and can end up by harming the potential of greater mobilisation of forces and of greater struggles. In his treatise *On Practice*, Mao Zedong wrote: 'We are opposed to die-hards in the revolutionary ranks whose thinking fails to advance with changing objective circumstances and has manifested itself historically as Right opportunism'. 'Their thinking is divorced from social practice, and they cannot march ahead to guide the chariot of society; they simply train behind, grumbling that it goes too fast and trying to drag it back or turn it in the opposite direction'.

The Maoist documents available with us describe the method of creating 'favourable circumstances'. They rely on the inner contradiction of the imperialist forces impacting the Indian ruling classes, creating political uncertainty and weakening administration. This will, according to the Maoists, lead to mass uprisings against the 'comprador ruling classes' and the police and the army will be affected. This, in turn, would lead to world war! If this is not day dreaming, what is?

CPI (M), in its Programme, has said: The struggle to realise the aims of the people's democratic revolution through the revolutionary unity of all patriotic and democratic forces with the workers-peasants alliance at its core, is a complicated and a protracted one. It is to be waged in varying conditions in varying phases. Different classes, different strata within the same class, are bound to take different positions in these distinct phases of the development of the revolutionary movement. Only a strong Communist Party, which develops the mass movements and utilises appropriate united front tactics to achieve the strategic objective, can make use of these shifts and draw into its ranks these sections. Only such a party bringing within its fold the most sincere and sacrificing revolutionaries would be able to lead the mass of the people through the various twists and turns that are bound to take place in the course of the revolutionary movement.

The CPI (M) believes that the flourishing and development of mass-revolutionary struggle is the primary task at this stage. To a true Marxist, simply making loud proclamations of armed struggle can never become a pre-condition for establishing one's revolutionary credentials. Since neither the working class nor the working masses would go in for violence on their own, what should be the stand of the Party of the working class? The CPI (M) Programme notes: The Communist Party of India (Marxist) strives to achieve the establishment of people's democracy and socialist transformation through peaceful means. By developing a powerful mass revolutionary movement, by combining parliamentary and extra-parliamentary struggle, the working class and its allies will try their utmost to overcome the resistance of the forces of reaction and to bring about these transformations through peaceful means. However, it needs always to be borne in mind that the ruling classes never relinquish their power voluntarily. They seek to defy the will of the people and seek to reverse it by lawlessness and violence. It is, therefore, necessary for the revolutionary forces to be vigilant and so orient their work that they can face up to all contingencies, to any twist and turn in the political life of the country.

The Reality

The Maoists guerrillas have stated that their task comprises providing encouragement to the masses for taking part in 'political and military programmes, including sabotage and annihilation of enemies'. The results are there for everybody to see.

Right from the earliest days of the Naxalite movement, the line of individual assassination has been adopted as a policy by the left sectarians. One has to pause and recall that on the eve of the arrest of Charu Majumdar, six Naxalite leaders, including Kanu Sanyal, Sourin Bose, C. Tejeswar Rao, and D. Nagabhusan Pattanayak, confessed that the CPC took great exception to the line of annihilation of the Naxalites. (This confession was later published in November 1972.) The CPC accused the Naxalites of mechanically following the people's war theory of Lin Biao, and pointed out that dipping the hand in the blood of a class enemy did not make a revolutionary Communist; on the other hand, it will ensure that the Party was no longer a Communist Party. The left sectarians, including the PWG, the MCC and the CPI (Maoist), have indulged in mayhem over the years. Between 1991 and 2001, 2,077 people, mostly ordinary citizens, were killed in Naxalite-related violence. The method of killing is gruesome with people being burnt alive or smashed into smithereens by exploding crude or sophisticated devices. In 2002, the Maoists killed 90 people, in 2003 the figure reads 136, in 2004 it was 70, and in 2005,

122. Despite the Maoists' penchant for identifying persons as 'police informers' before killing them, 80 per cent of those killed by them represented ordinary people who are not class enemies, even by Maoists criteria. Some of those killed were in fact members or supporters of rival Naxalite groups; this was internecine struggle, pure and simple. In Bengal, the Maoists' forays include killing 12 CPI (M) workers and 17 police personnel. They have also exploded landmines, destroyed isolated buildings in remote areas, and have tried to spread terror among the village folk. Spreading thinly across the borders of Orissa, Chhattisgarh, Madhya Pradesh, Karnataka, and Maharashtra, the Maoists have concentrated chiefly if not solely on spreading terror and causing mayhem in the name of 'revolutionary ways'. They prefer if they can to build up contiguous areas as 'zones' in the areas where they operate.

Lately the rate of attrition among the left sectarian elements has been notable. In Andhra Pradesh, the rate of surrender by the PWG averaged over 550 per year. The decimation was also evident in Bihar and Jharkhand. The Maoists utilise the increase of Maoist activities in neigh-bouring Nepal and the formation of a coordination committee of the South Asian Maoists to strengthen their terror tactics. They use the long and unguarded border between Bihar and Nepal to bring in illegal arms and to run training camps on both sides of the border. They keep in close touch with extremist outfits of Kashmir, the northeast India, and the LTTE from whom they get help with arms training. They may even have, as per reports published in the media in November 2004, links with the ISI of Pakistan.

However, the net political impact of the Maoists activities is very marginal and transient. For example, in Bihar and Jharkhand, ceiling surplus was neither taken away from the landlords nor redistributed among the landless and the rural poor. The chief source of income of the Maoists in the rural stretches is extracting levy from the landlords and the nouveux rich of the villages. They appear far from interested in protecting the interests of the rural poor or in preserving natural resources.

On the other hand, the Maoists are linked to a large and widening network of dishonest traders and businessmen. In Chhattisgarh and in Orissa, the villagers have clashed repeatedly with the Maoists who are involved in racketeering of forest resources including *tendu* leaves and *babui* fibres. Using the power of the gun to establish sway over villages and villagers, the Maoists has effectively become a source not of inspiration but of fear for the rural people. The shotgun justice of the Maoists' mass courts is well documented. The Maoists have also increasingly become the handmaiden of the bourgeois political parties. The Naxalite poet Varavara Rao has confessed before the advocates' committee about the links that the Maoists have with the Telugu Desam Party at the local level in particular. He has also said that both the Telugu Desam and the Congress have utilised the 'services' of the Maoists in exchange for lucre.

It was recently disclosed that a minister in the BJP-run Munda government in Jharkhand put to use the Maoists to win elections in exchange for a considerable sum of money. In Bihar, the adage goes that those who represent bourgeois parties during the daylight are Maoists by the night. The confession of a former state secretary of the PWG about the outfit being in hand-in-glove with the Trinamul Congress is another case in point in this regard.

DEVELOPMENTAL PERSPECTIVE

A running theme of the corporate media is that the Maoists could gain ground in Bengal because of lack of development. Each dastardly murder committed by the Maoists is being justified on the basis of 'lack of development'. A look at the Maoist documents will make it amply clear that they remain in the villages not because they are determined to work for the interests of the tribal people and the rural masses. They have chosen the areas precisely because it suits their 'terrain theory' of guerrilla warfare. The calculation is to utilise the isolated nature of the terrain to carry out terroristic acts.

The Maoist documents spell out how they do not believe in development within the existing framework and they are also firm in their conviction that any slogan of 'partial development' for the poorer section of the rural masses is revisionist and a betrayal of the revolution. They also claim that to raise the slogan of development without armed might is to placate the ruling classes as their lackeys. The principal aim of the corporate media in focussing attention on growth is to deny the rural growth and expansion under the Left Front government. To the bourgeois media, development means the widening of the scope for a luxurious lifestyle for the thin layer of the rich and the super rich. To the corporate media, then, the rise in the purchasing power of the capitalist, the top layer of the middles class, and the nouveux rich of the rural belts represent development. The CPI (M) has a class outlook on development in the evolving socio-economic reality.

The struggle for development to us denotes the struggle waged by the mass of the people of the country for improvement in their standard of living. The question of development loses significance devoid of issues related to land reforms, redistribution of rural resources, wage, employment, education, and health. The CPI (M) has been carrying forward the struggle for development within the restrictions imposed by the bourgeois-landlord framework. Another countervailing factor has been the present stage of globalisation. Yet it is important to struggle for development because it is the Communist Party that can be the real ally of the masses in the struggle for a better life, and to increase the window of minimum opportunity. The programme of the CPI (M) has made it clear that the 'Party will utilise the opportunities that present themselves of bringing into existence governments pledged to carry out a programme of providing relief to the people and strive to project and implement alternative policies within the existing limitations'.

The developmental perspective of the Left Front government has resulted in 15 lakh rural landless getting land. Five lakh families who have received land and patta documents belong to the scheduled tribes. The right of the sharecropper is well established here. The role of the panchayats has seen the correlation of forces in the rural belts change. In the urban areas, the right of the workers, the bustee dwellers, and the employees-middle class has been extended to the extent it is possible to do so. The Left Front government has progressed while establishing the difference it has in the policy outlook vis-à-vis other state governments. However, no one should labour under the illusion that in circumstances nationwide where the evil effects of the capitalist economic system and of liberalisation mount every day, this state will remain free of the adversities just because there is a Left Front government in office. The document entitled 'Left Front Government and Our Tasks' adopted at the 21st State Conference of the CPI (M) states that in the backdrop of the national scenario, the generation of income in the districts has fallen behind that of Kolkata and its neighbourhood. 4,612 villages have been identified as very backward. 46 lakh people live in great poverty.

The document also notes how unemployment has become a serious and worrying issue. In the rural areas, thus, the number of the landless goes on increasing. The agricultural production has gone down compared to the 1980s and the 1990s. The scheduled tribes and scheduled castes belong to the poorest sections of the people in the rural areas. Malnutrition in the rural areas is a worry. In 18 per cent of the villages, supply of potable water could not be arranged. To tackle the situation, the Left Front government has brought about changes in the priority of policy and implementation. The work of developing the backward areas is being given additional stress. The development of education, health, and self-reliance has been given the shape and character of mass drives. Industrialisation is viewed in the perspective of employment-generation. The CPI (M) never loses the perspective that development is an integral part of class struggle, and that it plays an active role in changing the correlation of class forces.

Involved in day-to-day activities of a developmental nature, the CPI (M) never shies away from identifying its points of weaknesses in order to enhance its class-conscious initiative. The Maoists are never willing to do this because of the nature of politics they cling fatuously to. They stand against developmental work, especially in the backward areas. They militate against the setting up of roads, water supply, health centres, and child education centres. They use explosives and guns to prevent development from happening. They swim against the tide, isolated and alienated from the masses. They want to encroach on forest resources from a purely commercially exploitative point of view. They fear that development will sweep away their pockets of isolated 'terrain'. The difference between the CPI (M) and the CPI (Maoist) is one of politics, and the question of development is a part of it.

The Maoists are a part of the social unrest generated by contemporary capitalism. The unrest is ideologically in favour of the status quo although in its outer exposition, it spreads anti-status quo thoughts and concepts. In these times, adventurism, extreme right reaction based on nationality and religion groups, terrorist activities, and anarchism can appear in various forms. Dialectically, and ideologically, all this emanates from contemporary capitalism. Each of these phenomena shares the same class basis. Rather than from the class-conscious struggles of working class, they emerge out of the petty bourgeois class compulsions. Thus Lenin:

A petty bourgeois driven to frenzy by the horrors of capitalism is a social phenomenon which, like anarchism, is characteristic of all capitalist countries. The instability of such revolutionism, its barrenness, and its tendency to turn rapidly into submission, apathy, phantasms, and even a frenzied infatuation with one bourgeois fad or another—all this is common knowledge. However, a theoretical or abstract recognition of these truths does not at all rid revolutionary parties of old errors, which always crop up at unexpected occasions, in somewhat new forms, in a hitherto unfamiliar garb or surroundings, in an unusual—a more or less unusual—situation.

There is no mistake in identifying the Maoist as an anarchist force.

UNDERSTANDING MAOISM IN INDIA

Origin of Maoism

The term Maoism comes from Mao Zedong of China who formulated a variant of the Marxist-Leninist communism in China. The main principle of Maoism is the armed revolt of the farmers against the ruling class. It is also known as the People's War wherein masses of the lower classes resort to guerilla warfare against the ruling parties and the government.

MAOISM IN INDIA

In post independent India, the government brought thousands of acres of land under development. This acquisition of land left thousands of tribal communities homeless. According to Dr. Walter Fernandez an estimated 60 million people were displaced between 1947 and 2004. These tribal people did not get adequate compensation and were deprived of their livelihood since they depended on the forests for sustenance. In 1967 in the Naxalbari village in West Bengal, tribals and peasants organized the first armed struggle against the government. Led by Charu Majumdar who was influenced by Maoist thought, the movement became known as the Naxalite movement. Today, the Communist Party of India (Maoist) is the political party representing the principles of Maoism. Its aim is to overthrow the government of India. The Maoist movement has infested almost the whole country in the past 40 years. It is now present in 23 of the 28 states. Every year, the Maoists are killing more people in order to fulfill their aims.

GOVERNMENT OF INDIA'S RESPONSE TO MAOISM

The government of India has banned the CPI (Maoist) party by labeling it as a terrorist organization and is constantly exploring military options to put an end to Maoism. This is because the Maoist organization is being funded chiefly through extortion, looting, abductions and poppy cultivation.

Solution to Maoism

According to the Peoples Union for Democratic Rights, the killing of the 76 men in Dantewada is an unfortunate fallout of the government's policy of military attack on the Maoists. Labeling the CPI (Maoist) as a terrorist organization based on its way of working masks the underlying issue of the tribal community which is an integral part of India. Unless both sides are willing to look in to the matter of land allocation, development and livelihood of the tribals, there cannot be a peaceful solution to Maoism in India.

10

Indian Maoists: Impact of Global Economic Crisis

PRESENT FINANCIAL CRISIS & THE IMPENDING GREAT DEPRESSION

India is one of the four exemplary emerging markets that were cited by neo-liberal imperialism as proof that global capitalism was the road to eventual prosperity. The reality is that India is one of the major centres for 'out-sourced' and 'off shore' super-exploitation, and hardly immune from the dysfunction of the big imperial centres. Last week, for example, came the revelation that one of the largest IT outsourcing firms, Satyam, had been methodically over-stating its annual profits (just like so many big US firms), leaving investors holding worthless stock shares and the company chairman under arrest for fraud.

Meanwhile, for the vast majority of the 1.1 billion people in India, life is characterized by brutal poverty. As one recent Reuters news item admitted "for all of India's optimism, it was a reminder that the country of sprouting shopping malls still must deal with the more than two-thirds of Indians who live on less than a dollar a day.

Impact on India

Take India (for more details see the following article), for all the exaggerated claims of the PM and FM the economy is already badly hit. Till end October the BSE share index has fallen 60% since its all time high of 21,207 in Jan 2008 as the

FIIs have pulled out a massive $ 12 billion. On November 21st it reached a 38-month low of 8,451. Real estate stocks have dropped by 90% and Mutual Funds (where much of middle-class savings are put) by 80%. Today, of the 2,699 quoted companies half are below the book value. Due to the big pull out of foreign funds not only has the stock market crashed the rupee declined by as much as 15% in the few weeks ending October 2008 to fall below the 50 mark. Exports have already been badly hit given that foreign trade and service comprises 40% of our GDP. So, for example, there has been a 50% drop in iron ore exports since August leading to a pile up of 4 million tones at the ports. Prices have crashed from $ 140 a tone three months back to $ 85 per tone. Tata Steel has been regularly closing its plant in Tatanagar since the last two months. Drop in cement orders has led to ACC laying off 25% of it staff. Small textile firms are collapsing and over 4 lakh garment workers are likely to be thrown out in the next few months due to cancellation of export orders. It has already suffered losses of Rs.400 crores since January due to a massive hike in prices of cotton yarn and other inputs. The Tirupur textile hub alone will loose 50,000 jobs in the next six months as 25% of its units will shut down. Ludhiana's hosiery manufacturers and exporters have already lost 30% of their business due to the meltdown seriously affecting the 35 lakh workers (15 lakh migrant) involved in the industry. In Meerut over 20% of the 30,000 gold artisans (mostly Bengalis) have gone home. In Surat 20% of the diamond units have closed down and those that remain have less work. They have been affected by the drop in exports and rise in costs of rough diamonds with the rupee falling against the dollar. In Mumbai's sprawling slum, Dharavi, export of leather belts have dropped from 70,000 per month to 3,000 per month.

Besides this, badly hit will be all the BPOs(1), IT enabled services and those dependent on foreign orders for their survival. Already many are facing closure and those that survive are cutting jobs, salaries and perks at a fast rate. Indian airlines industry like Jet Airways first retrenched on a big scale and later took back the staff with salaries cut to a faction of what they earlier got. ASSOCHAM, a top association of the business houses, has said in a report dated Oct.31 08 that Indian companies will slash 25% of its workforce "to sustain operations". It said that layoffs, to begin with, will be in the seven key industrial segments — steel, cement, IT-enabled services/BPOs, financial & brokerage services, construction, real estate and aviation.

And this is just the beginning. So far savings have not been hit particularly except in Mutual Funds as nationalized banks have not had significant exposure abroad. But ICICI Bank has been badly hit and there is strong possibility of bank and insurance failures, particularly in the private sector with those tied up with TNCs.. The ravages of the worldwide depression will hit countries like India badly as the imperialists will seek to push the burden of that crisis on the backward countries. Already the dalal Finance Minister has announced a slew of measures that increases enormously the concessions given to foreign capital. As we go to the press he announces that drastic changes are to be made in this sphere. This will only aggravate the situation further, though it may help the big industrialists and financiers — both Indian and foreign.

CRISIS OF NEO-LIBERALISM; KEYNESIANISM NO ANSWER

The Great Depression of the 1930s was finally pulled out of its crisis after World War II through Keynesian formulas of state intervention (nationalization) and the welfare state. In those days it also had to contend with a powerful socialist camp. But with the temporary collapse of socialism worldwide and the retreat of national liberation movements and a persisting economic crisis since the mid-1970s, the neo-liberal formulas were pushed to the fore. Reaganism, Thatcherism, et al became the fashion and Keynesianism, nationalization were much ridiculed, not to mention the socialist alternative. The 1990s saw neo-liberal economic polices peak where the market was the new god that determines everything. Fortunes were made on a scale never seen in the history of capitalism; of course, in the wake of immense impoverisation, with the rich-poor gap also becoming the widest ever. It was even portrayed as "the end of history", as though the 'golden' capitalist era is here for ever and socialism relegated only to history text books. Even welfare was now privatized with a massive mushrooming of NGOs funded by the moneybags and the state. Growth rates grew compared to the era of the 1970s and that became the irreversible alibi for the neo-liberal theoreticians. And with it was accompanied the gigantic leaps in communication technology in the form of the computer, internet, cell phone, TV, etc that gave it the glamour of a scientific inevitability. The high profile media portrayed none of the misery below the surface and only promoted the world of wealth and glamour. The middle class was brainwashed with this continuous bombardment, and a section even got an opportunity to eat off some crumbs from the imperialist/comprador table. The smallest dissidence was labeled 'terrorist' and callously dispensed with. Once so branded, one ceased to be human, it was as though a dangerous insect had been crushed. The poverty stricken masses too were a non-entity in this make-believe world.

But now the fantasy world of the neo-liberal bubble has burst; and burst in a way that it is unlikely to re-gain for long. Meanwhile it will pull down with it millions more into the mire and suck away lives in lakhs. With one financial bubble after the other bursting the theoreticians of neo-liberalism have no answers and seem totally helpless in the face of the continuing collapse of pillar after pillar of the financial establishment. The gods of power and wealth are tumbling down.

They have just their standard fiscal answers — reduction of interest rates is their main tool: to increase liquidity (i.e. money for capitalists) and make available easy credit for the masses to spend and revive the slumping market. But it is not working. On Oct 9th, for the first time ever several Central Banks acted in concert to stem the market panic. The US Fed cut interest rates by 50 basic points to 1.5%; while the European Central Bank cut interest rates from 4.25% to 3.75%. The Bank of England and the Central banks of Canada, Sweden, Switzerland and China also cut interest rates within seconds of each other.

But this was not able to stem the rot. The collapse of the banks, financial institutions and now even the industrial giants continue. Interest rates were reduced further and now in the US the rate stands at 1% and in Japan at 0.2%. On Nov 6th England once again slashed interest rates, this time by as much as 1.5% to bring it to 3% — a 53-year low. In desperation they have thrown all their neo-liberal theories to the winds and governments have intervened with gigantic bail-our packages to rescue the banks, investment institutions and even companies. This is defacto resorting to the much abused 'nationalization'. As long as they were making huge profits, privatization was the mantra; now when they are making losses and are in fact collapsing it is back to nationalization. But this Keynesian alternative is no real solution; it is a mere palliative to give immediate relief. The social democrats and the CPI/CPM type socialists may harp on these alternatives but they will have to explain the earlier failures of the Keynesian model of the 1960s resulting in the crisis which began in the 1970s, and still continues. Also they will have to explain the collapse of the Soviet Union (after capitalist restoration) and those of the then East European countries — all of which were built on a powerful state sector. The present crisis which is reminiscent of the Great depression is a systemic problem of the capitalist mode of production itself. The roots of the crisis lie in the capitalist system itself for which there is no solution within it. The only real solution to revive the economy is through the very overthrow of the system and its replacement with the socialist alternative

Why? To answer this let us go into the history and dynamics of the present crisis and see if there is any answer within the system.

Crisis of Over-production Endemic to Capitalism/ Imperialism

The Great depression of the 1930s was followed by the world war. The post-war years saw a relative boom in the worldwide economy with the US at the centre. But in the 1970s the world economy once again slipped into crisis, marked by the oil shock, removal of the gold standard (against the dollar), perennially slow (or even negative) growth rates, etc.

This crisis that began in the 1970s has continued with intermittent brief recoveries, right up to today. The crisis of over-production which is endemic to the capitalist system results from the intrinsic contradiction of the capitalist seeking to maximize profits (and capital accumulation) through depressing wages to the maximum possible. Continuous capital accumulation demands continuous growth of the market as the capital has to be invested somewhere (otherwise it is not capital, but mere money); but markets are always restricted due to the depression of the wages and low purchasing power of the masses. It is this contradiction that leads to regular cries of over-production. The capitalists can only operate within this limited framework, but are unable to resolve this contradiction. This results in regular crises and in the era of imperialism the Great Depressions.

So with the crisis setting in the 1970s there was a drop in the purchasing power of the people as all crises are accompanied by rising unemployment, wage freeze, etc. So the capital being accumulated has no outlet in the manufacturing sector for re-investment. So it sought other paths in the sphere of pure finance. In the 1980s the high levels of capital accumulation, specifically thrown up by the petrodollars, found a new outlet in lending to the third world. Through the 1980s this went on, on a huge scale helped along by the IMF and World Bank, giving gigantic returns to the investors and pushing these countries into deeper and deeper debt. Enormous profits were not only made through charging interest, but devaluation of the currencies and making the loans conditional to extract maximum tribute from the prey. Within a decade the loot was so acute that most of these countries were pushed to bankruptcy and, in fact, many of the loans had to be rescheduled. This period, though it had minor recoveries, witnessed regular economic crises as in 1973, 1979, 1985, 1987, and 1992. It also witnessed the bubble like growth of the Japanese economy (which briefly began to be a challenge to the US), and then its bust in 1989, from which it is yet to recover.

The 1990s and the present centaury witnessed what came to be called globalization as the solution for their endemic crisis since the 1970s. Now the surplus generated through capital accumulation, unable to find a growing market (except for the opening up of China) resorted to two means: massive Mergers & Acquisitions, on a scale never seen before creating giant conglomerates; second, resorting to high levels of speculation and finacialisation of the surplus being generated through the real economy. This was facilitated by the technology boom in computers, internet, etc.

As Raymond Lotta said in an article on the net: When we speak of capitalist accumulation, we are referring to the competitive production of surplus value (the source of profit) based on the exploitation of wage labor; and the investment and reinvestment of profit on an expanding, cost-cheapening, and technologically more productive basis.

When we speak of "financialization," we are referring to three particular features of the larger structure of capitalist accumulation in this period of imperialist globalization: a) the growing political and economic power of the financial layers of the capitalist class; b) the vast expansion of financial activities and of financial services, like organizing and financing corporate takeovers, insuring investments against risk, creating new financial instruments, etc.—activities in which profit-making involves the siphoning, centralization, and reinvestment of surplus value through financial channels; and c) the increasing separation of finance from production.

This process of financialization has gone the furthest in the United States, and it is a major factor in U.S. imperialism's ability to preserve and extend its dominance in international financial markets. Financialization is also a means through which wealth, and effective control over productive forces is centralized by the imperialist countries—even as production has grown more geographically dispersed and increasingly carried out within sub contractual networks in the Third World.

Financialization involves efforts to squeeze out more "value" from already created value. One measure of this is that in 2006, the daily volume of trading in foreign exchange markets and in derivatives (financial instruments) added up to $11.4 trillion—which almost equals the annual value of global merchandise exports that year. In terms of the shifts in the structure of the U.S. economy, the financial sector's share of total corporate profits has risen from 8 percent in 1950 to 31 percent last year.

So here the surplus value generated from the real economy was circulated again and again around the globe in the sphere of speculation, giving astronomical profits to the owners of the capital. But it was a bubble and had inevitably to burst as it had no solid base to it. Market expansion in the US was sought not by hiking wages but by pushing the entire populace into debt through excessive credit — housing mortgages, credit cards, etc. The US also became the most indebted country (in Oct. 2008 the external debt reached the gigantic figure of $ 10 trillion) with the largest trade deficit. This fragile situation was sustainable as long as the dollar maintained its supremacy resulting in large inflows form other countries (with most govts. holding their reserves in dollars — the largest today is that of China). If the collapse of the US financial institutions is accompanied by the fall of the supremacy of the dollar (which is rivaled by the euro) and shifting of reserves to another country the fragility of the US economy will result in total collapse. But with it, it will pull down other economies of the world, so that is why, as yet, no one wants to disturb the existing equilibrium by transferring their dollar reserves.

The crisis today is so deep that it is being compared to the Great Depression of the 1930s. But even in the boom years of the 1990s there was the crisis of 1997 (S.E. Asia and Russia as centre), the bursting of the internet bubble of 1999, and the recession of 2001. So, since the 1970s the crises continued with brief periods of recovery, in many cases artificially created through fiscal manipulations and creation of bubbles. This has now imploded on their face in a crisis, the magnitude of which is incomparable to the other downturns since the 1970s. It is in essence the crisis of over-production, and all fiscal stimulation is proving ineffective. There is no solution within the framework, but to survive the impending chaos the imperialists and their agents throughout the world will resort to horrors of unbelievable proportions, including wars, fascist massacres to quell the inevitable revolts, levels of exploitation not recently seen, etc. Such are the dismal days ahead, not to mention the massive distress created through the collapse of people's savings, earning capacity and purchasing power.

The Only Alternative

There are reports that in Europe Marx's writings have come onto the best-seller list. Even rulers are referring to Marx to understand the causes for the crisis. This is quite natural as it was only Marx that gave a scientific understanding of the capitalist system, building on the initial understanding put forth by people like Adam Smith and Ricardo. No doubt capitalism has changed its form in this era of imperialism (scientifically explained by Lenin) but the laws of its functioning remain in tact. The understanding of these laws will not only give an understanding to the present crisis (with all its new manifestations of financialisation, etc) but also the limitations to the solution within the existing system.

But Marx not only gave a scientific understanding of capitalism but also put it in historical perspective. Through a scientific understanding of history he traced its evolution from feudalism and its inevitable transition to socialism. Through his understanding of history from earliest times to now he showed that with capitalism it is far from "the end of history" but history will traverse through to finally reach socialism and communism. In addition he showed that history has shown no society transformed from one to the next peacefully, it always came through bloody battles as the rulers of the old do not voluntarily give up their benefits without a bitter struggle. They did not wage world wars for nothing. They resorted even to genocide when their interests were threatened. Numerous examples are there in history and contemporary Iraq is yet another example.

So amidst this chaos sanity and peace can only be brought by overthrowing the existing system and replacing with something that is more humane and rational — socialism. In backward countries like India it will have to pass through two phases but the direction is the same in all countries of the world. Communism has been much vulgarized by the revisionists of the CPI/CPM variety and much reviled due to the reversals of socialist systems the world over. In this 21st century communism must learn from the negative experiences of the past and incorporate all that is positive with a new creativity to catapult society into a real paradise that we all seek. For the present there is utmost necessity to fight the big back the big attacks being launched on the people's living standards by the capitalists/imperialists worldwide. There is also a dire need to organize powerful communist (Maoist, not revisionist) parties, for it is only they that can withstand the impending fascist attacks and show the light to a beautiful new future. Marxism is once again getting a new life, let us spread its scientific and revolutionary teachings widely so that the masses can get to the truth and understand the ongoing turmoil.

THE BLOODY NETWORK OF INDIAN MAOISTS

Continuous attacks by the Nassaliti rebels in the Indian states of so-called "red corridor". The exploitation of the claims of tribals and peasants, confrontation with the Marxist Communist Party that governs West Bengal, links with the rebels in Nepal. Indian Maoists continue their standoff with New Delhi and will not let go of 13 of the 28 states where they are present.

Mumbai (AsiaNews) - On the night of November 24th a group of 55 Maoist rebels have blew up a government office in Kharakpur in Munger district of Bihar state. It was the latest in a series of attacks by insurgents along the so-called "red corridor" that runs through the states of Maharashtra, Andhra Pradesh, Chhattisgarh, Orissa, Jharkhand, Bihar and West Bengal.

The Maoists have spread to 13 of the 28 Indian states and are considered the most serious threat to the country's internal security. The historic and strategic epicentre of the red revolt that has been sending shock waves through India for decades is West Bengal. For 32 years the *Communist Party Marxist* (CPM) has been in government in the state bordering Bangladesh, and has become a symbol of power. The opposition has been monopolized by the Maoists who are deeply rooted in tribal villages and forests.

The legal opposition, of course, is in the hand of the National Congress of Sonia Gandhi and the Trinamul Congress of Mamata Benerjee, but the defense of the most poor and needy tribals had been hijacked by the Maoists and many times in a violent way. Since November 2007, 69 CPM workers and 10 villagers had been killed in West Midnapore district alone. In June this year the Maoist raided the police station and kept under control the town of Lalgarh. Eleven companies of Central Reserve Police Force (CRPF) had been deployed against state government's demand of 50. There is no week without news of some ambush by the Maoists. On November 20 the Maoists threaten to kill Bihar ministers' kin since the Bihar police machinery are letting loose a reign of repression against the families of the top Maoist leader Arvind Kumar. On the same day the Tata-Bilaspur passenger train was derailed after the Maoist blew up rail tracks near Goelkera railway station. The Naxalite movement started in the sixties when Majumdar and Kanu Sanyal of the CPI (Marxist) inspired by Mao Zedong lead a violent Santhal uprising in West Bengal Naxalbari village. In 1969 the Communist Party of India (Marxist- Leninist) was born. The history of the communist movement in India went through a fragmentation that produced three communist parties.

In 1977, when the Congress Party lost control of the central government in New Delhi the Communist Party went to power in Calcutta (West Bengal) and is still in power now. For 25 years the mythical figure of Jyoti Basu held the reins of power, but his style of governance kept changing. When Deng Xiaoping in China embraced successfully the capitalist mode of development, the communist government of West Bengal follow suit, but the most poor of the poor felt betrayed and reorganized themselves in the jungle. After Jyoti Basu, came Buddhadeb Bhattacharjee who open up to many industrial houses and started expropriating agricultural land to build industrial estates alienating the farmers. "Calcutta runs after Shanghai" writes Federico Rampini. That was the occasion when the Maoists jumped in to the fray, organized the farmers and resisted the take-over. That is what happened in Singur and Nandigram. The Tatas had to shift their Nano plant to Gujarat. This success emboldened the Maoists who multiplied their attacks.

But the presence of Maoists is not confined only to the state of West Bengal. The red belt cuts across India, starting from Nepal in the North, through West Bengal, Bihar, Jharkhand, Chhattisgarh, Orissa, west Maharashtra and Andhra Pradesh in the South. They put their training camps on the border regions so that they can easily escape from the police of one state crossing over the border. Recent reports in the press give the origin of the supply of their arms from Nepal, Bangladesh and China. At least 30 different groups are active across the country with a combined membership of around 50.000 activists. But their differences over their perceived revolutionary roles often result in bloody battles. Many groups are accused of land grabbing and extortion. In 2004 the Maoist Communist Centre and People's War join hands to form the Communist Party of India (Maoist), which is now the biggest armed group ever to challenge the very existence of the Indian state. An estimated 20.000 are bearing arms, one fifth of India's forest is under their control. And they are active in 165 districts of the 604. Now the central government is in a fix. The state governments ask assistance from the centre and request also the help of the army particularly for military aerial survey. The helicopters are vulnerable also to small arms, but the central government does not allow to return fire.

The centre has extended its full support to the Left Front government in Bengal to combat Maoist terror in the state. The move could spark fresh tension between the Congress and UPA ally Trinamul Congress whose leader, Mamata Banerjee is keen on a dialogue between the state and the Maoist Red brigade. But the Interior Minister, Chidambaram and the Bengal Chief Minister Bhattacharjee agreed that there should be "no talks with the Maoists, unless they agree to completely surrender their arms and come for a dialogue under the constitutional framework". Bhattacharjee requested the Centre to start operations in the neighbouring Jharkhand as well, where the Naxals, on rum from Bengal, are taking shelter only to return later. But the Centre can not intervene unless it is called by the State.

But a day after Chidambaram's tough talk Maoists kill 17 cops in Gadchiroli district, at Laheri, in the neighbouring state of Maharashtra, 18 km from the border, on 8 October. Early this year, Maharashtra state cops lost 15 men in Maekegaon and 16, including 5 women, at Hattigota, both in Gadchiroli district. According to sources, the Maoist numbered more than 300 and comprised mobile military dalams that have recently moved from Chattisgarh. Police said there were many from Nepal among attackers who were equipped with sophisticated weapons and ammunition. In two days the Maoists struck three attacks, beside Laheri, they set on fire a gram panchayat building in Irupdhori village, and killed a farmer, Suresh Halami suspected to be a police informer. These three attacks have shattered the morale of the district police.

The Maoists are very vindictive with police informers. On the 5 October, in Taliban-style execution, they beheaded a special branch inspector, Francis Indwar, and threw his body on a branch road leading to National Highway 33 that connect Patna to Jamshedpur, 20 km from Ranchi.. The officer was abducted few days before and held hostage demanding a swap for arrested Maoist ideologues Kobad Ghandy in New Delhi and Chhatradhar Mahato in Kolkata and another captured leader Chandrabhusan Yadav.

On 21 Settember, Maoists launched a massive attack on CPM party office at Enayetpur, 15 km from Midnapore, triggering a gunfight that left at least 15 people dead. Witness say that at least 10.000 tribals took part in the assault. Going back in time the list of attacks is very long:-on July 12, twenty-three cops, including a DSP, were killed in ambush in Rajnandgaon in the state of Chhattisgarh;- on May 22, sixteen cops killed in Gadchiroli; on Feb 1, a party of policeman walk into trap laid in Dhanora, Gadchiroli district, to probe arson and 15 were killed; June 29 2008, 38 specially trained Greyhounds were killed in Malkhangiri in the state of Orissa.

There are, of course, successful police operations against the Maoists. On 16 September 8 Maoists had been gun down and a gun factory destroyed in Chinta Gufa of Dantewada district in Chhattisgarh state. But a real undeclared war is going on with success and defeat on both sides.

Also on the political scene accusations and contra-accusations are hurled at each other. The Trinamul Congress chief, Mamata Banerjee accused of being sympathetic with the Maoists returned the fire suggesting that the Maoists an the Marxists of the government were two sides of the same coin. "They are working together" she said. Mamata's outburst came a day after chief minister Buddhadeb Bhattacharjee asked her party to "sever links with the rebels". CPM veteran leader Jyoti Basu, too echoed his words, charging the Trinamul with joining hands with the Maoists to unleash violence in the state.

"Everyday our workers are getting killed. Our party offices are burnt. The Trinamul Congress an the Maoists are doing this together. They are taking law into their own hands" said Basu.

At the beginning of November, after being in the denial for months, the Nepalese Maoists admitted that they are extending "full support and cooperation" to the Naxals in India. A senior standing committee member of the Unified Communist Party of Nepal Maoist (UCPN-M) CP Gajurel, was quoted in a daily as saying: "We have extended our full support and cooperation to the Indian Maoists, who are launching armed revolt." The same newspaper had also earlier carried a report that a Maoist leader had met Indian leader Kishenji at an undisclosed place in October.

Faced with the Maoist menace the Left Front government in Bengal is now planning to spend Rs 1.600 crore for the development of the three Naxal-hit districts of West Midnapore, Bankura and Purulia. The chief minister of West Bengal, Buddhadeb Bhattacharjee, at the beginning of November paid a visit to Jangalmahal in Midnapore district. In sheer defiance of the huge police bandobast for the chief minister visit, the Maoists ambushed a patrol party 50 km from Midnapore town and just 30 minutes after the CM left, killing four soldiers. Eyewitness said the Maoists sprayed bullets from AK-47 rifles, looted arms from the vehicle, and walked away without any resistance.

On 27 October, tribal activists, backed by armed Maoists, under the name of local outfit People's Committee against Police Atrocity (PCPA) seized the Bhubaneswar-Delhi Rajdhani Express in West Midnapore district and detained it for five hours before security forces could free the hostages. The railways continue to be a vulnerable target.

What is shocking is that in these states where the Maoist revolt is burning the local governments are only busy rewarding their own cadres and forgetting the large populations. So it is with the CPM in West Bengal and also in Chhattisgarh a recent scandal has revealed that a former tribal chief minister, Madhu Koda, in four years as chief minister, has increased his declared assets of 20.000 Euro in 2005 to an estimated 60 million Euro today, with illegal investments allover the world.

Before becoming a deputy he was a daily wages earner. Corruption and police atrocity seem to be the upsetting causes.

INDIAN GOVERNMENT CONTINUES ITS OFFENSIVE AGAINST MAOIST INSURGENTS

Despite several cease-fire proposals from the Communist Party of India (Maoist), which is mounting a guerrilla insurgency in India's "tribal belt," and the Indian government, the latter is continuing a massive, multi-state military offensive dubbed Operation Green Hunt. Launched with considerable fanfare last fall, the Indian government's offensive is being spearheaded by tens of thousand of heavily-armed paramilitary troops. The Indian army is providing logistical support.

The ostensible aim of the offensive is to restore the state's writ over a large swathe of forest and hill territory—largely populated by historically marginalized tribal people and covering parts of the states of Jharkhand, Chattisghharh, Orissa, Andhra Pradesh, Maharashtra, and West Bengal—so that the government can bring "development." The truth is India's ruling elite covets these resource-rich lands for mega resource-extraction projects and wants to dispossess their tribal inhabitants and transform them into a cheap-labor workforce. No sooner had India's Congress Party-led United Progressive Alliance (UPA) government won re-election last May than it labeled the Maoist insurgency the country's greatest "internal security" threat, surpassing "jihadi terrorism" and the separatist insurgencies in Kashmir and the north-east. It vowed that suppressing the Maoists would henceforth be a top government priority.

In a speech last fall, Indian Prime Minister Manmohan Singh conceded that the Indian state has failed the tribal peoples, combining neglect and indifference with land-seizures and repression. But this admission was an artifice, aimed at rallying support for Operation Green Hunt with the claim that the government is now truly concerned about the welfare of the tribal people and only wants to suppress Maoist "terrorism" so it can right its past errors and promote socio-economic development. The size of the government offensive and especially the growing involvement of the Indian military in the planning and execution of the counterinsurgency campaign has caused some apprehension in ruling class circles. It is common knowledge that security forces and a Chattisghharh government-sponsored militia, the Salva Judum, have committed numerous atrocities, summarily executing insurgents and murdering and terrorizing tribal villagers.

Last fall several prominent members of India's military-security establishment criticized plans to use Indian military planes to transport troops, warning that this could ultimately result in strafing and widespread civilian casualties. This, they argued, would only further feed the Maoist insurgency.

In an attempt to shift responsibility for its Operation Green Hunt onto the Maoists, the government has said on several occasions that it would be willing to enter into talks with the Maoists if they abjure violence. In late February, Home Minister Palaniyappan Chidambaram went somewhat further, offering to initiate talks with the Maoists (who in India are commonly known as Naxals or Naxalites) if they suspended their military operations for 72 hours. Declared Chidambaram, "We never said to the Naxals that they [must] lay down arms or disband their organisation. Let there be no violence for 72 hours and we are willing to sit down to discuss the issues."

Previously, the Maoists had said they would be willing to enter into talks if the government unconditionally released several of their senior leaders, restored lands taken from tribal groups, and cancelled Memorandums of Understanding (MoUs) with various Indian and foreign corporations for further mega-projects in tribal areas. But in response to Chidambaram's late February offer, Maoist spokesman Koteshwar Rao offered a 72 day ceasefire, stretching from February 25 to May 7, with the only condition being that the government halt Operation Green Hunt. Rao suggested that the talks could be mediated by prominent intellectuals and human rights activists, suggesting among others the writer Arundathi Roy and Kabir Suman, a musician and Trinamool Congress MP.

After waiting several days, Chidambaram dismissed the Maoist ceasefire offer as "somewhat bizarre." He charged that barely three hours after Rao had floated his 72-day ceasefire proposal the Maoists had attacked a joint West Bengal police-

Central Reserve Border Force patrol in the West Midnapore district of West Bengal. This attack was not far from where a week before Maoist insurgents had overrun a paramilitary camp at Shilda killing 24 security personnel. On March 2, in an unexpected development, West Bengal police arrested one of the top CPI (Maoist) leaders, Venkateshwar Reddy. Reddy, who is also known by the *nom de guerre* Telugu Deepak, was the reputed mastermind of the Shilda attack.

In response to Deepak's arrest, Maoist spokesman Koteshwar Rao threatened a "full scale offensive" in West Bengal if Deepak and another CPI (Maoist) Politburo member were not soon released. He also said that the Maoists were prepared to spread their campaign of armed attacks into India's cities: "We will intensify our strikes if the government does not initiate talks. If need be, we will proceed towards towns and cities." Predictably, the UPA central government and the West Bengal state government, which is formed by the Communist Party of India (Marxist)-led Left Front, rejected the Maoists' demands and are using their threats to justify the intensification of the military offensive.

The Stalinist Communist Party of India (Marxist) or CPM is playing an utterly foul role in the Indian state's anti-Maoist counter-insurgency war. The CPM—which propped up the UPA government for its first four years in office and which in West Bengal is ruthlessly pursuing pro-big business "reforms," including banning strikes in the IT sector and expropriating peasants for Special Economic Zones—has repeatedly trumpeted Manmohan Singh's claim that the Maoists are India's greatest internal security threat. In their statements there is not even a suggestion that the current anti-Maoist drive is directed at consolidating the state's control over the tribal peoples so as to facilitate capitalist exploitation.

This puts them to the right of even much of the liberal corporate media. Thus the *Deccan Chronicle* in a February 24 editorial conceded that the Maoist insurgency is centered in an area that is "India's wealthiest mineral belt [and] which is being eyed by the government and by foreign and Indian mining interests" and that "there are instances of tribals being driven out of their homes so that the government can go ahead with its industrialization programme." Mimicking the rhetoric of the Hindu supremacist BJP, the CPM claims that the spread of the Maoist insurgency is due to violence and intimidation, not the deprivation and repression to which the tribal peoples have been subjected by the Indian state, including governments formed or supported by the parliamentary Left.

Indian workers and toilers must oppose the Indian state's counterinsurgency war against the Maoists. It is directed at upholding and intensifying the oppression of the tribal peoples. Moreover, the Indian ruling elite is using the purported threat of Maoist "terrorism" to justify the state repression of all manner of political movements. That said, the Maoists offer no progressive alternative for the working class and oppressed of India. The Maoists—like the mainline Stalinist parties, the CPM and the CPI or Communist Party of India—insist that the struggle for socialism is not on the agenda in India.

The Maoists make occasional ritual references to the revolutionary role of working class, but the thrust of their political activity is mobilizing the tribals and other sections of the rural population in support of "anti-feudal" measures and promoting various ethno-linguistic secessionist movements, which seek to reshuffle the boundaries of the capitalist nation-state system in South Asia. The Maoists' armed struggle, which often takes the form of "revenge attacks" on petty oppressors, goes hand-in-hand with maneuvers with various sections of the political establishment. Thus in West Bengal, the Maoists have established a quasi-public alliance with the Trinamool Congress (TNC)—a right-wing, Bengali split-off from the Congress Party and sometime partner of the BJP—and have justified this alliance in the name of fighting the "social fascist" CPM-led Left Front. At present the TMC is the second largest component of the UPA government. Similarly, the Maoists have indicated a favourable attitude to the current state government in Jharkhand, which is headed by the Jharkhand Mukti Morch, another UPA constituent.

While the Indian government's offer of "talks" to the Maoists was a propaganda ploy to rally public support for Operation Green Hunt, India's rulers are mindful that in India in the past and more recently in neighbouring Nepal, Maoists have been persuaded to forsake peasant-based insurgency for integration into capitalist parliamentary politics.

INDIAN GOVERNMENT SUFFERS REVERSAL IN ITS WAR ON MAOISTS AND TRIBALS

The Congress Party-led United Progressive Alliance (UPA) government, which has been on the warpath against a spreading Maoist insurgency, has been thrown into a serious crisis following a deadly ambush by Maoist guerrillas on April 6 that killed 76 security personnel in the forests of the eastern state of Chhattisgarh. The Dantewada ambush is far and away the largest reversal Indian state forces have ever suffered at the hands of the Maoists—who are also known as Naxalites—in the four decades that they have been attempting to develop a "protracted people's war" based on the peasantry and, more recently, India's oppressed tribal population.

The UPA considers the Maoist insurgency, which in recent years has spread to more than 200 of the country's 626 administrative districts, the country's "greatest internal security threat," because it stands in the way of the Congress Party's goal of seizing tribal lands on behalf of domestic and international capital. Soon after winning reelection to a second term in May 2009, the UPA government proclaimed suppression of the Maoist-led tribal insurgency a top priority. Sections of the tribal population in India's eastern jungle highlands have turned towards the Maoists out of desperation after enduring decades of repression, displacement and massacres at the hands of the Indian state.

Of the 76 dead, 75 belonged to the Indian government's paramilitary Central Reserve Police Force (CRPF) and one belonged to the Chhattisgarh state police. Two days after the ambush, Home Minister P. Chidambaram, the chief political architect of the government's military offensive against the Maoists, offered his resignation in writing. Unsurprisingly, this was promptly rejected by Prime Minister Manmohan Singh and by Congress Party President Sonia Gandhi, whom Singh acknowledges as the true head of the UPA government.

The government's offensive against the Maoists, which has been dubbed Operation Green Hunt, stretches across six states located mainly in the east and involves tens of thousands of heavily-armed central government paramilitaries and the police forces of the six states. The 80,000 or more paramilitaries that are mounting Operation Green Hunt are receiving logistical support and training in jungle warfare from the Indian army.

There is no doubt that the success of the Dantewada ambush has seriously dented Chidambaram's swagger and prestige. From the inception of Operation Green Hunt, the Indian Home Ministry has overseen its planning, with Chidambaram playing a major role in both coordinating and publicly promoting the Indian government's first-ever, nationally-directed, anti-Maoist counterinsurgency offensive. The *Times of India* observed that Chidambaram's very public role in promoting Operation Green Hunt had amplified the political fallout from the ambush. "[The] repercussions," wrote the *Times*, "are far more serious than they would have ordinarily been because of the blunt-speak Chidambaram engaged in to goad states to forge a common front" against the Maoists.

The government was gratified, therefore, that in the wake of the Dantewada ambush the major opposition parties—from the Hindu supremacist Bharatiya Janata party (BJP) through the Left Front—demonstrably rallied round the government and declared their continuing support for the counterinsurgency campaign. The official opposition BJP generally refuses to cooperate with the UPA government, which it brays against for purportedly being soft on terrorism and coddling India's impoverished Muslim minority. But in the immediate aftermath of the Dantewada ambush, the BJP rushed to Chidambaram's defence, hailing him as the best man for taking on the Maoist insurgency.

The Communist Party of India (Marxist) [CPM], the dominant partner in the Left Front similarly proclaimed its support for Operation Green Hunt and Chidambaram. In the days after the ambush, senior CPM leaders, including party General Secretary Prakash Karat, Politburo member and parliamentarian Sitaram Yechury, and West Bengal Chief Minister Buddadeb Bhattacharjee repeatedly endorsed Manmohan Singh's contention that the Maoist insurgency is the greatest internal threat facing India. Not long ago the

Stalinists were justifying their support for the UPA—the Left Front provided the governing coalition with its parliamentary majority for four years, ending in June 2008—on the grounds that it was the only way to prevent the "communal-fascist" BJP from returning to power. Now they join with the BJP in depicting the Maoist insurgency in veritable Bush "war on terror"-type terms, downplaying, if not outright dismissing, the misery and dispossession of the tribal peoples and the state violence to which they have been subjected.

Particularly noteworthy was Bhattacharjee's endorsement of Chidambaram. In early April the Home Minister had publicly reprimanded the West Bengal Chief Minister for the growing political violence in West Bengal, thereby signalling that the UPA government might in the future invoke article 356 of the constitution, which empowers it to place a state in which law and order have broken down under "president's" or central government rule. The Trinamool Congress, a Bengali regionalist party and the second largest member of the Congress-led UPA coalition, has been campaigning for the imposition of president's rule in West Bengal since last May's national election in which it dealt the CPM and Left Front a humiliating electoral defeat.

Still smarting from Chidambaram's rebuke, Bhattacharjee declared in response to the Dantewada ambush, "This is not a time to blame anyone. It is the time to work together. We must work collectively." "Work collectively" in waging war, that is. In an attempt to rally public support for Operation Green Hunt, Chidambaram had previously spoken about the government's willingness to enter into "peace talks" with the Communist Party of India (Maoist.) Now the ambush is being cited by the political establishment as proof that there can be no talks with "terrorists."

Indian security forces are notorious for their violations of human rights, including summary executions and torture, but Chidambaram seized on the ambush to proclaim, "This shows the savage nature of the Maoists—the brutality and savagery they are capable of." Home Secretary G.K. Pillai, giving voice to the ruling elite's thirst for revenge, vowed that the government would give "a fitting reply" to the Maoists. The central government has announced that 6,000 more CRPF troops will be mobilized in support of Operation Green Hunt. Meanwhile, the *Hindu* reports that the people of Mukram, a village of about 50 houses near the ambush site, have fled into the forest for fear of reprisals from CRPF personnel who accuse Mukram's residents of having provided information to the Maoists that made the ambush possible. The April 12 *Hindu* cited a villager as saying, "Everyone is terrified that the police will take revenge by attacking the village. They have already killed one person."

The Dantewada ambush has revived discussion within the Indian elite about directly using the Indian armed forces to suppress the Maoist insurgents. Several members of the UPA government including Prime Minister Singh and the Home Minister Chidambaram have told the media "all options are open." Although many in the political establishment are pressing for broadening the military's role in the counterinsurgency campaign, the army and air force chiefs have publicly expressed their opposition to such a course of action.

The recently promoted commander of the Indian Army General Vijay Singh said, "The Naxalite problem is a law and order problem, which is a state subject. It stems from certain issues on the ground, be it of governance, be it of administration, be it of socio-economic factors." Similarly the Air Force Chief commented, "The military–Air Force, Army and Navy–are not trained for limited lethality. The weapons that we have are meant for the enemy across the border. Therefore, I am not in favour of use of Air Force in situations like the Naxal problem."

India's military top brass fear being drawn into a low intensity war that would sap morale and undermine public support for the military. They also recognize that the militarization of the anti-Maoist campaign could well backfire, with atrocities and repression feeding antigovernment sentiment. The Dantewada ambush is indicative of the relationship of the Indian bourgeoisie and its state to the tribal peoples. Government officials are viewed as outsiders. Villagers shun contact with them, let alone with armed security personnel.

That said, the Maoist insurgency offers no way forward for the working class and oppressed masses of India. The Naxalites are a politically retrograde nationalist-Stalinist movement that long ago rejected the struggle for the political independence and hegemony of the working class, that is for socialist consciousness. Instead they have made the development of rural-based guerrilla warfare the focus of all their activity. Like the CPI and CPM to which its traces its origin and whose history it venerates, the CPI (Maoist) claims that the struggle for socialism is not yet on the historical agenda in India. It has combined armed struggle with the promotion of various caste, ethnic and tribal identities and opportunist maneuvers with parties of the bourgeois establishment. In West Bengal the Maoists have aligned themselves with the Trinamool Congress and assisted the efforts of this rightwing split-off from the Congress Party and frequent BJP ally to exploit the growing popular opposition to the West Bengal Left Front government.

In the immediate aftermath of the Dantewada ambush, the Maoists reiterated their call for peace talks with the government. The recent Naxalite resurgence is attributable to the desperate conditions that prevail in much of rural India, on the one hand, and to the criminal policies being pursued by the Stalinist Left Front, on the other. For decades the Communist Party of India (Marxist) and the Communist Party of India have subordinated the working class to parliamentary maneuvers with the parties of the Indian elite, becoming in the process an integral part of the political establishment. In the states, such as West Bengal, where they form the government, they are unabashedly pursuing pro-investor policies.

It is because the working class has been prevented from advancing a socialist solution to the social crisis—mobilizing India's toilers in a struggle to liquidate capitalist rule and thereby liquidating landlordism and casteism and completing the other unresolved problems of the democratic revolution—that the Maoists have temporarily been able to attract support from a section of India's impoverished tribals.

11

Maoism: Evolution and Development

Millennia are too long: Let us dispute over mornings and evenings. — Mao Zedong (1963)

The conventional wisdom of the day presents Mao as some kind of a "monster", for instance, in Jung Chang and Jon Halliday's 2005 book, *Mao: The Unknown Story*, which, in its obsessive intent to denigrate Mao, is least concerned with the known facts about the man. Indeed, in Li Zhisui's *The Private Life of Chairman Mao*, he is made out to be a "monstrous lecher" by a doctor, bent on disparaging Mao, shabbily doctoring the facts. It is evident that a "battle for China's past" is underway, with the elite intelligentsia leading the attack. The latter are Chinese, who were the victims, real or imagined, direct or indirect, of the Cultural Revolution, and some leading lights in the "China Studies" field the world over, who have always been prone to somersaults depending on the direction of the political wind in Washington. For instance, their positions have shifted from "disparaging" during the period of Cold War hostility to "grudgingly complementary" following Sino-US détente in the early 1970s, and then, to "Mao-was-all-wrong; Mao-is-to-blame" with the great reversal in China in the post-Mao period when the official view turned anti-Maoist, and the ideology of neo-liberalism took hold.

The credo of objectivity that is repeatedly claimed is a myth. It is not surprising that in a world where "the ideas of the ruling class are in every epoch the ruling ideas", the views of the beneficiaries of the cultural revolution, the peasants and the workers, who gained in terms of education, healthcare and other aspects of social welfare, as also, in the "voice" they got in the fields and the factories, and in the political arena, are not being heard (Gao 2008). With this necessary communication of the side I lean on, let me then get to the origins of Maoism, which got its lease on life in the immediate aftermath of the eventual rejection of the disastrous line of "united front from within" (leading to restraints on organisational independence), which was virtually forced on the CCP by the Third International (the Comintern) in 1923. It was claimed by the latter that the Kuomintang (KMT), led by Chang Kai-shek (after Sun Yat-sen died in March 1925), represented the "revolutionary national bourgeoisie" of China. This alliance was supposed to produce national liberation and the bourgeois-democratic revolution (revolution led by the bourgeoisie in alliance with the workers and peasants), but led only to the disastrous defeat of the communists at the hands of Chang's counterrevolution in 1927, leading to the civil war (1928-35).

But even in defeat there was a silver lining: no doubt the Chang-led KMT controlled the bulk of the armed forces; but the Fourth Army deserted in August 1927 to join the communists, which led to the founding of the Red Army. A new leadership of the CCP gradually began to coalesce around Mao; however, it was only by around 1932 that this budding "Maoist" authority gained legitimacy and the CCP could forge, and refine over time, its own strategy and path to achieve the goals of the "new democratic revolution" (NDR).

For our purpose over here, it must be mentioned that the Comintern had mechanically extended Marx's historical analysis of the transition from feudalism to capitalism in Europe to the colonies/semi-colonies/neo-colonies, merely adding on that imperialism had allied there with the feudalists to maintain and consolidate its power. It was then assumed that the national bourgeoisie would take the lead in the struggle against imperialism and feudalism/semi-feudalism, and therefore it was the duty of the communists there to rally the masses in support of such a project, for it would lead to national independence and bourgeois democracy, without which the struggle for socialism would have had to be indefinitely postponed. But, as we have seen, such a policy led to the disastrous defeat of the communists in China in 1927. The so-called national bourgeoisie proved to be nothing but the ally of imperialism against the communists.

It was the CCP under Mao that most effectively challenged the Comintern line by refusing to surrender control and leadership to those who could not be relied upon to carry through to the very end the struggle for genuine national independence or the fight against feudalism/semi-feudalism. The quality of the leadership was crucially important (Sweezy 1976: 10). It adopted the strategy of protracted people's war (PPW), which relied on the peasants, built rural base areas, carried out "land to the tiller" and other social policies (for instance, dealing with the gender question through the mobilization of women in the countryside) in these areas (run democratically as miniature, self-reliant states) thereby building up a political mass base in the countryside to finally encircle and "capture" the cities.

Here it needs to be emphasised that it was only during the anti-Japanese resistance (1937-45), when the contradiction between Japanese imperialism and national independence became the principal one (playing the leading role), relegating the fight between feudalism and the masses to a secondary and subordinate position, that the CCP managed to shift nationalist opinion progressively in its favour. It was in this period that it overcame its confinement in the rural areas to move on to the national stage, extend the PPW and capture the popular imagination. The CCP could not have successfully "captured" the cities, but for the massive nationalist upsurge in the course of the anti-Japanese resistance turning decisively in its favour due to its correct handling of the unity and struggle between nationalism and anti-imperialism, leading on to the successful completion of the NDR.

At the core of the NDR was opposition to the transformation of the society under the leadership of the bourgeoisie and its political representatives. The NDR — unambiguously led by the communist party — suppressed the big bourgeoisie because, even as it retained private capitalist enterprise, it was primarily meant to create the prerequisites for socialism. At the heart of the course of the NDR, from 1927 to 1949, was the building of base areas, involving the following (Gurley1976: 70-71):

1. achieving victory in the political struggle, thereby establishing the basis for running a miniature state in the base area;
2. winning the economic struggle — land to the tiller, land investigation, promotion of mutual aid and cooperation, and achieving the development of the productive forces (the material means of production and human capabilities) in agriculture and small industry; and,
3. carrying off the cultural and ideological struggle, with a great deal of overlapping among the three.

All of this — whether political, economic, or cultural and ideological — entailed following the "mass line", which is a distinctive feature of Maoism. This is a method of involving the masses in how, for instance, each of the above is to be done and then implementing what had been decided upon with their participation. The party leaders thereby correctly understand the opinions of the people, and so fashion the required policies in a manner the masses will support and actively implement. Mao summed this up pithily as: "from the masses, to the masses". Indeed, in the process of participating in the "land to the tiller", land investigation, and in the ideological struggles, the people understood the local class structure and the ideas and institutions bolstering the status quo (Gurley 1976: 71-72).

This brings us to three crucial dimensions of Maoist theory and practice in trying to enrich the democratic process in the Leninist vanguard party, the mass organizations, and the society. In the Maoist conception of the vanguard party, just like in Lenin's, centralised guidance by a revolutionary elite is at the core, and this elite leadership is drawn from intellectuals, workers and peasants, with the difference that workers and peasants are sought to be represented, over time, in greater proportion. What is however distinctive in Mao is the conscious effort to fuse the inner-party organisational principle of democratic centralism ("freedom of discussion, unity of action") with the mass line ("from the masses, to the masses"), the mass organisations under party leadership providing the crucial link between the two. However, a word over here about the claim of the vanguard party being led by the proletariat might be in order. Here, as Benjamin Schwartz (1977: 26) explains, in Maoism, the term "proletarian" refers to a set of moral qualities — "self-abnegation, limitless sacrifice to the needs of the collectivity, guerrilla-like self-reliance, unflagging energy ...iron discipline, etc" — as the norm of true collectivist behaviour. Proletarian leadership then comes to be constituted by a set of intellectuals, workers and peasants who excel in these moral requirements.

We are thus beginning to grasp some distinctive features of Maoism — the conception of NDR as opposed to that of bourgeois-democratic revolution; PPW; "base areas" and the way they are established; the principal contradiction (which may change over time) steering the course of the PPW; and, democratic centralism *plus* the mass line. It is then time to introduce what may indeed be the *differentia specifica* of Maoism, best done by illustration from Maoist practice in China. We have already alluded to the idea that the road to socialism was already entered upon and struggles to persist on that road were undertaken early on in the new democratic stage of the revolution itself. We said that the big bourgeoisie is suppressed during the NDR itself in order to lay the ground — create the pre-conditions — for socialism. Why?

Socialists, more than others, are well aware that there are definite limits to the compatibility of capitalism and democracy, that is, if the latter is understood as government in accordance with the will of the people (Sweezy 1980). But from a capitalist point of view, such democracy is acceptable and considered viable only if the majority continues to believe that the capitalist system is the best for them, or that there is no alternative but to live with it. The moment this belief erodes, democracy becomes a potential danger to capitalism, best illustrated in the case of Chile from 1970 following the coming into office of a party pledged to beginning the transition to socialism, whereupon the big bourgeoisie collaborated with Washington and the military took over to save capitalism there (Sweezy 1980). To circumvent such a possibility, a new type of democracy ("new democracy") has to be created which doesn't preclude the transition to socialism if the majority want it, for which, the big bourgeoisie has to be suppressed. In effect, the NDR doesn't do away with capitalism, but it confiscates the property of the imperialists and the big bourgeoisie — those at the apex of wealth, power and privilege — and hence stymies the anti-democratic opposition to socialism from their representatives and backers.

But let us elaborate upon the Maoist idea of steps within the new democratic stage, steps in the transition to socialism, and steps within the socialist stage itself, and the thought that the pre-conditions of a subsequent step/stage in the process of progressive change must be created within the step/stage that has to be transited from. The land reform program leading on in steps to communes can be used as an apt illustration. It may be best to take William Hinton's books, *Fanshen: A Documentary of Revolution in a Chinese Village* (1966) and *Shenfan: The Continuing Revolution in a Chinese Village* (1983), which together provide a rich documentary account of the land reform in Long Bow village of Shanxi province during 1946-48, onward to the formation of mutual aid teams, and from 1953, the merging of those teams into "elementary cooperatives", and from there to advanced cooperatives and further on into communes, and tracing developments up to 1971. They tell a whole lot of facts, even those that contradict what the author is trying to argue, but it is difficult to even propose a framework to look at this whole social canvas. However, fortunately, subsequently Hinton has helped provide such an enabling structure (1994; 2002; 2004), though he also revised his assessment of the Cultural Revolution following the publication of *Shenfan* (Pugh 2005).

Perhaps it would be best to begin where *Fanshen* concludes (Hinton 1966: 603): Land reform, by creating basic equality among rural producers, only presented the producers with a choice of roads: private enterprise on the land leading to capitalism, or collective enterprise on the land leading to socialism.

There is one more important insight that comes from *Fanshen* — that when one extracts rent and interest, and what is lost in "unequal exchange" from the net output of the poor peasant household, especially in a bad year, what remains is not even what wage labour would have got, that is, if one were to impute the respective wage rates for family labour. This suggests exploitation of a greater order under semi-feudalism than under backward capitalism, if both are at the same technological level. Marx had also referred to this, albeit, in a different context, when he discussed the plight of the Irish tenant farmer. This leads one to a dispute with those scholars, including Benjamin Schwartz (1951: 4) who hold that the CCP, though successfully having come to power essentially on the strength of its organisation of the peasantry, and not that of the urban proletariat, had inaugurated in China the "decomposition" of Marxism that Lenin began in Russia, and thus, the opposite of the significant innovation that some have attributed to it.

Let us then get to *Shenfan*. In 1948 itself, the peasants had begun to form mutual aid teams where a small number of households pooled resources other than land (tools, implements, draft power, occasional labour) but still cultivated the land on an individual basis. Then in 1953 the formation of elementary cooperatives got underway, in which land as well as other resources were pooled, but individual ownership rights were maintained. Incomes were based partly on property ownership and partly on labour time committed to cooperative production in ratios set to garner majority local support. Here dividends had to be paid on the assets, including land, made available, but the complaint of the middle and rich peasants was that this was not as much as they would otherwise have got, that is, if they had cultivated individually by hiring in labour. But when crop yields began to increase because of more intensive use of labour in the cooperative mode, the conflict regarding how to divide the income as between the labour contributed and the assets pooled became sharper (Hinton 1983:142-43). The resolution usually took the form of moving from something like a labour to capital share of 40:60 to 60:40, for, over time, it was living labour that had created the addition to assets. A time would then come when the new assets created by labour overwhelm the original assets pooled at the time of the formation of the cooperative, when it then became appropriate to abolish the capital share of the net output, that is, move to "advanced cooperatives".

The latter entailed a definite socialist advance, involving all peasant households being incorporated in such producer cooperatives, with common ownership of all productive resources. As Hinton (1994: 6-7) puts it: When the new capital created by living labour surpasses and finally overwhelms the old capital with which the group started out, then rewarding old shareholders with disproportionate payments amounts to exploitation, a transfer of wealth from those who create it by hard labour to those who own the original shares and may, currently, not labour at all.

Of course, with one more step on the collective ladder, the advanced cooperatives were turned into larger units of collective economy *and* government — the communes. The point however is that in each step of the ladder leading up to collectivization, the preconditions of the next step were introduced, which helped resolve the old contradictions and smoothed the transition to the next step/stage.

But, it is alleged that the strategy of the Great Leap Forward (GLF) (1958-61) and the organisation of the people's communes, and the left deviations of that period led to a massive famine in which up to 30 million people are said to have died. Then, there have been the excessive violence and the personal tragedies of the Cultural Revolution (CR). For both, the excesses of the GLF and the CR, Mao and Maoism have been held entirely responsible. Hinton however disagrees. To get to the truth, he explains the context — that of "protracted political warfare" (Hinton 2004: 51). The NDR was a revolution of a new type, new in that it was meant to create the preconditions for the socialist road, unlike bourgeois-democratic revolutions that open the road to capitalism. Following 1949, however, the resolution of the contradictions with semi-feudalism and imperialism brought the contradiction between capitalism and the Chinese working people to the fore — the latter became the principal contradiction.

Right from the time of the launch of the NDR, the CCP had been divided into two major factions — a "proletarian" one, headed by Mao, and a "bourgeois" one, headed by Liu Shaoqi and Deng Xiaoping; pre-liberation, the former was based in the liberated areas, while the latter was in the KMT-dominated cities. After liberation in 1949, the two factions "merged as one organisationally, but they never did merge ideologically" (Hinton 2004: 54). This led to a fundamental split over development strategy and policy ever since Mao took China decisively on to the socialist road. It was on the eve of the GLF that Mao declared on 27 February 1957 ("On the Correction Handling of Contradictions among the People"): "...the question of which will win out, socialism or capitalism, is still not settled". As Hinton put it: "No policy, from either side, could be applied without contest", which meant extreme friction between the two factions. He goes on:

To blame Mao, then, for the struggle that ensued and for its outcome is unwarranted, unrealistic, and unhistorical. Mao did what needed to be done given his social base [the rural poor and the workers in the alliance he cultivated], while Liu did what he had to given his social base. After a decade of conflict things came to a head in the Cultural Revolution.... Mao had the upper hand politically. He was able to speak directly and mobilise hundreds of millions of peasants and workers. But Liu had the upper hand organisationally...

...in 1958, ...severe disruption ...coupled with very bad weather in 1959, '60, and '61 ...produce(d) a shortage of crops, hunger, and even starvation. Mao's initiatives failed temporarily but were well conceived...

...During the Cultural Revolution similar extremes arose. ...However, the movement as a whole was a great creative departure in history. It was not a plot, not a purge, but a mass mobilisation whereby people were inspired to intervene, to screen and supervise their cadres and form new popular committees to exercise control at the grassroots and higher.

...The principal contradiction of the times was the class struggle between the working class and the capitalist class expressed in the party centre ...unless it was resolved in the interest of the working class the socialist revolution would founder. ...the method must be to mobilize the common people to seize power from below in order to establish leading bodies, democratically elected organs of power was ...summed up by the phrase "bombard the headquarters"... the target of the Cultural Revolution [was] "party people in authority taking the capitalist road".

Basically, in order to resolve the contradiction between the "proletarian line" and the "bourgeois line" within the party in favour of the former, the Maoists, in the CR, tried to plant the seeds of a later stage of socialism in the earlier stage itself, thus doing away with a mechanical separation of the two stages and concentrating instead on their interrelations (Magdoff 1975: 53). The two stages of socialism, supposed to follow chronologically, are the phase where distribution of the social product is according to the principle "from each according to her/his abilities, to each according to her/his work" followed by the phase where distribution is according to the norm "from each according to her/his abilities, to each according to her/his needs". Magdoff explains that Maoists focus on the interrelations between the two, and therefore emphasise the need to create the preconditions for the transition within the earlier phase itself, the main prerequisites being the way the social product is distributed and a change in human relations. If one doesn't do this, the inequalities produced and reproduced by the current stage will lead to the emergence and consolidation of a new privileged elite that will gradually transform itself into a new ruling class. And, they derive their justification of this with reference to Marx's *Critique of the Gotha Programme*, with its forceful description of the necessary persistence of inequality in a socialist (but not communist) society. One can thus understand why the major concerns during the CR were "measures that tend[ed] to reduce differences arising from the division of labour between city and country, manual and mental labour, and management and employees", knowing very well that their attainment was "in the far distant future and will involve many political struggles in the years ahead".

It is then clear that Maoists reject Stalin's mechanical interpretation of Marx's 1859 Preface to *A Contribution to the Critique of Political Economy* as a deterministic theory of history. Mao accused Stalin of emphasising only the forces of production (the means of production and human capability) to the neglect of the relations of production (relations at work, and ownership relations that bestow control over the forces of production and the product), and the superstructure (institutions such as the state, the family, religion, education, and the law, and culture and ideology). Even among the productive forces, Stalin — Mao alleges — in a relative sense, neglected the growth of human capability, which should have constituted the core of the forces of production. Again, Stalin essentially viewed the direction of causation as a one-way route from change in the forces of production to alteration in the relations of production, and thereon to revamp of the superstructure (Mao 1977).

Mao instead argued that elements of the superstructure are transformed only with a considerable lag; the old culture hangs on long after the material base of the economy is radically altered. But, if a conscious effort is made to change the elements of the superstructure, this, in turn, affects the economic base (the productive forces and the relations of production). Hence, Mao was bent on ushering in the people's communes even before the modernisation of agriculture, for the former, in his view, by changing the relations of production and elements of the superstructure, the latter with a lag, would, in turn, spur the productive forces. Hence, also the stress upon the stifling economic effects of the prevailing class structure of the factories during the CR, or of the domination of landlords and "comprador-bureaucrat" capitalists in the pre-liberation period, or on the liberating effects of smashing the superstructure (for example, Confucian culture). How apparently open-ended the interrelations among and between the forces of production, the relations of production, and the superstructure are in Mao's conception of Marx's theory of history?

MARRYING THE VARIOUS STRANDS

We have seen in this essay that, at its best, Marxism leads one to expect a close interrelationship between theory and practice; where either is scarce the other will be acutely disadvantaged. Maoism, by and large, has privileged practice over theory — it views practice as the foundation of theory. But what does the Maoist dictum "seek truth from practice mean"? At its best, and if one reads Mao's July 1937 definitive *On Practice: On the Relation between Knowledge and Practice, Between Knowing and Doing*, he takes on both, the dogmatists and the empiricists, the "right opportunists" and the "leftists". As he puts it: "Practice ['class struggle, political life, scientific and artistic pursuits'], knowledge, again practice, and again knowledge.

This form repeats itself in endless cycles, and with each cycle the content of practice and knowledge rises to a higher level". And, in his outstanding August 1937 essay *On Contradiction* he holds that contradictions — the struggle between functionally united opposites — cause continual change. Development stems from the resolution of contradictions and strategy involves choice of the form of struggle most suited to resolve a contradiction. But the desired qualitative alteration can be brought only through a series of stages, where the existing stage is impregnated with the hybrid seeds of the subsequent one, thereby dissolving the salient contradictions of the former and ushering in the latter. Mao's Marxism was of the Leninist school, albeit tending closer to its Stalinist version (which, as we have seen, is a decomposed version of Leninism), but struggling to overcome and go beyond Stalinism.

We have traversed a wide canvas with some wild strokes, covering the ground from Marxism to Leninism, and from there to its Stalinist revision, and then to Maoism in terms of its evolution and development in China from the late 1920s to the late 1960s, focussing on its *differentiae specifica*. The latter, we have found, are:

- the poor peasantry of the interior of a backward capitalist/semi-feudal society rather than the urban proletariat constitute the mass support base of the movement;
- theory of revolution by stages as well as uninterrupted revolution, implying a close link between successive stages;
- the stage of NDR, which makes capitalism much more compatible with democracy, thereby aiding the transition to socialism;
- the path and strategy of PPW, which relies on the peasants, builds rural base areas, carries out "land to the tiller" and other social policies in these areas (run

democratically as miniature, self-reliant states) thereby building up a political mass base in the countryside to finally encircle and capture the cities;

- the conception of "base areas" and the way to establishing them;
- "capturing" (winning mass support in) the cities by demonstrating a brand of nationalism that is genuinely anti-imperialist, thereby re-orienting an existing mass nationalist upsurge (as during the anti-Japanese resistance, 1937-45 in China) in favour of the completion of the NDR;
- democratic centralism *plus* the "mass line", ensuring that "democracy" doesn't take a backseat to "centralism" and making sure the people are involved in policy making and its implementation;
- the central idea that contradictions — the struggle between functionally united opposites — at each stage drive the process of development on the way to socialism, which is sought to be brought about in a series of stages, where the existing stage, at the right time, is impregnated with the hybrid seeds of the subsequent one, thereby dissolving the salient contradictions of the former and ushering in the latter;
- open-ended interrelations among and between the forces of production, the relations of production, and the superstructure; and
- the idea that political, managerial, and bureaucratic power-holders entrench themselves as a ruling elite and, over a period of time, assume the position of a new exploiting class, and that the people have to be constantly mobilised to struggle against this tendency.

"Materialist dialectics" as a way of thinking and a guide to doing was a powerful tool in Mao's hands, but its weaknesses were perhaps inherent in its very strengths; in the end, the very method led him to hugely overestimate the pace of change and vastly underestimate the obstacles to change. Marx too fell into the same trap when his very method of analysis led him to believe that revolution was around the corner, immensely underrating the huge barriers to progressive change. Does the very application of the method of materialist dialectics lead its practitioners to err on the side of "voluntarism" in their practice?

If one looks forward from the vantage point of 1969 — the year marks the beginning of the end of the Maoist era — the great reversal from "socialism" to capitalism (Sharma, ed. 2007) lay ahead. But 1969 also affords a good look back in time. It might help to begin from an incident from Mao's childhood when he was in school, which he related to the American journalist Edgar Snow (1972). One day he and his fellow students were witness to the decapitated heads of rebels strung to the city's gates as a warning. The insurrectionists had led starving peasants in an uprising to find food. The savage repression of the rebellion was obvious, and the incident left a profound impression on the boy and he never forgot it, deeply resenting the treatment meted out to the rebels. Clearly, from a very young age Mao came to view the prevailing social order as quite simply intolerable and to expect a revolutionary high tide sooner or later. "A single spark can start a prairie fire", he told his close comrades in January 1930; twenty years later, he is said to have declared: "The Chinese people have stood up!" There is a touching story of Mao's triumphant entry into Beijing which is worth recounting:

There were a million Chinese present to welcome him. A large platform, fifteen feet high, had been built at the end of a vast square, and as he mounted the steps from the back, the top of his head appeared and a roar of welcome surged up from a million throats, increasing and increasing as the lone figure came fully into view. And when Mao ...saw the vast multitude, he stood for a moment, then suddenly covered his face with both hands and wept. But in the years after 1949, even in the mid-1960s, as we have seen, the question of whether it will be capitalism or socialism in China was still unsettled. At the age of 72, the guerrilla in Mao stirred again — better to burn out than to hit the skids. As Jerome Ch'en (1968: 5), quoting Mao the poet put it: The Chinese revolution was at a cross-road. It could "look down the precipices" and beat a retreat or "reach the ninth heaven high ..." and then "return to merriment and triumphant songs." The choice, according to the poet, depended entirely upon one's "will to ascend." Four years later, all that remained were the embers — the time had come to just fade away. Not much later, his closest comrades, Zhou Enlai and Zhu De passed away. The Bard of Avon's idea that "all the world's a stage" has acquired the status of a cliché, but it must surely have been one of the great pleasures of Mao's life to have been on the same stage with the two of them. The time was now up for one of the greatest Marxist revolutionaries of all time to ascend to the stars to join them, and Marx, Engels, Lenin, Trotsky, Stalin, the 20 million soldiers of the Red Army who had died in the war against fascism, the many ordinary peasant-guerrillas of the PLA who sacrificed their lives in the long march to a better world.

Maoism, however, needs to be taken to task; one cannot but ask: Why the peasants and workers didn't resist the great reversals to capitalism in China and the Soviet Union — the counter-revolutions? Were these regimes, as long as Mao and Stalin were around, really socialist, as has constantly been the claim of latter-day Maoists? The truth could only be highly disappointing, that is, if one were to judge Maoism, as is only fair, by the fruits of its project of taking humanity along the road towards equality, cooperation, community, and solidarity. In China itself, Maoism didn't succeed on this score — all the united actions of the workers and the poor peasants, all the mass education of the Maoist period didn't seem to have brought about their intellectual development to a point where, when it came to taking on the "capitalist roaders" after 1978 to uphold the ideas of equality and cooperation as against hierarchy and competition, they did precious little. Maoism failed to provide a successful working model of socialism in the 20th century. What's worse, even as Mao was in his last years, People's China entered into an accommodation with US imperialism against the Soviet Union — Mao's *On Contradiction* was misapplied to justify the arrangement. In a blatant violation of an important Maoist tenet, nationalism got the better of anti-imperialism when in 1974 Deng Xiaoping used so-called "three worlds' theory" to rationalise the "right-wing" turn in China's foreign policy. But despite all these shortcomings, there can be little doubt that over the longer period, from the late 1920s to the late 1960s, Maoism did something unprecedented in human history — it brought about a drastic redistribution of income and wealth in China; it radically reordered the way Chinese society's economic surplus was generated and utilised, all for the better. aaa

MAO'S LEGACY AND THE FUTURE OF MAOISM

It's time then to talk of Mao's legacy. As we have seen, Maoism has a definite view about how to get to socialism, and about what needs to be done to meet the basic needs of everyone in a poor country. Development is to be on an egalitarian basis — we are all in it together and everyone rises together. What then of Mao's legacy, Maoism? Surely, this is open to all who share his Weltanshuuang, his method of analysis — materialist dialectics — his values, his vision, and choose to embark together on the long march to socialism, knowing before hand, that the journey is fraught with considerable peril. aWhat then of Maoism in India, one might ask? Maoist China did its best to feed, clothe and house everyone, keep them healthy, educate most of them. Contrast this with the deplorable conditions in India at the end of the 1960s and even today — the tragedy of India ruled by her own big bourgeoisie — and one gets wind as to why there are some in India who look to the Maoist model of development as the way to a richer and fuller life for all. Anu — whom we started this article with — was one of them.

However, while one may have deep respect for such people, one needs to ask the question: Are the basic path and strategy of revolution that were necessary in China in the 1930s and 1940s right for India in the 21st century?a Well, India differs very significantly from the China of those times, more so in its history, geography, class and social structure, traditions, and in the nature of its "semi-feudalism"/backward capitalism, the accommodation of the big bourgeoisie with imperialism, the strength of the repressive apparatus of the state, the nationalities question, and so on. And, importantly, while Chinese history is replete with periodic widespread peasant uprisings, Indian history, in a comparative sense, is scarce of such rebellions, which perhaps can be explained in terms of caste — it is fundamentally antithetical to any meaningful unity of the exploited and the oppressed.a Recall that Mao adapted his Marxism-Leninism to the realities of China's history, China's potentialities; "learn truth from practice" was his message. Surely a party [CPI (Maoist)] that stems from a political tendency that, over the last 40 years, has done its best to take the Indian revolution forward might like to take a hard re-look into the abyss that is India — its history, its potentialities.

The Maoists must keep in mind that the scientific validity of the Maoism they uphold will be judged in the first instance in India by its contributions to correctly explaining Indian social reality. There is a lot they have had a hand in this respect, for instance, in emphasising the parasitical reliance of Indian capital on the state for its self-expansion, expressed in the notion of *bureaucrat* capital. Or, in stressing the powerful role of the state in the very making of the Indian big bourgeoisie (of course, the "state's" fostering of the ruling classes more than the other way round, going back to ancient times, is an insight from the eminent historian D D Kosambi). The Maoists have also helped us to see the post-1956 official "land reforms" as having led to the partial amalgamation of the old rural landowning classes into a new, broader stratum of rich landowners, those not setting their hands to the plough, including an upper section of the former tenants, all of whom, despite the various markets, have yet to rid themselves of various "semi-feudal" practices and pre-capitalist elements of culture. Also, it is the Maoists who, in their practice, correctly do not even try to differentiate the rural poor into "agrarian proletariat" or "landless peasantry", knowing very well that the same very poor household can be categorized in one or the other at various points in time. And, in organising the "agrarian proletariat"/"landless peasantry" along with the poor and middle peasants, and a section of the rich peasants, they insist on factoring in the caste question, despite their knowing how highly problematic and painfully difficult such a getting together can be. Also, it is the Maoists more than others who first grasped the brutal character of the dominant classes and the leaders of the political parties they have co-opted, the very same categories whose forebears had taken power in the name of Gandhian non-violence. All this is knowledge essentially derived from their practice; and, needless to say, in keeping with Mao's legacy, the content of practice and knowledge has to go on continuously rising to a higher level.

The party [CPI (Maoist)] has come in for a lot of condemnation for its violent activities, including killings. The violence however has to be viewed in the context of the undeclared civil war that is underway in the areas of its influence, for instance, in Dantewada in the state of Chhattisgarh (PUDR 2006). The government is implementing a barbaric counter-insurgency policy, which includes the fostering of a network of informers and combatants among the civilian population, right from the village level upwards — a state-supported, state-sponsored, and even state-organised so-called people's resistance [called Salwa Judum (SJ)] against the Maoists. Entire villages have been evacuated and the villagers forcibly dumped into relief camps, and this, in the circumstances of large-scale acquisition of land by private corporations in what is a mineral-rich region. The last four years have witnessed violent attacks, loot, destruction, intimidation, rape and killing on an unprecedented scale principally by the SJ; indeed, the latter has even forcibly mobilised the displaced into its ranks. Undoubtedly, the killing is by both sides, but the big difference is that the Maoists, generally when they target specific state representatives, or even informers, they first warn them to desist from the anti-people activity they are undertaking. Those guilty of rape, torture, deaths in custody, or responsible for "encounter" killings are singled out so that others may, out of fear of such reprisals, desist from acting thus. As far as the SJ representatives are concerned, any person who joins them is targeted, not because of any personal enmity, but because of the role that the SJ has been playing in the undeclared civil war.

More generally, the violence also has to be seen in the context of the close de facto nexus between economic and political power at the local and regional levels; the dominant classes, through various means, exercise a degree of control over the police and the judiciary, which increases the chances of violent confrontation between the contending classes.

Those who deliberately, falsely depict the Maoists as "devotees of violence", choose to suppress the fact that the violence of the oppressed (and the Maoists who now lead them) has been always preceded and provoked by the violence of the oppressors (and the state and private forces that back them). To claim, as some liberals do, that the violence of the oppressed is "morally equivalent" to that of the oppressors, is to endorse the reactionary state, which backs the oppressors. And, in this age of the management of public opinion, the "programming" of what the public thinks, sees and reads, the "facts" that are disseminated are artificially separated from a whole host of other relevant facts, never allowing the public to discern the "real" present.

But, while acknowledging that antagonistic contradictions between hostile class-based organisations will lead to violence, it is a Maoist tenet that guerrilla actions ought to be subordinated to "mass-line" politics — the Maoist guerrillas should give precedence to winning over the mass of the people in their base areas and, in consequence, in the surrounding areas — and work towards a better balance ("proportionality") than ever before between means and ends. Regarding the resort to violence in the revolution, to the extent that I have absorbed their writings, it would be fair to say that Marx and Engels might not have disagreed with the use of violent methods by the revolutionary forces in India today. The dominant classes could never be expected to give up their control without employing all the repressive power at their command. It is useful perhaps to recall that Marx's response to the "crimes and cruelties alleged" against the "insurgent Hindus" of 1857 was to set out an account of the daily violence "in cold blood" of British rule in India (Marx 1857).

As to the false claim that the Maoists have no mass support in their areas of influence, one has only to listen to perceptive yet sensitive, independent observers who know the situation on the ground. The state forces are much stronger (as far as armaments and numbers go) than the Maoist guerrillas, and yet the tribal peasants support the latter. Why do these peasants take the risk of supporting the underdogs, even when they know that when the guerrillas are vanquished, they, as their supporters, will be at the mercy of the state forces, and will most probably perish? If, at the risk of death itself, the peasants choose the guerrillas, surely there must be something more significant going on over here.

Besides India, Maoism is a political force to reckon with in Nepal, the Philippines, and Peru. The Nepali Maoist leaders have been imaginative — their ideas of some combination of the "Chinese" (triumph in the countryside and spread to the cities) and the "Russian" (victory in the cities and spread to the countryside) models of revolution, and of "21st century democracy" (multi-party competition as long as all agree by the goals of "new democracy") are appealing. But these theories are being put to a severe test in practice. The Unified Communist Party of Nepal (Maoist), given its relative strength vis-a-vis "the enemies" of democracy and their friends and masters outside the borders of that small country (above all in India), seeks to utilize the bourgeois republic as a stage in mustering the force of the impoverished masses and nationalist intermediate strata to proceed towards NDR.

What then of the future of Maoism and the renewal of socialism that it promises? Frankly, "whatever chance there may have been that the revolutions of the 20th century could or would provide successful working models of socialism" have long since been extinguished; "socialism, we are told, has been tried and failed". But, as Marx was the first to show, the obstacles to a better future cannot be meaningfully addressed within the framework of capitalism. The challenge then is to revive and renew the legacy of socialism. In this, can Maoism illuminate the way?

Maoism has its roots in Marx who was, above all, a *radical* democrat — he demanded the reincarnation of community and mass solidarity; he dreamed of the communion of human beings with nature; he stressed the dialectic of liberation; he looked forward to a just society alongside "rich individuality"; and, as Paresh Chattopadhyay (2005) reminds us, he insisted on the removal of commodity exchange, the division of labour, the state,... But, then, Lenin too, in his *State and Revolution* appeared as a thoroughgoing democrat, though he introduced into his conception of socialism elements that are antithetical to the "association of free individuals" — wage labour and state (Ibid).

Mao and the Chinese Maoists too gave the impression of being revolutionary democrats, that is, if one were to go by the 20 million people marching through the streets of various Chinese cities in the last week of May 1968, the demonstrators mainly chanting the slogan: "long live the revolutionary heritage of the great Paris Commune". Indeed, Marx's interpretation of the Commune was then deemed relevant to the revival of the revolution in China, something that found a place in the famous "Sixteen Points" of 8 August 1966. "Let a hundred flowers blossom, let a hundred schools of thought contend" was not merely intended policy for the promotion of progress in the arts and sciences, but one of ushering in a flourishing socialist culture, at least that was the claim.

Thus, given the *radical* democratic streak running from Marx to Mao, the best thing that Maoism could do is to commit to the promise of *radical* democracy; after all, while it is true that there cannot be liberty in any meaningful sense without equality, for the rich will certainly be more "free" (have more options) than the poor; so there also cannot be equality without liberty, for then some may have more political power than others.

So far, all revolutions inspired by Marx have only enjoyed the support or participation of a significant minority. Can the commitment to *radical* democracy up the tide to get the help of the majority? Will the means then be carefully chosen so that they never come to overwhelm the socialist aspiration?

12

India Falters in Combating Maoist Guerrillas

Active Maoist Guerrilla warfare and passive expansion of the ideology of capturing power through the barrels of the gun is swinging imagination of masses living in the fringe areas of the society-the rural have-nots, forgotten forest dwellers and the exploited masses in different parts of the country. Statistically the Maoist headed movement has affected several states right from West Bengal to Maharashtra and Andhra Pradesh.

The units in Kerala, Karnataka and Tamil Nadu are yet to start organized armed violence. Recent visit to certain areas in Punjab-Sangrur, Faridkot and Bathinda etc areas and certain pockets in Haryana educated me about existence of strong Maoist groups in these so called prosperous states also. Delhi, Kolkata, Patna etc cities continue to be the hub of intellectual sympathizers and promoters of the movement.

The speed with which the movement is spiraling has not been analysed in the correct perspective by the political decision makers, intellectuals, intelligence agencies and law and order implementing agencies. The reasons are many, parts of which I had shared with the readers in my article Maoist Apparatus and Bridging Old Fault Lines, published in this portal. It is proposed to outline some more details in this essay concluding the last essay. It is better to have a peep into the efforts of the Union and State governments in the direction of meeting the menace with approximated correct prognosis.

Some readers of the Part 1 of the essay asked me to explain Mass Control and its cyclic effect. Mass Control is both physical and psychological control on the people in a given area, who look up to the STATE for means of livelihood, basic amenities, protection of lives and properties and ensuring upward movement of the people from poverty to prosperity. In vast areas of rural India, forested areas inhabited by the Advasis (aboriginal tribes) and in mining, industrial areas huge segments of people live under extreme penury.

In certain areas (including prosperous Punjab) peasants commit suicide in large numbers, marginal landholders become landless, forest areas are denuded by timber tycoons, Tendu leaf (for making bidi) cultivation is hijacked by the moneylenders, forest lands are forcibly grabbed for mining purposes and most of the government schemes to help the rural people with monetary help land up in the pockets of politicians, bureaucrats and middlemen. Over period such people lose confidence on the STATE and it is gradually replaced by the revolutionary group who seek emancipation through violence.

This inevitably follows by armed conflict between the STATE and the Revolutionaries; in this case Maoists. Gradually Law & Order takes priority over other mandatory duties of the STATE. Gradually the conflict takes the shape of guerrilla warfare between the STATE and the Maoists.

The STATE tries to retain Mass Control by using police forces and that alienates people to greater degrees. Sometimes the Maoists deliberately attacks police posts located in villages. This invites increased retaliation on the village from the STATE. Under STATE pressure the people surrenders to Maoist Mass Control and the chain of STATE and MAOIST violence continue to haunt the people.

Once small areas are "liberated" by the Maoists they run their own government and paralyze all government establishments including schools, health centres lines of communication and even stoppage of payment of revenue to the STATE. The economy of the area is paralyzed and the STATE continues to depend on force as a multiplier ingredient to smash the Maoist movement. Use of the expression Fringe People is an inclusive exercise for incorporating poverty stricken, landless, jobless, uprooted mass of people. The level of poverty, as per unreliable government data is also alarming. It is estimated that 456 million Indians (42% of the total Indian population) now live under the global poverty line of $1.25 per day (PPP). This means a third of the global poor now reside in India. The Planning Commission of India uses different criteria and has estimated that 27.5% of the population lived below the poverty line in 2004–2005, down from 51.3% in 1977–1978, and 36% in 1993-1994. The source for this was the 61st round of the National Sample Survey (NSS) and the criterion used was monthly per capita consumption expenditure below Rs. 356.35 for rural areas and Rs. 538.60 for urban areas. 75% of the poor are in rural areas, most of them are daily wagers, self-employed householders and landless labourers.

Indian economy has grown steadily over the last two decades. Its growth has been uneven when comparing different social groups, economic groups, geographic regions, and rural and urban areas. Between 1999 and 2008, the annualized growth rates for Gujarat (8.8%), Haryana (8.7%), or Delhi (7.4%) were much higher than for Bihar (5.1%), Uttar Pradesh (4.4%), or Madhya Pradesh (3.5%). Poverty rates in rural Orissa (43%) and rural Bihar (41%) are among the world's most extreme.

The India State Hunger Index 2008, by the International Food Policy Research Institute, Punjab has the best nutritional situation, whereas malnutrition in Madhya Pradesh is worse than in Ethiopia or Sudan. Worse is the condition in tribal areas of Chattisgarh, Orissa, Garhchiroli area of Maharashtra, plain and hill regions of Jharkhand, rural areas of West Bengal and Bihar.

These are areas where the Maoists or Naxals have stepped up their Guerrilla warfare. On a given map the compact area looks like a liberated zone. The State response basically veered around restoration of law & order, battling the guerrillas, decimating them through live action and forcing them out of the "liberated areas." The nucleus of police response is the Police Station. For example Dantewada district in Chattisgarh has 21 police stations and 2 police outposts. Number of Police outposts has gone up during last two years. In addition to state police force a few central police force encampments have also been established. The hill district having 9046.29 Sq kms area has only 478.93 kms tarred road. Police mobility is extremely limited. Average strength of a police station is about 10-15, except on occasions Special Forces are attached to a police station for raiding Maoist hideouts. Previously most of the police stations were located in makeshift or dilapidated structures without any watch tower, perimeter defences and faster communication facilities. The phone lines are unreliable and are generally deactivated by the Maoists. Wireless communication is being improved and in recent times some police officers have been given mobile phones. The problem with mobile phones is that towers are very few and often some existing towers are blasted out by the Naxals.

A police station is supposed to dominate an area of over 450 kms. With the given available strength in a working day (normal average is 7 out of 10), poor motor transport facility, inadequacy of wireless communication and supply of antiquated rifles the presence of normal police force is considered insignificant; not fit for fighting Maoist rebels equipped with modern arms. The inventories of the Maoists include Kalashnikov rifles, Light Machine Guns, 2" mortars and assorted rapid firing weapons. In addition to these they possess several kinds of landmines and IEDs. The Maoists are well trained in guerrilla warfare, jungle warfare and tactics of ambush. Their encampments are mobile. The guerrillas have no fixed HQ. In fact, a given guerrilla group do not spend nights in the same village. The groups are mainly composed of compatible tribe members.

Most of these tribal inhabited areas are extremely poverty ridden. Cultivation, harvesting forest resources etc are main sources of livelihood. In most cases funds provided under Integrated Rural Development Programme, NREG, Sampoorna Gramin Rozgar Yojana and other social security programmes do not reach the real people. For example, if an amount of 300 is sanctioned per family under NREG the fortunate family may get rupees 100, if they are lucky. In most cases out of 100 about 7-9% people actually receive the amount; rest goes to pockets of the bureaucrats, local politicians, leaders of local self government and even petty clerks. The STATE government sanctions the amounts to the district collectors, allocated by the central government. From that point downwards the money develops wings and the real recipients remain where they were. Same is the fate with Anganwadi system introduced in some of the areas. Right from the district office to the lowest governing tool in the panchayat and certain elements in the Anganwadi institutions share the money and the real education and total child development system remain where they were.

We will discuss these aspects in later parts of the essay. Police operations have three basic formats: group patrolling (often in platoon strength, rarely in company strength); village searches, and rare ambush parties. In group patrolling the general trend is to march in a column with 15-20 feet distance between two sepoys. These parties do not have mine sweeping vehicles and mostly they are not equipped with handheld mine detecting devices. This results in frequent mine explosions and police casualties. The information that a police party was planning patrolling in a particular direction somehow or other reaches the Maoists through their information network, interception of VHF radio talks. They plant antipersonnel mines on the likely routes to be taken by the patrol parties.

My experience in Nagaland and Manipur and the experiments conducted by army and paramilitary units indicated that instead of a single column patrol party or area domination party it was safer to send out two other parallel parties (smaller in size); one on both flanks of the main party. This tactics paid good dividends and guerrilla parties waiting in ambush were often taken by surprise.

Village searches are mostly perfidious. Police and Salwa Judum parties often enters homes, violate privacy of women and forcibly take away eatables including fowls, goats etc. Often the villagers are made to assemble in one place and some are tortured to obtain information. Police commanders do not realize that such tactics and illegal plundering and faulty operational methodology alienate the people more and they prefer the Maoists to buy protection.

Deployment of ambush parties are not done on the basis of precise human intelligence. This is the weakest area of anti-guerrilla operations. The tribesmen have basic distrust for

State administration; they are alienated by malpractices of timber-tycoons, Tendu leaf contractors, loan sharks, Mahajans (who advance money against crop) and of course against police, whom they consider as ambassadors of State repression. The normal state intelligence outfit and its district detachments are burdened with multifarious-political errands to normal terrorist-jihad activities. They are supposed to keep track of dowry killing, starvation death by agricultural workers, village feuds and most law & order problems. They have no focused training and resource to gather human intelligence (HUMINT) about the Maoists.

It is high time the State governments create special intelligence cells for Maoist problems. In a State like Jharkhand a special intelligence cell should consist of minimum 500 officers and men, specially trained by the Intelligence Bureau and other outfits handling commando and guerrilla warfare. Several meetings of the Union Home Minister with the State police chiefs and advisories to the Chief Ministers have not been able to make them understand that without high quality HUMINT it is not possible to carry out successful armed actions against the Maoists. Every district of the affected states should have a contingent of the special intelligence unit. These units should have attached compliments of trained commandos, who can move with lightening speed to intercept the Maoist group informed upon by the human assets. The DG police and the Operations Chief in each district may order immediate planned action without waiting for bureaucratic shenanigans. Unfortunately, in States like Chhattisgarh (despite an efficient DG Police) and Jharkhand such modern anti guerrilla concepts are yet to be implemented. Neither the Union and State governments have looked into the old British model in Malaysia, US model in Vietnam, and the models practiced in Greece and Italy nor they have gone for any other innovations improving upon India's own experiences in insurgency infested areas. The politicians talk for the sake of befooling the people.

Even if some Central paramilitary forces are inducted they cannot operate without help of local police and intelligence. As newcomers they are more vulnerable. Central forces can only succeed if battalions are allowed to dig in the affected areas for years together, build up defences, sanitize the villages and develop their own HUMINT potential. Temporary visiting units are guests; they are not effective operative units. Delhi must understand this and persuade the States to borrow Central forces for at least ten years. Units may change, but CRPF must be replaced by CRPF for the sake of continuity and force-homogeneity. A contingent of CRPF to be replaced by a contingent CISF after three months is a useless exercise. Minimum rotation of forces can ensure better operational capability.

While on Chattisgarh the issue of Salwa Judum is required to be briefly examined. Pro-Maoist intellectuals have painted pictures of "village grouping" by the government in the name of mobilising villagers against the Maoists. "Village Grouping" was successfully tried by the army in Mizoram. The principle was to deny water to the fish and make them vulnerable to lack of oxygen. There is no doubt that the villagers, either out of "Mass Control" factor or fear of decimation provide help to the Maoists. Once the villages are "grouped" (temporarily) the Maoists would be denied the water to swim about freely. Human rights groups and even the judiciary have intervened in the matter. The system of VVF (as in Manipur), Village Guards (as in Nagaland) and Special Police Officers (as in Punjab) for deployment after sustained training by a paramilitary force in guerrilla warfare and handling of medium and heavy weapons.

The Constitution has bestowed rights on the people to defend themselves. No court can rule against this fundamental right. Besides Chattisgarh, the readers to visit Lalgarh, Jangalmahal etc places in West Midnapore of West Bengal. Maoist activities (Naxal) are not new in this district of West Bengal bordering Bihar/Jharkhand. The Naxalite movement in Debra, Gopiballabhpur in mid-1969 had wrought the mass-killing violent movement for over 7 years, before the peak of the movement could be blunted. In fact, Debra, Gopiballabhpur, Jhargram, Shalboni, Jangal Mahal, Lalgarh etc areas are in West Midnapore district. These are most backward areas of Bengal. Except Haldia ports complex, Kharagpur and a few pockets nearer to Kolkata rest of the district is as backward as the adjacent districts of Purulia, Birbhum and Bankura are.

Some efforts were made, too late in the regime of the CPM, to start industrialization in Singur (Nano factory of TATA) and Nandigram (chemical complex of Salim group). Here is another classic case of political rivalry between the CPM and Trinamool Congress feuding over industrialization in agricultural area and politicization of land acquisition on the plea of displacement of the rural people.

This feud helped TMC, Jamiat-ul-Ulama-e-Hind and several NGOs, and indirectly the Congress to create severe disturbances. The government had expressed intention of acquisition, the Haldia ports authority had issued a notice about likely acquisition, but no government action had been taken to forcibly occupy the land for the proposed SEZ at Nandigram. The TMC led agitation helped the Maoists to walk into the vortex of tornado created by political rivalry. There is no denial of fact that the issue of acquision of agricultural land for industrial use in Nandigram (Midnapore) and Singur (Hooghly) had kicked off bloody trails of political tornado, but these politicized movements might have had earned a few more votes for the TMC and the Congress, but the momentum had encouraged the Maoists to slip into Jhargram, Shalboni, Lalgarh and even Midnapore Sadar areas with arms and explosives. In Nandigram and nearby Singur area the Bhumi Uchhed Pratirodh Committee and Jami Rakkha Committee etc bodies were organised and were highly infiltrated by the Maoists.

Nandigram and Singur were the stages where TMC and Congress rehearsed political revival and the Maoists initiated a new phase of sustained movement in west Midnapore, basically a forested single crop area, mostly inhabited by the tribal people-Santhal and Oraon, Majhi, Mahato, Ho, Munda etc and sprinkling of lower caste Hindus. Here also a front organisation was floated styled as Peoples Committee against Police Atrocities. This mass organisation was headed by CPM's local committee member Chatrdhar Mahato. Besides this front organisation the Maoists also organised Solidarity Forum for Lalgarh, Shramajivi Swastha Udyog, Utsha Manush, Janaswastha Committee, and Janaswastha Swadhikar Mancha etc. These front organisations received support from Bengali intellectuals, writers and film makers.

The apex social organization of the Santhals, the Bharat Jakat Majhi Madwa Juan Gaonta took up the leadership of the struggle, although the leader of the organization, the "Disham Majhi" Nityananda Hembram openly professed that they were being guided by the people's movement and they had no control on it. The upsurge of adivasis is continuing unabated and is also spreading to newer areas. They laid siege of Jhargram and only after discussion between the Bharat Jakat Majhi Madwa Juan Gaonta and the administration, the siege of was partially lifted. The blockade on the road connecting Jhargram and Dahijuri was lifted on 14th November but the Bharat Jakat Majhi Madwa could not convince the protesters to lift the blockades of the other roads connecting Jhargram. Besides Lalgarh, the movement has now spread to Binpur, Jhargram, Jamboni, Shalboni, Belpahari, Garbeta and Gopiballavpur. People's response to joint State and Central operation was so spontaneous that the movement had spread to the last two blocks of the Jhargram sub-division, Nayagram and Sankrail. Nayagram block was disconnected by piling tree trunks on the roads in Dhankamra and Barpat. Dhankhori, Gajashimul, Mudakati and Kungarda areas of Sankrail block have also been blockaded. On the other hand, all connections to police stations and camps in the Belpahari block of Jhargram sub-division has been cut off. A group of around 500 armed tribal blockaded the Neguriya police camp near Chakadoba in Belpahari. The local shopkeepers and traders have declared that they would not supply anything to the policemen in the camps.

The West Bengal government cannot deny its responsibility for neglecting the area. While Below Poverty Line index in the state is 27% in West Midnapore areas the index is 43% to 37%. There are about 12 government aided schools in the tribal area, but hardly any teacher is available, The Health Centres are almost nonexistent. There is no regular doctor, least speaking of free medicine supply. Some sample study was made about a few central funded welfare projects in the Jhargram-Lalgarh areas. People have not even heard about Sampoorna Gramin Rojgar Yojana (SGRY), Rural Housing, Self Employment Programme, Berozgar Bhatta (unemployment allowance), and National Rural Employment Guarantee (NREG) etc schemes.

A sample study of Belpahadi indicated that the CPM leaders offered some NREG facility to their cadre. Only 7% of rest of the tribal people received some NREG support. Some sampling was made of Anganwadi (rural school) scheme in Sankrail and Nayagram areas. It was found that only 5 to 7% benefit reached the targeted people. Rest of the money was misappropriated by the village authorities, Block officials and even top notches of the Aganwadi scheme. A sample study of the Integral Rural Development Programme (IRDP) was made in Belda area. The findings were disheartening. The amount received by the district and Block authorities and the Panchayats were distributed amongst the political sharks. The real tribal people received nothing (CPM supporters excluded). It is not possible for one person to study the entire developmental activities. But the if samples are any indicator, it must be said that the governmental tools were misused and the benefits offered by Delhi were either eaten by the political-bureaucratic cartel and very little trickled down to the deserving tribal population.

The magnitude of the national problem of sharks eating up the smaller fries was horribly exemplified in a publication of the Times of India (Nov. 26, 2009) about 22,853 ghost employees drawing pay for decades from the Municipal Corporation of Delhi to the tune of Rs. 17 crores per month. Statistics about only one agency has been dug out. There are about 10 such departments under Delhi government which maintain ghost employees costing the tax payers about Rs. 50 crores per month.

What is happening in the rural areas and in the forested tracts as well as in vast mining tracts in different parts of the country, where India's shining global economy is yet to shine even for fractions of days in any given year. Nearly 30% of India's population goes to bed in empty stomach and about 40% can barely manage two square meals in any given day. In Lalgarh area the same misfortune of the people was noticed by non-partisan observers.

Militarily the government of West Bengal failed miserably to control the Maoist movement. Local formations of the CPM (notoriously known for motor cycle groups) dominated the area and maimed all political opposition and even reasonable ventilation of genuine grievances. They were, at many places, supported by the local police. The ordinary people lost touch with the administration and the administration was blissfully ignorant about the Maoists building up local committees, arming the people, bringing in improvised explosive devices and building up comprehensive people's fronts. Obviously, these fronts received support from Trinamool Congress and Congress, who thought of Nandigram like exploitation of the Maoists for retrieving political ground. This was a miscalculation. The Maoists are very active in adjacent Jharkhand, Orissa and Bihar. The borders are open. When chased the Orissa and Jharkhand Maoists slip in Midnapore and Purulia districts of West Bengal. Similarly, the Maoists also recruit their cadres from West Bengal tribal population. The intellectual brains of Bengal, Andhra Pradesh and Orissa guide the movement. Local leaders are also emerging in Jharkhand, Chattisgarh and other parts of the country.

Let us look into the military formation in Lalgarh and Jangal Mahal area of West Midnapore. The Maoists have organised village level squads for cutting of road connection, planting IED or anti-personnel and anti-tank mines (to hit mine proof vehicles). These village committees are also assigned the task of attacking isolated police posts. Major police stations are at West Midnapore Kotwali, Sankrail, Jhargram, Lalgarh, Shalboni (also EFR headquarter) Manikpara (near Kalaikunda airbase) etc. Besides the District HQ the average strength of police stations were (before joint operations) 10-15. The police were armed with .303 obsolete rifles. One jeep per police station was the only means of communication. Phone lines were unreliable and cell phones were not in profuse use because of lack of towers. Wireless communication was also generally absent. The police depended on muscle support from the CPM cadre.

Once the organised Maoist activities started in Lalgarh, Jhargram, Shalboni, and Jangal Mahal etc areas police resistance evaporated. The State did not deploy sufficient numbers of the crack Eastern Frontier Rifles (EFR) and other State Armed Police Battalions. Kolkata depended on ramshackle police forces and party cadre. Once these efforts were blunted by the front organisations the trained Maoists' reserve arms caches in the hill areas were brought in. This is proved by the daring attack on Sankrail police station by 100 Maoists and kidnapping of the officer in charge. The Maoists have attacked government establishments in West Midnapore Sadar (planting of mine), Jhargram sub-divisional HQ, Shalboni, Nayagram and other places.

The joint Central and State police operations (seen on TV) were mainly conducted in plains areas of Lalgarh, amidst populated segments and in some cases under pan of TV cameras. My enquiry with local people, not connected with the Maoist movement, mostly apolitical, some owing allegiance to CPM, revealed that the State government first tried to augment ridiculously low strength in the police stations. They also depended on the trained party cadre to build up local resistance. However, backed by other tribal organisation, Trinamool Congress and Congress the Peoples Committee against Police Atrocities (PCPA) organised sustained opposition to police incursion. The main Maoist guerrillas provided support by planting mines and opening fire on the Central and State forces under cover of deep forested areas. The joint operation was limited to regaining government control on the Lalgarh tract and no sustained and planned operations were conducted in the hills adjoining Jharkhand and Orissa. The hardcore Maoist cadres infiltrated from Jharkhand and Orissa and revived the Naxal movement in West Midnapore areas along with pockets in Birbhum and Bankura. If a bird's eye view is taken of the compact Maoist affected areas in this region it would seem that the belt between Birbhum (home district of Union Finance Minister), Bankura, West Midnapore, Jharkhand and Orissa is painted either red or pink. This is what the Maoists call "liberated zone."

What are the preparations of the West Bengal government? It is a sad and shady story. Without going into the political skullduggery it can be safely concluded that the CPM and other Left partners had built up groups of Banditos, often armed with lethal weapons and homemade bombs. After about 25 years other political groups, such as the Trinamool Congress and its passive partner the Congress have also started organizing groups of Banditos, who gradually gathered the courage of physically clashing with the Left opponents. Both the sides made West Bengal into a political killing field. The Maoists are known for taking advantage of such mass chaos and side with one or the other to progress in their planned advance in selected pockets. Working in conjunction with the violent political forces they establish their own bases.

Historically the CPI (ML), the hardcore Charu-Kanu-Jangal faction was against the CPM line. My personal experiences in Naxalbari operations gave me impressions that Charu Majumdar was vehemently opposed to any negotiation with the Left leaders like Hare Krishna Konar. However, later in 1972 elections elements of the Naxals supported the Congress in districts like Midnapore, Bankura and Birbhum, Jalpaiguri, Burdwan and Hooghly etc. Besides the Bangladesh war effect support from the Naxals also resulted in resounding victory for the Congress. That CPI (M) should crash from 113 in 1971 to 14 in the 1972 was totally unexpected so was the Congress party's tally of 216 seats. The point made is that the Maoists are not averse to side with political parties of their choice to augment their own agenda. They enter a new area as tails of political parties and later establish bases of their own. If it were Congress in 1972 to seemingly exploit the Maoists, it is Trinamool Congress and its appendage, Congress in 2011. Political parties forget the universal lesson that the tiger they often ride devours the rider sooner than later.

The State government's dependence on local police and party cadre misfired. The Maoists initially took advantage of anti-SEZ proposals of the government and often violent agitation started by TMC and its allies. Nandigram to Singur to West Midnapore was not reached in one lap. It took the Maoists and their political allies (tactical allies only) to build up movement in West Midnapore around the Union and State government's proposal to allot 4,500 acres of land near Shalboni to Jindal Steel Works SEZ factory. The chain of events started after the 2nd November, 2009 land mine explosion targeting the convoy of West Bengal chief minister Buddhadeb Bhattacharjee and union steel and mines minister Ram Vilas Paswan as they were returning from the inauguration of the Jindal Steel Works SEZ. It was alleged by the Maoists and their political allies that the land in question belonged to the government and was earmarked for distribution among the tribals. The chain of events resulted in violence between CPM cadres on the one hand and Trinamool cadres supported by Maoist front organisations on the other. Unable to resist the "occupation" of Lalgarh, Jangal Mahal etc areas the State government requested for central forces and they seemingly "reoccupied" the tract from the Maoists.

The fact is that the government of West Bengal still does not have any plan to build up forces to fight the Maoist guerrillas. They, in collaboration with guerrillas from Jharkhand and Orissa have started hitting at targets even in the heart of the district head quarter. Some semblance of law and order is being maintained by the State police and the Central forces deputed to help the local authorities. There are plans to start another combing operation. But the holes in the government nets are so big that small Maoists Pisces swim in the area unhindered. The State governments in West Bengal, Jharkhand and Orissa are yet to prepare a joint blueprint for fighting the guerrilla forces. The Central governments often announce certain offensive joint actions. However, except deputation of certain elements of central forces in the affected States no Joint Command has been conceived as yet.

There is no intelligence coordination between the State governments and the central intelligence agencies. Police stations are the best bases from where local intelligence is collected for tactical operational purposes. The intelligence networks in the rural and urban police stations have dried up. The area chowkidars, dafadars, lower revenue officials, gram sevaks, and other rural government employees have ceased to feed the police stations. Human intelligence is appallingly poor. Even the central intelligence agencies have not been able to build up HUMINT resources in the affected areas. Anti-Guerrilla warfare cannot be fought by wild goose's chase. Forces have to act on precise intelligence.

As the Maoists often use cell phones it is not impossible to locate the GPS coordinate of the phone under use. Once located helicopter borne forces can raid the area and neutralize the target. This aspect of coordination between signal intelligence (SIGINT) and airborne attack has not been conceived as yet. On the other hand the Maoists have excellent HUMINT assets from amongst the villagers and even educated sympathizers. Villagers not cooperating with the Maoists and suspected to be informers of the police are mercilessly punished. Recent incidents of cruel killing of police officers and innocent villagers prove that Mass Control mechanisms of the Maoists are near complete.

It is understood that the Maoists in Chattisgarh, Jharkhand. Orissa and West Bengal have obtained VHF communication sets from former LTTE members. These are used for communication between the Command with the Squads. VHF communications are able to transmit to shorter distances. If transmitted from a higher location the signals can be received even at a distance of 40 kilometers. Often the desired height is achieved by hanging an antenna on high rise trees. The State police are yet to install array of VHF monitoring instruments to pick up signals from the sophisticated VHF transreceivers used by the guerrilla forces. The police forces often use VHF sets in analog mode and not in automatic digital encryption mode. These can be easily intercepted either by identifying the frequency or by scanning the frequency logs. Police forces have not taken security precaution while using VHF sets during operations. These limitations are required to be attended forthwith.

The government agencies have just started thinking in terms of using Unmanned Aerial Vehicle (UAV) to survey the affected areas, locate hideouts and send the live broadcasts to the nearby forces to mount counter attack. Use of UAV in forested terrains may not yield expected results, unless the government acquires infrared equipped cameras for the UAVs to enable these flying machines to look down at precise targets through thick foliage and often mist covers.

Sample studies in Chattisgarh and West Bengal (broader study in all affected areas is necessary) it is found that the State police in Chattisgarh is better prepared and their mechanism of operations are more scientific. There has been marginal increase in HUMINT assets, but paucity of force prevents the State from comprehensive area domination. In

West Bengal the police forces are yet to wake up to the reality that the Maoists of today are not ragtag Naxals of seventies and eighties. These guerrillas are well trained, well armed and indoctrinated. They follow the Maoist principles of guerrilla warfare scrupulously. Bengal police forces, paralyzed by political pressure, have not been exposed to anti-guerrilla warfare.

The thin police forces are so inadequate that they are not enough in numbers to take on sustained anti-guerrilla warfare, they lack in weaponry and training in anti-guerrilla warfare. Even the Central forces are not trained to fight the guerrillas by organizing them into effective counter-guerrilla forces. Some States have designated certain numbers of policemen as Special Forces with fancy names like Cobra Force etc. The Centre and the States may like to consider assisting each affected State to raise minimum 7 battalions of anti-guerrilla Special Forces trained in the army's anti-insurgency warfare school. The present model of training some policemen in the model of National Security Guard (NSG) training manual may sharpen the efficiency edges. But the NSG is basically a static operations force for tackling static incidents like Mumbai incident of 26/11. It is not meant for deployment in anti-guerrilla warfare. The specially trained anti-guerrilla warfare police forces, like the VVF mentioned earlier live on and in the ground divided into strike squads coordinated by the battalion and higher commands. To fight guerrillas the forces have to adopt guerrilla ways of life.

The Central government often announces coordinated joint operations. This constructive idea can better be enforced if the entire mobilized forces (from different colours) are fused into a single operational force put under command of a Special Divisional Command (like the army) and operationalised in allocated territories for specializing in that territory till they are successful to retrieve the given territory from the Mass Control and military control of the Maoists.

However, it must be added that police action cannot alone eradicate the Maoist problems. An integrated and balanced approach and inclusive action plan is necessary to implement developmental works, providing employment, remodeling rural economy, education, health care and agricultural activities.

Mushrooming of enrooted corruption in different welfare schemes, as discussed in this essay are required to be probed. The government must ensure that minimum 70% of the welfare funds and yojanas benefit the people. At present only 10-15% benefits reach the real affected people. Combating Maoist guerrillas require total attention of the political decision makers and bureaucrats at macro and micro levels. Otherwise, present efforts would prove to be a war exercise between the State and certain segments of the people, who may ultimately be 25-35% of the population in the affected areas. The Guerrillas accrue new territories trough continued mass action. The present red and pink map may get enlarged sooner than later if corrective measures are not adopted NOW and NOW.

THE SPRING AND ITS THUNDER

The mainstream media is full of stories and analysis about the so-called "Naxal menace" - and the alleged attempt by Maoists to create a contiguous liberated corridor cutting through the tribal dominated belt from Andhra Pradesh to Bihar through Chhattisgarh, Orissa and Jharkhand.

Maoist activities have been reported in over 160 districts around the country in many of which they are trying to establish "liberation zones" where they dispense state functions of administration, policing and justice. (Here the reference to Maoists is exclusively to the CPI (Maoist) formed through merger of the People's War Group and the Maoist Communist Centre in 2004. There are other equally important streams of the Naxalite movement, chief among which is the CPI(ML) Liberation group with strongholds in Bihar and presence in many parts of India.)

What is also worrying many in the Indian establishment is the growing profile of the Maoists in neighbouring Nepal in recent months and its implications for the movement's growth in India. While the two Maoist movements have good relations with each other, it is not clear to what extent they have any kind of active collaboration on the ground.

The Naxal Terror Watch, a right wing blog site that supposedly monitors Naxalite activity in India claims (quite ridiculously of course) that the "PWG's current goal is to destabilise India and the subcontinent by a well coordinated strategy with international revolutionaries, and support from Pakistan and China". The repeated use of the term "menace" (as in "Dennis the Menace") by both the Indian government and media shows that the Indian state does not want to project the Maoist movement as too grave a threat as yet or at least does not want to acknowledge this in public. Another and more sinister implication of this term however is that Naxalism is to be considered a nuisance or a problem at the same level as malaria or encephalitis and the "infectious" Naxalites are to be stamped out like mosquitoes! (All the millions of tonnes of DDT used over the decades have not eradicated malaria in the country, so maybe there is a lesson in that somewhere.)

In a status paper on the "Naxal problem", placed in Parliament by union home minister Shivraj Patil on March 13 this year the UPA government spelt out a policy to combat the challenge posed by the "Naxalite menace". The 14-point policy stresses the urgency for the states to adopt a collective approach and pursue a coordinated response to counter the Naxalites. It emphasises that there will be no peace dialogue by the affected states with the Naxal groups unless the latter agree to give up violence and arms.

At the same time the paper acknowledged that the spread of Naxalism was not merely a law and order problem. "The policy of the government is to address this menace simultaneously on political, security, development and public perception management fronts in a holistic manner", it said.

Another component of the policy is that it asks political parties to strengthen their base in Naxal-affected areas so that the youth could be "weaned away" from the path of Naxal ideology. More ominously the paper says "Efforts will continue to be made to promote local resistance groups against Naxalites but in a manner that the villagers are provided adequate security cover and the area is effectively dominated by the security forces".

The paper is however silent on the recent upsurge in violence between the state-sponsored vigilante group Salwa Judum and the Maoists in Chhattisgarh, which has been dubbed by the media as a virtual "civil war".

At one level, as even its critics acknowledge, the presence and growth of the Maoist movement today is essentially due to the dire socio-economic situation of people living in the "affected" parts of the country. Like at the time of the original Naxalbari upsurge 39 years ago, even today it is this combination of stark poverty, an indifferent or even exploitative state machinery and oppressive feudal/business elites in different parts of the country that has been at the heart of the Maoist insurgency.

Tribal Belt Focus

It is no coincidence at all that the tribal belts of Andhra Pradesh, Orissa, Chhattisgarh and Jharkhand, where the Maoists are most active, are also among the areas in the country that have the lowest development indicators. Though information on the socio-economic profile of the adivasi population in India is quite sketchy available data shows that maternal mortality (between 8 and 25 per 1,000) among them is more than double the rates in the advanced regions of the country.

Similarly, the infant mortality rates are between 120 and 150, which is more than double the all-India average of 55. All these adverse health indicators are largely due to inadequate access to the right foods - iron, protein and micronutrients such as iodine and vitamins - and lack of access to healthcare services. A decade ago, the World Development Report observed, "The cycle between hunger- disease-low levels of productivity (measured both in terms of absence from work as well as duration)-low wages-indebtedness-reduced consumption levels-disease-is reflective of how the development process has largely bypassed the tribals".

Instead of being the harbinger of any kind of meaningful and participatory development, the Indian state since independence in 1947 has been basically predatory in the experience of the indigenous people. The state and its various agents have exploited them, violated their rights at whim and robbed them not just of resources but of their very human dignity. The marginalisation of indigenous people (and dalits) in this ancient land of ours has been happening over several millennia with the various waves of migration from outside thriving on their outright conquest, displacement or co-option. (To put it in the framework of Hindu mythology what we are talking about is that almost 3,000 years after the Aryan prince Ram co-opted the indigenous Hanuman to help him defeat the Dravidian Ravan – the descendants of Hanuman are still being treated like monkeys!)

Defenceless against the predations of the modern Indian state and its agents the tribals have naturally come under the influence of the Maoists, who offer them protection and mete out instant justice to their exploiters. Whatever objections one may have to the kind of violence employed there is no getting around the fact that the spread of the Maoist movement among indigenous populations - in the absence of equally effective alternatives - is a natural outcome of the situation on the ground in these areas. The point about available alternatives is important because in most - though not all - areas where the Maoist insurgency is making its impact felt, they are often the only real counter to the exploitation of the indigenous people by other organised groups such as state officials, businessmen and plain criminal elements.

This is all a bit simplistic of course and it is true that the Maoists have also made several mistakes; for example the destruction of transport and educational infrastructure in some of the tribal areas apparently in a bid to keep Indian security forces at bay. This has deprived local populations of whatever few benefits they ever derived from the Indian state.

Maoist Violence

More serious is the problem of the Maoists killing "informers" and others deemed to be their opponents when other methods of dealing with them could have sufficed. The recent report by a group of intellectuals and activists who went as part of an independent fact finding mission to Dantewara district in Chhattisgarh had this to say about nine widows they met whose husbands had been abducted and killed by Maoists for going to the government sponsored refugee camp: "Whatever their husband's alleged crimes for which they were given a summary death penalty, these widows were hardly oppressors, pathetic defeated women, helplessly thrusting out their passbooks without knowing what they contained or what they might do with the money, now that their husbands were gone." These kind of lapses are all reasons today for the alienation of the Maoists from a section of their own constituencies, both among the urban intelligentsia as well as the tribal people themselves. Such a rift is dangerous and as we see in the case of the Salwa Judum operations in Chhattisgarh it gives the Indian state and other vested interests opportunity to try and pit ordinary people against the Maoists.

There are also other important criticisms made of both the theory and practice of the Maoists - from within the broader left movement and outside it - that they need to heed carefully. One has to do with their dealings with the indigenous people themselves. Writing in The Hindu recently E A S Sarma, former secretary to the government of India, who was also part of the same fact finding team to Chhattisgarh mentioned earlier says: During the last two decades, the Maoists gained a mass base among the adivasis by taking up cudgels on their behalf against corrupt government functionaries, exploitative traders, and moneylenders.

The trouble began for the Maoists when they started dismantling the traditional political structures of the adivasis at the village level and began tinkering with landownership. Those that did not belong to their "sanghams" in the villages were considered anti-Maoist and dealt with firmly, sometimes brutally. The headmen of the villages and others intimidated by the Maoists, along with the non-tribals, started grouping together and working out ways to sabotage the Maoists' efforts.

Without "exoticising" the indigenous people one can safely say that the few remaining parts of the country, which still have indigenous/tribal populations left in a majority and where the Maoists are active are really the last bastions of their entire civilisation.

It is not clear to what extent this happens, but it seems that the Maoist intervention has certainly upset several aspects of traditional tribal life, customs and beliefs, the value of which can be decided only by the indigenous people themselves, and not outsiders - even those with revolutionary intentions.

This is a very important point because while the Maoists have chosen to act as the protectors and liberators of indigenous people from exploitation they should not, as outsiders, impose values completely alien to the local culture. There are many aspects of the project of "modernisation" promoted by the progressive and radical left that despite all good intentions have many negative implications in the long run. (In fact leave alone "teaching" the tribals anything the Maoists, with some humility, can probably learn a few things from the people they are helping resist oppression and spread these values to the rest of the country. While it is true that indigenous societies have become easy victims to the machinations of outside forces that are technologically better equipped and unscrupulous to boot they are far superior in social, moral and ecological terms to those who conquer them.)

Bibliography

A.N. Sharma: *Bihar: Stagnation or Growth*. Delhi: Spectrum Publishing House.

Banerjee, Sumanta: *In the Wake of Naxalbari: A History of the Naxalite Movement in India,* Calcutta: Subarnarekha, 1980.

Barmé, Geremie R. *Shades of Mao: The Posthumous Cult of the Great Leader*. Armonk, N.Y.: M. E. Sharpe, 1996.

Bonner, A.: *"Averting the Apocalypse"*, Duke University Press, London, 1990.

Bottomore, Tom: *A Dictionary of Marxist Thought,* New Delhi, Maya Blackwell, 2000.

Chalmers, Johnson. *Autopsy on Peoples War*. Berkeley: University of California Press, 1973.

Conway, G. 1992. *Sustainable Rural Livelihoods: Practical Concepts for 21st Century*. Sussex: Institute of Development Studies.

Dasgupta, B.: *The Naxalite Movement*, Bombay: Allied Publishers, 1974.

de Haan, A. 2000. *Migrants, livelihoods, and rights: the relevance of migration in development policies*. UK: Social Development Department.

Debray, Regis. *Revolution in the Revolution*. New York: Grove Press, Inc., 1993.

Dietmar Rothermund. *A History of India*. Totowa, New Jersey: Barnes and Noble, 1986.

Duyker, E.: *Tribal Guerrillas: The Santals of West Bengal and the Naxalite Movement*, New Delhi: OUP, 1987.

Ellis, F. 2000. *Rural Livelihoods and Diversity in Developing Countries*. New York: Oxford University Press.

Gao, Mobo: *The Battle for China's Past: Mao and the Cultural Revolution,* London, Pluto Press, 2008.

Ghosh, Suniti : *The Historic Turning-Point: A Liberation Anthology*, Calcutta, 1992.

Gurley, John G: *China's Economy and the Maoist Strategy,* New York, Monthly Review Press, 1976.

Kalyan Mukherjee and Rajendra Singh Yadav, *Bhojpur: Naxalism in the Plains of Bihar*, New Delhi, 1980.

Kapuria, R.S. *The Indian Rupee: A Study in Retrospect and Prospect*. Bombay: Vora, 1967.

Kay, Geoffrey: *Development and Underdevelopment: A Marxist Analysis*, London, Macmillan, 1975.

Kumar, Ashwani: *Community Warriors: State, Peasants and Caste Armies in Bihar*. New Delhi: Anthem Press, 2008.

Index

□□□